D0065676

MICHAEL DUFFY

AND

DAN GOODGAME

MARCHING IN PLACE

THE STATUS QUO
PRESIDENCY
OF GEORGE BUSH

SIMON & SCHUSTER
NEW YORK   LONDON   TORONTO   SYDNEY   TOKYO   SINGAPORE

SIMON & SCHUSTER
SIMON & SCHUSTER BUILDING
ROCKEFELLER CENTER
1230 AVENUE OF THE AMERICAS
NEW YORK, NEW YORK 10020

COPYRIGHT © 1992 BY MICHAEL DUFFY AND DAN GOODGAME

DESIGNED BY EVE METZ
MANUFACTURED IN THE UNITED STATES OF AMERICA

1   3   5   7   9   10   8   6   4   2

LIBRARY OF CONGRESS CATALOGING-IN-PUBLICATION DATA

DUFFY, MICHAEL, DATE.
MARCHING IN PLACE: THE STATUS QUO PRESIDENCY OF GEORGE BUSH/MICHAEL DUFFY
AND DAN GOODGAME.
P.   CM.
INCLUDES BIBLIOGRAPHICAL REFERENCES AND INDEX.
1. UNITED STATES—POLITICS AND GOVERNMENT—1989–   2. BUSH, GEORGE,
1924–   .   I. GOODGAME, DAN.   II. TITLE.
E881.D84   1992
973.928′092–DC20   92-20036
                                                            CIP

ISBN 0-671-73720-1

FOR DEMETRA AND MARCIA

CONTENTS

ABOUT SOURCES

This is not an "authorized" book. Much of the information and many quotes were provided to us on the condition that the sources remain anonymous.

Most of the officials quoted in this book are still working in the White House, at the Bush–Quayle campaign, or elsewhere in the administration.

Where we have relied on the reporting of others, sources are cited in endnotes listed near the index. We also have cited, wherever possible, the public statements of the president.

INTRODUCTION

Fascination with George Bush is a taste acquired slowly. It began for us in the summer of 1988, when *Time* magazine assigned us to report on the Bush and Dukakis campaigns, and it deepened over the next four years as we covered the White House. We watched as the man who had been derided as a wimp revealed himself to be a ruthless and resourceful campaigner, overcoming a 17-point deficit in the polls. Then, as president, Bush displayed facets of his personality that he had submerged during eight years as Ronald Reagan's loyal understudy. He was smart. He was calculating. He was remorselessly deceitful when it served his purpose. He knew his way around the diplomatic parlors and back alleys of Washington and the world, and amazed aides with his detailed familiarity with subjects ranging from the tax code to village-level politics in the Middle East. He was sunny, funny and energetic, and he won record approval ratings.

At the same time, however, Bush was defining no real priorities, for the nation or for his cabinet and staff. After a few months, we began to wonder: how can Bush be so popular if he isn't *doing* anything? Bush and a few close aides, we discovered, had carefully analyzed poll data and focus groups and learned that while Americans were concerned about the sorry state of public schools, pollution of the air and water, and the swelling federal debt, they also feared that any sweeping attempt by Washington to address these and other issues might only make things worse: it probably wouldn't work, but would create new bureaucracies and push up their taxes. The comfortable country club Republicans who formed Bush's base had always been suspicious of government crusades, but now they were joined by a larger group of middle Americans who, after a decade in which Washington raised their taxes while cutting their services, just wanted to be left alone. To be sure, they expected the president to say the right things about the homeless and education reform and the emerging democracies in Eastern Europe and Latin America—so long as it didn't cost them anything.

Bush was popular, we finally realized, not despite his lip-service approach to domestic policy but *because* of it. Public opinion, at least among the better paid half of the public that votes, was in a holding pattern, and Bush's presidency would be a holding action.

The president's minimalist strategy dovetailed with his core beliefs. Though he projected an image of political moderation, Bush is deeply conservative in his fear of change, his skepticism toward government's attempts to promote social progress, his caution and reactiveness. When faced with a decision, Bush often concluded that the best course was to do as little as possible: to "do no harm," rather than attempt reform at the risk of making things worse. The same fear of change drove his foreign policy. As demands for political and economic freedom rose across the communist world, Bush warned repeatedly of an enemy named "instability." But while Bush practiced quiet stewardship at home, he believed the status quo abroad required a bold and vigorous defense, as in the invasion of Panama or the Persian Gulf crisis.

This book is a critical assessment of the Bush presidency at home and abroad: how he won it and organized it; for what purpose and to whose benefit. We judge Bush's performance not against the expectations of critics on the right or the left, but by the standards of his own promises and rhetoric, with an eye to the opportunities and challenges that he seized or ignored.

The chapters are organized thematically, but also in a rough chronology, emphasizing the episodes we found particularly telling—for example, Bush's response to the August 1991 Soviet coup—while omitting others almost entirely. We begin by tracing the roots of Bush's victory in the 1988 campaign. We examine his domestic and

foreign policies and his class assumptions. We conclude with his attempts four years later to run at once *on* his record and *against* it.

In assessing Bush's odds for reelection, we are reminded that we
are finishing this book at a moment when he is nearly as unpopular as
he was when we started covering him in mid-1988. This is a cautionary
note, because political opponents and pundits have underestimated
his abilities throughout his career. As his old mentor, Richard Nixon,
put it recently, "You want to remember, every time you tend to write
off George Bush, he makes the big play."

—Michael Duffy and Dan Goodgame
May 1992

1

"THE HONOR OF
IT ALL"

Some obvious questions awaited George Bush on Wednesday, November 9, 1988, his first day as president-elect of the United States of America.

What were his plans? Would he move quickly to make good on his vows to clean up the nation's skies, fully fund Head Start, and broaden opportunities for disabled Americans? How would he convince lawmakers to go along with such proposals after a long campaign of ugly attacks on Democrats and considerable Congress bashing? How would Bush's kinder and gentler promises mesh with his concurrent oaths to halt regulatory red tape, keep Washington off the backs of business, rein in the federal government, and reduce the deficit? How would Bush do all that and still uphold his often repeated "no new taxes" pledge? And what about those other "issues"—the Pledge of Allegiance and those "card-carrying members of the ACLU"? Would he relegate to the ash heap of campaign history the case of convicted murderer Willie Horton's hideous rape of a Maryland woman while on a weekend pass?

After rising early to attend church, and then jogging in a Houston park with campaign manager Lee Atwater, Bush appeared in public to name his transition team and announce that James Baker, his campaign chairman, would be his secretary of state. Bush thanked his supporters, reminisced briefly about the campaign, and then took

15

questions. Asked to describe his mandate, Bush replied, "Well, I don't know whether I want to use the word *mandate.* . . . I would simply say the people have spoken, the verdict was clear, and therefore I will take what I think the prime issues of the campaign were and work constructively with Congress to attain the will of the people."

Bush was forecasting a great deal when he eschewed the word "mandate." His campaign had been a bewildering and sometimes furious fugue of mixed messages designed to woo and hold together an unlikely coalition of mainstream Republicans, activist conservatives, Reagan Democrats, and independent suburbanites. Bush won with a coalition whose demands were so contradictory that it would prove almost impossible to govern. But then a mandate had never been Bush's objective. Getting elected was. He had assembled a coalition not to govern, but simply to acquire the 270 electoral votes he needed to win the presidency.

Base + Swing = 270

In the vernacular of political consultants, 1988 did not seem to be a Republican year. To be sure, the economy was humming along amid the longest peacetime expansion in history. After the 1981 recession eliminated thousands of industrial jobs, particularly in the Midwest, the subsequent recovery sparked a boom in the Sunbelt and on the coasts. The shamans of supply-side economics credited massive, deficit-financed tax cuts with fueling the boom. But the rebound also was powered by two other forces: an explosion in personal computers and microprocessors and the businesses and management efficiencies it spawned; and a trillion-dollar defense spending spree. The former sparked an entirely new industry; the latter revitalized an older, long-subsidized sector. The Pentagon buildup benefited not only weapons makers, but the hundreds of local economies supported by the nation's refurbished military installations. In some areas, such as New England and California, the two booms combined to create an extraordinary, supercharged growth.

Despite the cuts in income taxes on the best-paid Americans, taxes on the middle class nonetheless crept up, due to higher regressive payroll taxes for Social Security and Medicare and state and local income and sales taxes. Only half of America's families managed to maintain their living standards in the 1980s, and many did so only by working longer hours, taking second jobs, and sending record numbers of women into the workplace—most of whom told pollsters they would rather stay at home or work part-time. Spawned by a colossal drug epidemic, crime had reached epidemic proportions in many large cities and had spread so far that neighborhood watch programs and private security patrols had become commonplace in suburbs and even rural towns. At the same time, the nation's schools were producing students whose test scores placed them well below their counterparts in other industrialized countries—a result that did not seem likely to stem the flow of skilled jobs to overseas markets. If things weren't bad enough, the very seas and skies seemed to be revolting. The summer of 1988 saw a record number of fires break out in the western forests, medical wastes wash ashore along the Atlantic coast, and a drought scorch the Great Plains.

While Americans coped with these challenges, many of the people in whom they entrusted responsibility suddenly seemed to be entirely undeserving of it. Scandal brought ruin to such financiers as Ivan Boesky and had begun to cast a shadow over Drexel Burnham Lambert and its whiz-kid bond trader, Michael Milken. Allegations of financial mismanagement engulfed hundreds of suddenly insolvent thrift institutions. Religious figures, such as Jim and Tammy Bakker and Jimmy Swaggart, would be defrocked in the wake of tax fraud and sex scandals. The federal government seemed a school for scandal, ranging from military procurement frauds to the tangle of arms sales and intrigue known as Iran-contra, which had ensnared President Reagan and crept to the threshold of the vice president's office.

These unsettling changes were reflected in the warped but often revealing cultural mirror. A sense of retribution stoked the decade's blockbuster books and movies. *Bonfire of the Vanities,* Tom Wolfe's huge best-seller, told the story of a powerful Wall Street stockbroker whose financially secure but morally bankrupt life is destroyed by an impulsive confrontation on an exit ramp in the Bronx. More bad things happened to bad people in *Fatal Attraction,* the hot movie ticket of late 1987, which told the story of a crazed woman who turns a yuppie's poor judgment into a nightmare. Perhaps it was no wonder that 1988's breakaway single recording—a witless reggae jingle called

"Don't Worry, Be Happy"—became the virtual theme song of the Bush campaign, as it played on *Air Force Two* between campaign events.

A vague sense that something was rotten seemed to stalk the land. The Roper organization reported in February 1987 that only 31 percent of the nation believed the country was on the "right track." Rising budget and trade deficits, among other factors, sparked a one-day 508-point run on the Dow Jones Industrial Average in October 1987 that shook the nation's confidence from coast to coast. Following the crash, the "right track" numbers dipped again (though these would bounce back). Pollsters detected other shifts in the public mood: between 1986 and 1987, the country's definition of "national security" began to change. No longer did Americans measure their nation's strength solely in terms of missiles, submarines, and armored divisions. Increasingly they told pollsters that America could be "secure" only if its economy was sound and its products were competitive. Some Americans linked the sense of misdirection to the growing evidence that America was falling behind Japan and Germany economically; others merely worried that whatever had once made America great had been lost in a microwaved, overleveraged MTV age.

Historian Arthur Schlesinger, Jr., has written that history can be measured in thirty-year intervals, during which the public mood swings back and forth between "public purpose," or liberalism, and "private interest," or conservatism. "There are already indications," Schlesinger said in December 1986, "that the private-interest conservative phase is running its course, including the outcome of the recent elections and the apparent weakening of the evangelicals. . . . All of this suggests that we're beginning to move into a time when public action will be dominant again as those who came of age in the Kennedy era take over political leadership." Democrats took heart from these predictions, thinking that history might finally deliver them an office they couldn't win by themselves.

Robert Teeter, George Bush's longtime pollster, saw it differently. Teeter realized that the nation was alienated by the excesses of the Reagan era but recognized that it was also unwilling to embrace the Democratic alternative. He felt that the public wanted only a minor course correction. Teeter sensed that the nation's general unease masked an overall satisfaction with individual voters' own personal lives. Surveys throughout 1987 and 1988 revealed that the public was unmoved by any single issue; Americans worried about drugs, crime, education, and the environment, but their concerns resembled a low-grade fever. Asked in 1987 to name "the most important problem facing the country today," only 12 percent of Americans agreed on the most-cited answer: "unemployment/recession"; no more than 9 percent named any other issue as the most important facing the nation. During 1988 these percentages actually decreased.

Teeter agreed that the public began to look inward during the final two years of the Reagan second term—but only so far. "The Reagan era was dominated by foreign and economic issues," Teeter said. "It had gone on so long and so well that by 1986 people became concerned about domestic issues. The country just shifted." But Teeter detected clear limits to this new concern for the country's well-being. One poll, taken in February 1987, revealed that the public broadly favored additional spending in only a few selected areas, such as on the environment, for the homeless, and on health care for the poor and aging. But support for additional spending on housing and food stamps, much less space exploration or the military, was much thinner.

In what is breezily described as "the national mood" lurked the potential to achieve false consensus. Teeter saw little agreement: even if voters knew some things were broken, few agreed on how best to make the repairs. Many voters feared the cures would make things worse: dumping more money on the poor and special interests might mean higher taxes, cuts in middle-class entitlement benefits like Medicare, or limits on such middle-class tax subsidies as the mortgage interest deduction. "We've only had fundamental changes five or six times in our two-hundred-year history," he said. "In 1980 there was this fundamental change. In 1984 people said, 'We like the change.' So by 1988 there was no desire to make a 180-degree turn. They said, 'What needed to be done is modify it, build on it.' They said, 'We like it, but what about the next eight years?' "

Already by 1988 a veteran of five national campaigns, Teeter liked to think of presidential elections as a simple counting game. On one level, getting elected was simply a matter of amassing the 270 electoral votes required by the Constitution. Republicans, by virtue of history and geography, started with a base of 150 to 200 electoral votes; Democrats began with a smaller base of roughly 100. In the scrimmage for the remaining electoral votes, six states—California, Illinois, Michigan, Missouri, New Jersey, and Ohio—were the key "battlegrounds" where the presidency was lost and won. In the beginning of

1988, Teeter figured Bush needed to win three of the six; Dukakis needed to win five. In gambling terms, the Massachusetts governor was drawing to an inside straight.

While the Dukakis campaign foolishly tried to contest Bush in every state, Teeter had no intention of spending much money or time in such traditionally Democratic states as Minnesota or Massachusetts —or doing much more than the minimum in states where Dukakis had no prayer of victory. He kept a list of all fifty states in his office, ranked in rough order of their likelihood to go Republican. It began with the obvious ones—Wyoming, New Hampshire, Nevada, and so on. Teeter kept track of the polls in each state and continually redrew a red line through the list where the Republican-leaning states totaled 270 electoral votes. The chart helped Teeter and Atwater identify where Bush and Quayle should and shouldn't campaign and where money should and shouldn't be spent. "A lot of people think presidential campaigns are national in scope," explained a Bush official later. "They're not. They're fifty one-state campaigns. Dukakis never figured this out."

"Getting to 270" required three steps: First, identify which voters constitute your base and secure them. Then, identify which voters constitute your opponent's base and attack them if it will energize your base or attract undecideds. Finally, determine which elements of the remaining swing voters are most persuadable in places and numbers sufficient to provide a majority when added to the candidate's base. Reduced to a mathematical equation, Teeter's strategy was relatively simple: Base + Swing = 270. Bush would make whatever promises were required to whatever groups of voters he needed to get to 270 and hope the whole contraption held together until the election.

THE RULING CLASS Bush began with his only real base: the roughly ten million Republicans who identified closely with Bush's background, experience, wealth, and breeding. If Ronald Reagan's base was in the party's right wing, Bush's home turf was peopled by voters who in various ways resembled the candidate. They were corporate executives, entrepreneurs, investors, country club members, professional men and women, wealthy retirees, and other members of the affluent class who had either climbed a long ladder to success or landed on the top rungs by happy accidents of birth or inheritance. Many of these voters had watched George Bush for more than twenty

20

years. They had seen his name floated for the vice presidency in 1968 and 1973, when Richard Nixon had briefly considered him to replace Spiro Agnew, and many had voted for him in 1980. Remarkably, many knew Bush, or had met him, or knew someone who had. They lived in plush Republican enclaves outside every large city in the nation, from Rye, New York, to Palos Verdes Estates, California, and they voted in unusually high proportion to their numbers. They represented roughly 10 percent of the electorate.

Bush was never more at ease on the stump than with the country club set. It was to this group that he could make his most genuine, heartfelt appeal. As president Bush would try to do the right thing, case by case. He wasn't passive or indolent, but he was a deeply reactive man who has always been less interested in doing anything specific as president than in just *being* president. He had entered politics without a desire to accomplish anything, but rather just to *serve*. He had wanted the job, as he once said, because he was taken with "the honor of it all."

These voters saw little wrong with the American condition. The 1980s had been good to them, and they had a natural stake in Bush's defense of the status quo. If Bush spoke disproportionately about foreign policy in campaign speeches, often stating flatly that overseas affairs would demand most of his time and energy, that was as it should be: most of the nation's biggest problems seemed far from home. Bush promised to steer America through an uncharted age when the Soviet Union would be changing, Europe would be consolidating, and foreign competition would be increasing. "Domestic policy can get us thrown out of office," he once said, quoting John Kennedy. "But foreign policy can get us killed."

Bush's approach to domestic affairs was in many cases a mere extension of his approach to foreign policy. His plan for economic growth turned as much on expansion of markets overseas as it did on a reduction in the capital gains tax. His plan for boosting American competitiveness overseas centered on seeking trade agreements with foreign leaders. Bush's plans for winning the war on drugs relied on expanded cooperation with governments of drug-producing countries. And he repeatedly mentioned that environmental improvements would need to be internationalized. Bush often said, "Building a better America doesn't stop at the water's edge." In many ways for Bush, it began there.

The ruling class did not expect much from Bush beyond steward-

21

ship, and Bush's original campaign promises were consequently neither dramatic nor particularly substantive. His announcement speech
carried few specifics beyond "outstanding education" and a revived
ethic of voluntarism. He promised to boost tax credits for oil and gas
drilling, signaling that he, far more than Ronald Reagan, believed in
using the tax code to favor particular industries and reward political
supporters. But on the whole, Bush could simply coast with this
group. "Initially," a senior administration official said later of the
precampaign days, "the instinct was not to do anything. The biggest
single factor was whether Ronald Reagan would turn the nation over
in good shape. If he did that, Bush was home free." Or as Bush
himself said in his campaign kickoff speech: "We don't need radical
new directions. We need strong and steady leadership. We don't need
to remake society, we just need to remember who we are."

THE RIGHT WING   Winning over the Republican party's right flank
would require more ardent courtship. Conservatives had never liked,
nor trusted, Bush. Reagan was their candidate, and everyone else was
just a cheap imitation. The vice president's Eastern Establishment
roots, his membership in the Trilateral Commission, and his failure to
project strength, especially on television, made him an imperfect
torch bearer for the Reagan Revolution. Bush had once backed the
right to an abortion and had decried Reagan's supply-side theories as
"voodoo economics." Those markers would be hard to ignore in a
fight for Republican nomination, particularly with such genuine conservatives as Pat Robertson, Jack Kemp, and Pete du Pont also in the
race.

Despite its image, the Republican Right was no more homogeneous
than any other part of the electorate. It comprised religious fundamen-
talists and evangelicals who had been active in politics for more than
a decade; it included old-fashioned "paleoconservatives" who had
long found the mainstream Republican party wanting in terms of backbone and direction; and, increasingly, younger, activist conservatives, many of them libertarians, who wanted to get the government
out of the expensive and, by their lights, counterproductive business
of housing, feeding, and supporting the underclass. Though remarkably diverse, these hard-line elements did possess some common
identifying marks. They were united in their opposition to government
regulations that were costly to business. Most, though not all, were

steadfast in their opposition to abortion, and all were virulently anti-tax. Members of both factions could be found in every state in the nation and in both rural and urban areas. They constituted roughly 10 percent of the electorate.

The Right was too important for Bush to write off or ignore—either in the Republican primaries or later. Atwater knew conservatives would exert a tremendous influence on the choice of nominee and had to be won over early and completely if they were to vote in large numbers in the fall. "The number one rule of politics," said Atwater, a man fond of rules, "is tend to your base first. Always protect it. Never, never abandon it." Starting in 1986, Atwater pushed Bush hard to starboard in a year-long campaign to bolster his conservative credentials. In a series of five carefully crafted speeches to five care-fully chosen groups, Bush began a pilgrimage that took him to all the stations of the right-wing cross. Bush backed constitutional amend-ments for a balanced budget and school prayer and two different constitutional amendments restricting the right to an abortion. He boned up on his religious reading so he could speak intelligently about the works of Robert Schuller, Adrian Rogers, and Jerry Falwell. Bush's top aides encouraged a religious writer named Doug Wead to author a book explaining Bush to conservatives, especially evangeli-cal Christians, who saw little of themselves in the Episcopalian vestry-man from St. Ann's of Kennebunkport. In the book, *Man of Integrity,* published in February 1988, Bush describes the peacemaking role of the United Nations as "minor at best" and professed that he was a born-again Christian. "If by 'born again' one is asking, 'Do you ac-cept Jesus Christ as your personal Savior?' then I could answer a clear-cut 'Yes,' " said Bush. "No hesitancy. No awkwardness."

Bush was no stranger to this sort of accommodation. He had em-braced the right wing to get his start in Texas politics in the early 1960s, when the nascent state Republican party was nearly controlled by the John Birch Society. Bush resisted the rightward shuffle in 1986, but Atwater explained repeatedly that it was simply the price of ad-mission. "He took a lot of heat for it," said a top 1988 campaign official, "and he didn't like it. But it had the effect of putting enough deposits in those accounts so that we didn't have to worry about them anymore."

The Right's continued devotion to all things Reaganesque hardened Bush's determination to say as little as possible of substance during the campaign. He knew that if he were elected he would have to clean up several megamesses left by Reagan. His own vow of loyalty—and his tacit, if not active, complicity in these fiascoes—made them the invisible agenda items of the Bush campaign. He kept quiet throughout the campaign about the savings and loan scandal and a mindboggling breakdown in nuclear weapons production facilities, each of which would require tens of billions of dollars to repair. Notwithstanding Bush's vow of tax celibacy, the deficit loomed over the next presidency. But his need to hold his right flank made these topics political unmentionables. Explained a senior Bush administration official later, "It was awkward for Bush to follow Reagan and claim success. We couldn't say that we'd be cleaning up the Reagan mess. We would just have to do it without talking about it."

Together, the country club set and the party's right wing represented the Republican party's most loyal core groups. But even with good turnout they constituted no more than about 25 percent of the vote. To win, Bush would have to reach out to two additional sets of swing voters, who together could provide the margin of victory.

THE REAGAN DEMOCRATS   Bush first needed to retain the loyalty of rebellious Democrats who had bolted their party in 1980 and 1984 to vote for Ronald Reagan. This shouldn't have been hard; though born and raised on Democratic party politics, Reagan Democrats had over the previous 20 years voted more and more reliably for Republican presidential nominees. The disaffection stemmed almost entirely from a volatile mix of economic and racial resentments. Like their hero, Reagan Democrats professed themselves weary of the Democratic party's high-tax, coddle-the-minorities policies. They had seen higher taxes consume a growing share of their weekly paychecks and resented the way it appeared to subsidize nonwhites on welfare. They had watched as busing to achieve desegregation and racial balance forced their children to go to schools far from the neighborhoods in which they lived—or brought blacks and other minorities into the all-white enclaves where they had scrimped and saved to live. And they resented what they perceived was a growing effort on the part of Democratic officials to put the interests of minorities—blacks, gays, radical feminists—ahead of the interests of the majority.

In general, these loosely affiliated voters were white, middle-aged children of the New Deal. They were, in the view of pollsters, liberal on economics but conservative on "values": they supported federal

24

entitlement programs from which they stood to gain, such as Medicare, Social Security, and unemployment benefits. They were at least prone to protectionism on trade matters and worried that the country was losing ground economically to the Japanese and Europeans. They were deeply patriotic and favored a strong defense. But they took a dim view of abortion, resented affirmative action, and saw nothing wrong with school prayer or the death penalty. They earned between $20,000 and $40,000 a year, in service or blue-collar jobs. They lived almost everywhere in the South, and in the North were clustered in suburbs like Parma, Ohio, outside of Cleveland; Warren, Michigan, outside of Detroit; and parts of Cook County, Illinois, outside Chicago's city limits. They were susceptible to emotional appeals, economic nationalism, anti-intellectualism, patriotism, and thinly veiled racism. They represented about 10 percent of the electorate.

They were also suspicious of Bush. The privately schooled vice president, after all, was nothing like Reagan. He lacked the Gipper's hardscrabble roots, his reflexive convictions, his dominating presence. The blue-blooded Bush grated their populist impulses. In fact, by nature Reagan Democrats were deeply suspicious of all Republicans. Many reported to pollsters in 1987 that they felt bad about abandoning the party in 1980 and 1984 and wanted a reason to come home. Atwater said that if Reagan Democrats "didn't see any differences or particular differences between the two candidates, guess what? They would have gone back and been Democrats again. They're always looking for an excuse to be, because they *are* Democrats."

Atwater moved in the spring of 1988 to retain them. He ordered Jim Pinkerton, his top opposition research aide, to dig up social and cultural "issues" that Bush could use to differentiate himself from Dukakis, label the governor a "Massachusetts liberal" and thus reposition the Democratic front-runner outside the mainstream of voters. "We need five or six issues, and we need them by the middle of May," Atwater recalled telling Pinkerton. "I gave him a three-by-five card and I said, 'You come back to me with this three-by-five card, but you can use both sides.'" Atwater was delighted with Pinkerton's excavations. Dukakis had vetoed a bill that would have made the Pledge of Allegiance mandatory in all Massachusetts schools; he was a member of the American Civil Liberties Union; he had delayed efforts to clean up Boston Harbor; and he favored gun control. When Atwater learned that the state of Massachusetts had allowed a black

25

convicted murderer named Willie Horton to take a weekend furlough from prison, during which he raped a white woman in Maryland, he said of Dukakis that he would "strip the bark off the little bastard" and make Americans believe Horton was the Democrat's "running mate."

Atwater's approach to the Reagan Democrats transformed the campaign from a race about issues into a race about values. For most voters, Atwater believed, choosing a president came down not to position papers and issue proposals, but to the cultural and personal cues a candidate transmits to explain to voters who he is and how he thinks. A candidate's "values," Atwater believed, told a voter more about how he would behave as president than a lengthy party platform. This was particularly true in a year when no single issue attracted voters' attention. Moreover, many swing voters felt unqualified to make an intelligent judgment about which candidate had the best approach to deficit reduction or helping the underclass. As a result, they based their vote instead on a candidate's overall approach to problems, his personal concerns and habits, his relationship with his spouse, or even the music and movies he liked. Bush's criticisms of Dukakis—expressed as patriotism, dislike of liberalism, belief in God, love of country music, and the like—resonated with an electorate that increasingly regarded a presidential election as a place to express its values, too. Or, as Bush once said, voting for president was like deciding who "you'd like to have sitting across from you at the dinner table."

By hammering for four months on the "big five," as the red meat issues were known inside Bush headquarters, Bush not only defined Dukakis in voters' minds as an unreconstructed liberal, but he transformed himself from a latent wimp into a hard-charging aggressor who could take on all comers and who would not be pushed around. Bush entered the 1988 race saddled with some of the highest negative ratings political pollsters had ever seen in a Republican front-runner. Eight years in Ronald Reagan's shadow had taken its toll: Bush was perceived as an uncaring, at-all-costs loyalist. As late as June of 1988 40 percent of the public had an unfavorable opinion of Bush, higher than Barry Goldwater's, George McGovern's, or Walter Mondale's at comparable times in earlier contests. The red meat attacks, while not capable of lowering Bush's negatives, drove Dukakis's to comparable levels, particularly with Reagan Democrats.

But they were not enough. Even if all the Reagan Democrats held,

Bush could not rely on them to provide the margin of victory. Between 1980 and 1988 they had declined as a percentage of the electorate. Thus, even as Bush worked hard to retain those who remained, Atwater and Teeter were positioning Bush to appeal to a second group of regular ticket splitters that was overtaking the Reagan Democrats in size and strength.

SUBURBAN INDEPENDENTS   If Reagan Democrats were liberal on economics and conservative on values, this group was their polar opposite: conservative on economics and liberal to moderate on values. Like the Reagan Democrats, the suburban independents were opposed to new taxes. But at that point their views of government and economics parted company. Where the Reagan Democrats generally believed in a large role for government, suburban independents were deeply suspicious of it. They questioned the need for a broad range of federal spending, from entitlements of all kinds to perks and high salaries for federal officials to wasteful defense spending. They didn't think much about Social Security beyond the dollars it sapped from their paychecks for what seemed like a pipe-dream public pension. Where the Reagan Democrats were working-class, the suburban independents were by and large professionals, managers, and small-business owners, with higher incomes, better educations, and white-collar jobs. Trade issues did not cut with them at all; protectionism seemed an escapist response to bigger problems like education and mismanagement of business. Most had attended college, and many drove small, foreign-made cars. Where the Reagan Democrats were likely to return to the Democratic fold in the event of a recession, the suburban independents believed themselves to be virtually recession-proof.

On the other hand, these voters were far more moderate than the Reagan Democrats on social issues. Though they were very tough on crime, many opposed the death penalty, believed in affirmative action, and backed the right to an abortion. Because so many had young children, they were concerned most about education, the environment, and child care. When Atwater, dying from a brain tumor, rushed a note to Bush in August of 1990 urging the president to sign a pending civil rights bill, it was this group of voters that Atwater was concerned about alienating. Civil rights was not a priority issue with independents, yet they wanted a candidate who shared their pride in

27

the racial gains made since the 1960s. Recalled Atwater's campaign deputy, Ed Rogers, "Lee always knew the Bush coalition was not necessarily the Reagan coalition. It had changed a lot in eight years. He was struck by how much the blue-collar group had shrunk. Their kids were not blue-collar."

The suburban independents were generally suspicious of politics and politicians. They had little use for political parties at all and would not support a candidate who they believed "played politics" with key issues. If the Reagan Democrats suffered from perhaps too much pride, this group, being more self-conscious, seemed to feel too keenly America's shortcomings; they were embarrassed by Vietnam, by Watergate, by Carter's fumbling foreign policy, by Reagan's fumbling manner in general. They did not want to be embarrassed again. They lived in better neighborhoods or houses than the Reagan Democrats, but often in the same county or city. Atwater at times called them "our yuppie base." If they weren't so antipolitical, they might be known as moderate Republicans. Depending on age, income, and politics, they represented anywhere from 12 to 20 percent of the electorate.

To woo these voters, Bush adopted a fourth pose. After careful study of their hopes and fears, he broke with Reagan in late summer of 1988 and unleashed an array of programs designed to improve the environment, education, and general welfare. Bush's "kinder, gentler" agenda was aimed squarely at the independents in the suburbs. In the space of six weeks Bush proposed new Clean Air Act amendments and released proposals to reduce acid rain, halt destruction of the nation's wetlands, end the contamination of the country's groundwater, and ban ocean dumping of medical wastes. He called for federal tax subsidies to support child care, vowed to "fully fund" Head Start, unveiled a college savings program, and pledged to offer broader Medicaid coverage to the poor.

One campaign official explained the burst of initiatives more pragmatically. "These issues were specifically designed to say 'If we stick our head in the sand, suburbanites are going to vote against us. But if we do these issues, they might not.' "

As Bush said repeatedly throughout the fall, "We are the change."

"Totally Schizo"

By late August, Bush was moving adroitly in several directions at once. His base intact, he spent most of his time after the Republican convention chasing the two groups of swing voters. On August 25, for example, he flew to San Antonio to round up Reagan Democrats. In a moment of relative candor, Bush explained that he needed to convince blue-collar voters that he shared their concerns. "Although I've said—I'll repeat it—it has not been difficult to be vice president, but in doing my job that way, there has been a sublimation of my passions and my convictions. . . . What I have to do is make them understand I really feel this in my heart." After a barge ride down the San Antonio River, Bush told one thousand sweat-drenched supporters that Dukakis was bad news for Texans. "I can't help but feel that his fervent opposition to the pledge is symbolic of an entire attitude summed up in four little letters: ACLU. . . . He says—here's an exact quote—he says, 'I am a card-carrying member of the ACLU.' Well, I am not and I never will be." Bush went on, citing another magazine article that quoted Dukakis as saying that "only the police and the military" should own firearms. "That is not the American way," said Bush. "That is not the Texas way. And I feel just the opposite." Bush then turned to abortion and voluntary school prayer. "I believe in the right to life," said Bush, "and encouraging adoption instead of abortion, and he's on the other side of that." He charged that his Democratic rival "seems to oppose the development of every new weapon since the slingshot."

But at the same time Bush was wooing Reagan Democrats in San Antonio, his advisers were busy ripping up his briefing book in Washington. In a single meeting that morning, James Baker and Richard Darman jettisoned Bush's stand against parental leave and adopted a more moderate approach favoring voluntary leave policies. They tossed out his standing opposition to raising the minimum wage and signaled that a small rise might be acceptable. They also completed the finishing touches on a speech later that week in which Bush would finally break with Ronald Reagan on the environment. The specifics of the proposals were far less important than their general thrust: Bush, not Dukakis, was positioning himself as the agent of change for a group of voters who were, at best, only fuzzy about how much change they themselves favored.

Bush would spend entire days juggling the various blocs in his coalition, winking at one while courting the other. He had to remain
loyal to his country club and conservative Republicans while wooing
both the Reagan Democrats and the kinder and gentler souls in the
suburbs. There was room for cross appeals: many of the same hot-
button issues Bush used to woo Reagan Democrats gratified the Republican Right. Similarly, many of the education and environment
initiatives aimed at moderates in the suburbs resonated with the president's affluent Republican base. Bush's push for yuppie philanthropy
—bidding high school students to volunteer for a year before college
—was carefully calibrated to appeal both to the moderates who disliked the selfish tone of the Reagan era and those in his ruling class
base with a history of noblesse oblige and a resistance to paying for
more welfare programs. Explained one official at the time, "There are
a whole lot of issues where the politics are mixed or difficult to parse,
and on some issues, Bush is as conflicted internally as his coalition
is."

For a time Bush would spend mornings in the kinder, gentler mode,
pursuing the independents with a weird amalgam of pragmatism and
idealism. Bush exhorted a breakfast audience in Sacramento on October 4 about the need for young Americans "who wear fifty-dollar
jeans and forty-dollar sneakers" to get involved in the lives of inner-
city kids. After polls showed that voters believed Dukakis was more
caring than Bush, the vice president mused aloud about the "sense of
unease" many better-off Americans had expressed about their own
children's dim awareness of minorities and the poor. "I want our
affluent to help our poor. I want the young men and women of our
tree-lined suburbs to get on a bus, or the subway, or the metro, and
go into the cities where the want is," he said. "We have prosperity,
and we have peace, but we also have unfinished business."

In the afternoon, Bush waved good-bye to the moderate voters in
the Sacramento Valley and flew to more arid Riverside, California,
and Reagan Democrat country, where he was endorsed by a local
police association and predicted that the "liberal governor" of Massachusetts would raise taxes and bring about economic doom. "Let
me give you some advice," Bush added. "If you fall overboard in
Boston Harbor, keep your mouth closed." This yo-yoing led cartoonist Garry Trudeau to introduce his fans to Bush's evil twin, "Skippy,"
a disembodied character who said all of the nasty things his more
gallant brother never would. Even Bush's advisers were somewhat

30

embarrassed to watch as the vice president alternated each day from
Dr. Jekyll to Mr. Hyde. "We were totally schizo," said one top campaign official.

Bush's television ads reflected this split. For every independently
produced ad featuring the face of the furloughed Willie Horton, the
Bush camp aired a slow-motion shot of Bush cuddling his grandchildren. None was more disarming than one that featured Bush's young
granddaughter Ellie LeBlond. As gentle music played in the background, the adorable little girl ran across the lawn at Walker's Point
into "Gampy's" arms. The screen dissolved to Bush walking with
other children, then catching Ellie in his arms—all in slow motion.
Then the screen faded to Barbara Bush, who reported this about her
husband: "I wish people could see him as I see him. I always loved
the time someone said to George, 'How can you run for the presidency? You don't have a constituency.' And George said, 'You know,
I have a great big family and thousands of friends.' And that's what
he has."

In this way, Bush's withering attacks on Dukakis's values were
doubly effective. Reagan Democrats might suspect Bush of trying to
cut their Medicare benefits or make the workplace less safe. But since
Dukakis might raise their taxes, the two men were awash in economic
issues. But because Bush was in touch with the Reagan Democrats'
values, he was holding nearly half of them in the GOP fold. Bush's
ads had an opposite but equally salient effect on suburban independents: he had matched Dukakis on the kinder, gentler agenda step for
step, but what tipped the scale in his favor was his firm "no taxes"
rhetoric. By late September the unlikely coalition was largely in place.
Bush had moved from seventeen points behind Dukakis in late July
and early August to more than ten points ahead by mid-September.

But over the next month Bush's multiple-personality act began to
wear a little thin. The various messages began to clash, as Bush's
kinder, gentler themes warred with the tone of his pit bull attacks.
Bush was running one of the nastiest negative campaigns in memory.
There was also a question of credibility, which bothered the independents in particular. The man who was born in Massachusetts, reared
in Greenwich, who summered in Maine and had wintered in South
Carolina, was "born country"? The man who had attended Andover
and Yale was damning the elites at Harvard? The politician who had
asked a waitress in New Hampshire several months earlier for "just a
splash more" coffee was now campaigning with macho men Chuck

31

Norris and Arnold Schwarzenegger? When skeptical reporters asked Bush to describe his favorite television show, his answer aptly summed up his cynical strategy: "I'd tell you 'Hee Haw,' but you wouldn't believe me and it's not on anymore anyway."

In late October the polls began to move again—this time against Bush. The combination of his relentless attacks on Dukakis and his mixed messages began to take a toll. Simultaneously Dukakis seized on a populist theme after weeks of listless campaigning, hammering the Reagan-Bush era as self-indulgent and making an issue of Bush's negative tactics. Polls, particularly in Teeter's crucial battleground states, began to tighten.

Bush was stumbling over his own message. In Missouri, for example, Bush had inundated voters with a bewildering array of mixed messages. To hard-core Republicans, particularly in the southern reaches of the state, Bush was pitching the party line: a mix of pro-defense and anti–gun control messages. To the state's large pro-life community, he was preaching strong moral foundations and a clear antiabortion message. He had also targeted moderates in the suburbs of St. Louis and Kansas City with literature touting his proposals on education and the environment. It was a volatile mixture, and it began to bubble ominously: what was in the mail didn't always jibe with what was on the television and the radio. Bush's unabated attacks on Dukakis did not sound kind or gentle. As the campaign wound down to the final days, sourness seemed Bush's dominant theme. Reagan Democrats, lured by Dukakis's populism, began to peel away; independents, confused by Bush's attack-dog tone, began having second thoughts. Explained Tony Feathers, Bush's Missouri organizer, "A lot of people just started to think that the bashing had gone on too long. Bush was relentless and maybe didn't need to be."

Atwater responded by scheduling a last minute campaign stop by Bush in suburban St. Louis on the day before the election. But the same thing was happening elsewhere. Illinois and Pennsylvania were closing to within five points. Three days before the election, Richard Wirthlin's tracking surveys for the California Republican party showed Bush slipping to two points behind Dukakis in the Golden State—statistically still a dead heat, but scary nonetheless. There, too, Bush's attacks on Dukakis for neglecting the mess in Boston Harbor and his support for prison furloughs—ads that had virtually destroyed Dukakis's 17-point lead two months before—were now beginning to backfire. Bush's California organizers realized this and pulled an ad slamming Dukakis for opposing the death penalty and replaced it with a simple no-frills spot on Bush's crime record. Bill Lacy, Bush's campaign manager in California, scheduled joint appearances by Bush and Ronald Reagan in Long Beach and San Diego in a last-ditch attempt to boost turnout.

Thus, with just hours to go before the polls opened, key states worth more than one hundred electoral votes suddenly moved into the too-close-to-call column. Not even Atwater was confident. As he commented to co-workers in Washington the night before Bush flew to St. Louis, "If this sucker lasted forty-eight hours longer, I'm not sure we would make it."

"That's Over"

Bush won walking away, posting 48.8 million votes to Dukakis's 41.8 million. He won forty states to Dukakis's ten, taking 426 of 538 electoral college votes. The president held his base, the Right, nearly half of the Reagan Democrats, and a broad majority of the suburbanites. Bush rolled over Dukakis in rural areas, attracted many new voters, and despite rumors of an incipient gender gap, did as nearly well among women as among men. In some states Bush even reached deep in Democratic turf and snared half of all voters earning between $12,500 and $25,000.

But George Bush was no Ronald Reagan. In only four high-growth states—Arizona, Georgia, Nevada, and New Hampshire—did Bush best Reagan's 1984 tally. Even against the amateurish Dukakis campaign, the GOP under Bush attracted 5.4 million fewer voters than it did under Reagan; in some states, such as Oklahoma, Iowa, and West Virginia, Bush dropped more than 20 points to Reagan's 1984 tally. In key states, such as Texas, Illinois, California, and New York, more than 400,000 Reagan votes jumped ship to Dukakis. Bush suffered enormous defections in farm states—even in those he carried. Compared with Reagan's showing in 1984, Bush dropped 18 points in Kansas, 17 points in North Dakota, 13 points in Nebraska, and 15 points in Illinois. He lost five hundred counties Reagan had captured. In a memo prepared for the Bush 1992 reelection campaign, Richard Nixon would note that a swing of 566,000 votes in ten states would have deprived Bush of victory. Stated Nixon, "We should not base our hopes for victory in November on the assumption that Bush had a landslide in 1988."

Bush emerged from the campaign not so much as a spokesman for the country's aspirations, but as a shrewd oracle of its uncertain mood and conflicting desires. He had come to represent different things to different people. To traditional Republicans, comprising business interests and the country club set, Bush was a card-carrying member in perpetually good standing. To conservatives he was an acceptable, if imperfect, torch carrier for the Reagan revolution. To disaffected Democrats, particularly older and ethnic refugees from the party, Bush was a take-no-prisoners American who wasn't afraid to use force against outlaws at home and abroad. And to moderate independents Bush was the kinder, more competent chief executive.

The many faces Bush adopted to woo his winning coalition would place considerable restraints on his presidency. As he sought to hold the line against government intrusion in the lives of Americans, he would run headlong into the demand for change from his new supporters. As he tried to make marginal improvements in the health and welfare of Americans, he would take heat from conservative members of his coalition. When he opted to do nothing at all, he would come under pressure from all sides to do more. Bush would slalom back and forth between political poles to maintain his fragile coalition. It was the legacy of his campaign.

Within hours of his victory Bush began to pivot, wheeling from "politics" to "governing." To Bush, the two are as different as the Civil War and Reconstruction. What happened during the campaign had nothing to do with what would take place in the White House because "politics" exists in a realm entirely separate from "governing." Politics—the silly, ignoble, unpleasant things one has to do or say to get elected—was the price one paid for being in public life; it was what you had to do to win. The only goal of campaigns, and the disagreeable politics they demanded, was victory.

The reward for wallowing in the dirt of politics was the consent of the governed. If, after four years, the public disapproved of his performance, Bush recognized, it could vote him out of office. "I can't keep everybody happy," he admitted early in his term. "I have the underpinning on knowing that I was elected, and if the people don't like it, then they're not going to elect me again. So you have, you get a certain comfort level, even in this big a job, from that fundamental little civics exercise. Not that you want to get arrogant about it."

The dichotomy Bush saw held several advantages. What a candidate did, or said, along the campaign trail shouldn't be held against him because voters themselves don't take such actions or comments seriously. Instead, Bush believes, voters recognize that manipulation of symbols is part of the game. They expect politicians to wrap themselves in the American flag. They cut candidates plenty of slack to say one thing but do another. As a result, Bush calculated, hard feelings would pass. On the morning after the election, reporters asked Bush to explain how he would unify the country after the sour campaign. "The American people," Bush said, "are wonderful when it comes to understanding when a campaign ends and the world of business begins. . . . This campaign is over."

No sooner had the 1988 campaign ended than Bush dropped the themes he had employed and adopted a conciliatory tone and style. Gone were the ugly advertisements, the demagogic mudslinging, even many of the advisers who had helped him win the job he'd sought for decades. Surrounding himself with grandchildren and puppies, he would undergo a personal makeover designed to blot out the memory of a sour campaign. Several weeks later Bush dismissed the campaign completely. "That's history," he said on the eve of his inauguration. "That doesn't mean anything anymore."

2

"I REALLY LOVE
MY JOB"

Americans sensed that they had elected a different sort of president when George Bush let it slip that he showered with his dog.

This was something new: an emperor who admitted that he (at least for a few minutes every morning) had no clothes. Coming amid countless other hints and reminders—most of them from Bush himself—that the forty-first president of the United States was not a bit like his predecessor, the disclosure was not as startling as it might have been. Bush, America knew, or would soon learn, owned a bowling ball. He hated broccoli. He delighted in organizing gag photos. He had trouble finishing his sentences. He had a fancy estate at Kennebunkport, Maine, which had been in his family for generations, but he ran errands to town and invited just about everyone to lunch. He preferred country to classical music. Like a lot of Americans, Bush took in baseball games in the summer, went fishing in August, disappeared on a hunting trip after Christmas. The anecdotes about Bush's "normal" habits tumbled forth from White House staffers like so many talking points. Even if not all of this was genuine—and some of it wasn't— the message was obvious: the president is a regular Joe. "This is the first normal guy to hold this office in twenty-five years," a senior official said.

"A Certain Liberation"

Of course, there was nothing normal about a guy who had been running for president for twenty years. But "normal" was a word heard frequently around the White House during the first six months of 1989 to describe the new occupant. Bush didn't have Jack Kennedy's embarrassing proclivities. He lacked Lyndon Johnson's crippling ego. Nothing in Bush could compare with the dark moods of his old mentor, Richard Nixon. He was neither as dour nor as idealistic as Carter. But most of all, "normal" was White House code for "not Ronald Reagan."

For the first several months of his presidency, Bush's task was tricky: while he had to distinguish himself from Ronald Reagan, he couldn't criticize his predecessor without criticizing himself. He had campaigned as the experienced co-pilot and took credit for the prosperity of the Reagan era. Moreover, Bush did not intend to steer the country on a different course. White House chief of staff John Sununu called Bush's succession a "friendly takeover." Bush said in April 1989, "We didn't come in here throwing the rascals out." Nonetheless, Americans had grown weary of the Reagan era, with its trademark mismanagement of government and the environment, its shallow excesses, its legacy of debt; although the new president had no interest in dismantling the house that Reagan built, he knew he would need to do some renovating: to sand down the roughest edges and slap on a new coat of paint. That Bush intended to do so little substantively different only heightened the need to distance himself stylistically from his predecessor.

This he did quickly. He ordered the Secret Service to stop his motorcade at traffic lights and slip through the federal city silently, without sirens. He went jogging at 5:30 in the morning and turned up in his office, ready to work, before 7 A.M. Bush and his wife went for walks many nights, slipping down to the South Lawn to chat with tourists through the wrought-iron fence. Reagan had been gone but a few days before Bush declared "National Ethics Week" and gave his first post-inaugural speech on the proper behavior for public officials. Asked if this was an implicit judgment of the Reagan team's ethical lapses, Bush replied with a curt "No."

Bush's strategy was simple: soar where Reagan had stumbled, exude competence where Reagan had displayed incompetence. In the three months between his election and his inauguration, Bush gave more press conferences than Reagan had in the previous two and a half years. After eight years of Reagan's uninformed and fanciful answers, Bush's performance at these sessions seemed comparatively miraculous. He was well informed, thoughtful, and funny. With only ten minutes' preparation, and often with none at all, he could handle questions on almost any subject. By 1989 he had turned this forum into his preferred lever of leadership. Press conferences became Bush's way of showing his stuff and signaling to Americans that their country was in good hands.

The subtext of Bush's briefings was more important than the answers themselves. With each question he fielded, he was telling Americans, "Reagan is gone, I am here. And I know what I'm talking about." White House pollsters discovered in focus groups during 1989 that nothing Bush did in his first year of office impressed Americans as much as his handling of questions in presidential press conferences. David Demarest, the president's communications director, later explained, "Those sessions were about candor, about being on top of his job, about humor, about being knowledgeable, about comfort and banter with the press and being confident, about liking it. Those qualities are the qualities that got through." After watching Bush during the transition, Ron Brown, the Democratic party chairman, was sobered: "Our party has a lot to be worried about," he said.

Although Americans had watched Bush dart on and off the national stage for nearly twenty years, they saw a very different person during these first months in office. For eight years, as vice president, Bush had placed himself under wraps while Reagan ran up the budget deficit, trashed the environment, and secretly diverted proceeds from the Iranian arms sales to the Nicaraguan contras. Bush said later that he opposed, to varying degrees, the excesses of the Reagan era, but he never let his personal views as vice president become widely known. One top Bush official marveled at Bush's discipline during those eight years. "When you realize how he runs his administration now, and you recognize what an anathema the previous administration must have been, then you recognize what an extraordinary act of self-discipline his eight years of loyalty and silence under Ronald Reagan was."

Bush maintained a brave front all those years, despite endless insults about his bland subservience. He was called a "lap dog" by George Will and a "wimp" on the cover of *Newsweek*. Cartoonist

Garry Trudeau accused Bush of placing his manhood in a "blind trust." But Bush saw in his forbearance not spinelessness, but fealty and self-control. To him, the eight-year straitjacket was a test he had passed, not a humiliation he had suffered. He had survived the ordeal, his loyalty to Reagan unquestioned and his links to the right wing strengthened. The sacrifice had been well worth it, for the reward for his patience was the presidency itself. While his critics condemned his performance as vice president, Bush believed that the American people watched him closely, admired his loyalty, and then rewarded him based on his steady, low-profile performance.

Thus, being elected president was emancipating for Bush, and he celebrated his new freedom with exuberance. Bush attacked his job in almost maniacal fashion. Consider "the longest day" of Bush's presidency. His official presidential papers commemorate April 25, 1989, as follows: "The president declared that a major disaster existed in Texas as a result of severe thunderstorms and flooding that occurred March 28 to 29. He directed the Federal Emergency Management Agency to provide assistance to supplement state and local recovery efforts. In the afternoon, the president attended a baseball game between the California Angels and the Baltimore Orioles at Anaheim Stadium in Anaheim, California." In fact, after signing the relief papers in the morning, Bush attended a fund-raising breakfast in San Jose, California, then moved to a speech and fund-raising luncheon in Silicon Valley. He flew to Orange County to view the confiscated ranch of a busted drug dealer; a meeting with Hispanic Republicans at UCLA followed. As reporters and aides slumped visibly, Bushy, crisp and chipper as ever, ordered in choppers to take his party to the Angels game, where he ate everything in sight: boiled shrimp, nachos, beer, hot dogs, and popcorn.

He was restless to the point of being, in his own words, "too hyper." Bush wore out his aides and the reporters who trailed him. One Sunday in Los Angeles in 1991, the president was in such a hurry to leave church and get on the tennis court that he left behind a military aide toting the briefcase that contains codes for launching a nuclear strike. Aides yearned for a few days off to go home, pay bills, do laundry, and cut the grass. Pool reporters on *Air Force One* often just ran out of questions for the president on flights home to Washington, permitting Bush to digress into long monologues about puppies and exercise machines. Fitzwater, in a March 1989 speech was only half joking when he told his audience that Bush "got home from the

39

inauguration after midnight, and held an open house at 8 A.M., led a tour of the mansion at eight-fifteen, shook hands with tourists for a half hour, was in the Oval Office at nine, held a press conference at nine-fifteen, and by ten had the press shouting, 'Stop him before he speaks again!' " One Herblock cartoon depicted a female television correspondent catching some badly needed sleep at the White House while Bush, hovering over her, says, "I'm here to answer your questions." As a state dinner for Poland's Lech Walesa was winding down in March 1991, Bush slipped upstairs, changed clothes, and went jogging around the South Lawn while some of his guests continued to enjoy his hospitality on the state floor of the White House. (Few top aides were surprised when, less than two months later, doctors discovered Bush's thyroid was overactive.)

What Americans saw in the first six months of the Bush presidency was the man old friends had always prized—a generous, winning, high-spirited host. "What you saw before was fake," said one old pal. "This is the real thing." Bush himself admitted that the election had been a kind of release. "There's been a certain liberation," he said a few days before he was sworn in. "When you're vice president, you vow to conduct yourself in a certain way . . . it's less clear to outside observers what you're really like. When you're calling the shots, it's easier."

Three years later Bush was able to be a bit more forthcoming about his imprisonment as he watched his own vice president, Dan Quayle, take some of the slings and arrows that had just a few years before been aimed at him. "My view on Don Quayle is he's done a good job. He is getting the most unfair rap from his critics of anybody that's been in this job. And you're talking to the wimp. . . . And now some that saw that we can react when the going gets tough maybe have withdrawn that allegation. But it wasn't pleasant. The job doesn't lend itself to high profile and decision making. It lends itself to loyally supporting the president of the United States, giving him your best judgment, and then when the president makes a decision, supporting it."

Less Is More

Bush's eight years at Reagan's side taught him a great deal about how to be president and about how *not* to be president. He learned that a well-liked commander in chief, which Reagan was for most of his two terms, would be forgiven many a political gaffe or unpopular policy initiative. Bush also learned that a president who promised too much, who raised expectations for sweeping change, would, like Reagan, in the end be seen to fall short of the mark. So Bush set out to endear himself to the American public while at the same time working to lower its expectations both of him and his presidency.

To the task, Bush brought something special: an ironic, self-mocking approach to the job. He went through the motions of being president that tradition dictated, but often with his tongue visibly planted in his cheek. He had always had a good sense of humor: he mocked his own stultifying oratory at the Republican convention in 1988 with the wooden paraphrase of Dirty Harry, "Make my twenty-four-hour time period." He cued up exploding golf balls made of chalk for unsuspecting visitors at Kennebunkport. On Halloween 1988 he donned a rubber George Bush mask and walked through his campaign plane exhorting passengers to "Read my lips! Read my lips!"

As president Bush went beyond self-effacement to self-parody. He resisted what he called the "show-biz" aspects of his job: when NBC News came to film a "Day in the Life" of Bush in 1989, the president greeted Tom Brokaw in the Oval Office and, while the videotape rolled, launched into a conversation with the unnamed, unknown, and obviously unseen camera crew—a gesture to remind viewers that Ronald Reagan's successor regarded such half-staged charades as silly. When Bush shook hands in crowds, news photographers placed behind him by White House advance teams would ask him to turn around and smile so they could shoot something more appealing than the back of his head. Bush often refused, or jerked his head back and forth, thinking it rude to greet one person while he looked at someone else. Visiting the Acropolis in 1991, Bush turned to photographers and asked, "You want your basic Parthenon shot?" Six months later he got down on his hands and knees and crawled into an oversize wooden doll house to play "telephone" with four-year-olds at a Head Start center in Maryland. Afterward he deadpanned, "I learned an awful lot about bathtub toys."

Winking at the political stunts expected of a president became, for Bush, a kind of theater in itself—a new kind of political pantomime. For nearly every time Bush noted the respect he had for the office, he would do or say something that suggested, sometimes explicitly, that he didn't take the job too seriously. He once gathered his advisers in the Oval Office, placed a crystal ball on his desk, and widened his eyes over the orb as a photographer snapped the picture with a Polaroid. (An aide later forwarded the snap to a *Time* reporter, saying, "The president wanted you to know how he *really* makes decisions.") At Kennebunkport in August 1991, Bush said he would spend his vacation playing "a good deal of golf . . . a good deal of tennis, a good deal of horseshoes, a good deal of fishing, a good deal of running —and some reading. I have to throw that in for the intellectuals out there."

Bush was inventing the postmodern presidency, pointing with near perfect nineties irony to the little absurdities that went with the job of being the most powerful man on earth. Melanie Griffith, the movie star and actress-wife of Don Johnson, recalls standing on the road outside her home in Aspen, Colorado, and watching the president's motorcade go by one day in August 1990. In fact, it wasn't just *any* day; it was August 2, 1990—the day after Saddam Hussein invaded Kuwait. But Bush, seeing Griffith, stopped his car, activated the special speaker in the rear of his limousine—Bush calls this device "Mr. Microphone"—and barked at Griffith's one-year-old daughter, "What's the matter, Dakota? Never seen a talking car before?" Bush invited Dana Carvey, whose "Saturday Night Live" imitations of the president were frighteningly convincing, to the White House. There, during a fifteen-minute Oval Office chat, Bush and Carvey stood in front of the massive fireplace and talked simultaneously at each other, one being Bush, the other doing Bush. When Carvey began chopping the air with one hand and talking about "Daaaan Quaaaayle—getting stronger, learning ev-er-y daaay," Bush doubled over in laughter. By the end of 1991 Bush was doing imitations-of-Carvey-doing-imitations-of-Bush during televised press conferences, whipping back his hand and sometimes suggesting that he had begun to resemble his impersonator.

This downsizing of the presidency served a dual political purpose: Americans came to like Bush and to expect less of him. It was as if to say "Like me? Trust me." And it was hard not to like a man who, surrounded by grim-faced Secret Service agents, howled with laughter when he played the twenty-dollar-bill-on-the-end-of-a-string trick on unsuspecting waiters at the Chinese embassy; who would greet visitors to the Oval Office by placing a wind-up mechanical bumblebee on the floor and letting it buzz around; who walked around the White House with a voice-activated stuffed monkey that socked itself on the head whenever the commander in chief began to talk. Bush's image-as-anti-image dance appealed to many voters who, even if they regarded Bush's priorities as misplaced, could see that he was at least tuned in to their sarcastic David Letterman sensibilities. Bob Teeter noted that many baby boom voters who neither agreed with nor voted for him seemed nonetheless to appreciate Bush's self-conscious skepticism about his job. "Bush is very appealing from a stylistic point of view," Teeter said. "He acts like a president when he has to, and when he should lighten up, he lightens up."

Indeed, the personality offensive worked so well that Americans began to forgive Bush his shortcomings. Halfway through his first term even Democratic pollsters admitted with some frustration that voters were attributing few of the nation's problems to Bush himself. But most significant, Bush's overall approval rating was almost always higher than his narrower showings on his handling of the economy, the environment, or education. Though Americans retained numerous criticisms about the country, griping about economy, crime, and the general irrelevance of government and politics, they were reluctant to pin much blame on Bush. Pollster Paul Maslin, who held focus groups around the country in June 1991 in order to probe Bush's liabilities for House Majority Leader Richard Gephardt, who was then pondering a run at the White House, discovered few weak spots. According to Maslin, voters saw so many political and economic problems on the national and international horizons that they seemed to root for Bush simply because he was earnest, cheery, and likeable. "What we hear a lot of," said Maslin, "is that 'at least he's trying.' They like him. They don't feel great about him. But they don't think he's personally corrupt. And he's benefited from the contrast with Reagan. He is more moderate, he isn't extreme, and everybody loves Barbara Bush as much as they hated Nancy Reagan.

"And when you ask them if he bears any responsibility for these problems, they say, 'What can one man do?' They've lowered their expectations." As his old friend from Yale, Thomas "Lud" Ashley, liked to say, "It's easy to underestimate George Bush because he's so damned genteel and nice."

43

To be sure, if Americans underestimated Bush, it was in part because Bush worked so hard at it. When he emerged the surprise victor of the Iowa caucuses in 1980, he told reporters in an unusually candid moment that he would disparage any national poll that suggested he was ahead. "If somebody comes out with something that shows me way out front, I'll be poor-mouthing it. I'll say 'This is ridiculous. God, how could you expect that from a little guy like me?' " Eight years later, as president, Bush would play down the significance of big speeches just hours before he delivered them. He claimed that he had no agenda for meetings and summits at which he would later unveil twelve-point proposals. In fact, sandbagging the press was standard operating procedure for Bush. "Politics is no profession," Bush once wrote, "for people who don't like surprises."

In a further attempt to diminish expectations and shrink the role of the presidency, Bush made a concerted effort to lower his public profile—which meant cutting back on the amount of time he spent on television. Like most Americans, George Bush likes to watch TV. By his own admission he watches "quite a bit." He sits in his private study upstairs at the White House and video surfs, flipping through the fifty-seven-channel television system by remote control. But Bush's is no ordinary set—nor ordinary remote control. Inside a large wooden cabinet are four normal-size screens mounted around a fifth big-screen model. Each screen comes with its own, always loaded videocassette recorder. ("So you can record all four going at once while you're watching," Bush once explained.) The contraption can be controlled by a giant, clipboard-size remote-control device or a combination of any of *eleven* other, smaller clickers. The arrangement has been known to embarrass the president: "I don't like to tell you this," he once said, describing the setup in his usual herky-jerky syntax, "because you'll think I'm into some weird TV freak here." His wife accused him of watching too much: "Not too much, but plugged into TV too often, put it that way," he allowed. When Ellen Warren of Knight-Ridder News Service happened upon the setup during a mid-1991 tour of the White House residence, guide Barbara Bush described it as the ultimate boy's toy. "This," she said, "is why wives leave their husbands."

The miniature version of the "Nightline" set helped Bush keep track of how his administration was being beamed to voters. But it was also a daily reminder of the medium's power. TV had always been a problem for Bush. In a way he was too real for TV, too "hot" for a medium that seemed to favor a calm and cool persona. Bush had trouble sitting still. He waved his hands and arms too much. He was given to awkward gestures and ill-timed smiles. His tortured syntax, charming perhaps in conversation, was baffling on the tube. The combination made him seem more like a loopy, distracted, jargon-mad creature than the leader of the free world. During practice sessions for debates during the 1988 campaign, media wizard Roger Ailes despaired of Bush's mannerisms, which rather than conveying an image of strength often made him look a bit daffy.

But because he had campaigned as a caretaker and arrived in office with only the most marginal mandate for change, Bush had no need to carve out a large public role for himself. A high-profile presidency would only raise public expectations at a time when any president would be hard-pressed to satisfy the country's complex and conflicting political demands. Bush instead sought to dial back his exposure, particularly on substantive issues, trimming the role of the presidency in the lives of most Americans. In this way he was making a virtue of necessity: his inability to affect a swaggering leadership style dovetailed with his minimalist agenda.

Before his inauguration, the president-elect and Marlin Fitzwater huddled to discuss ways to showcase his strengths but guard against overexposure. In an eyes-only memo, Fitzwater suggested that Bush refuse to make statements at the three or four daily photo opportunities that clog his daily schedule. He proposed holding frequent press conferences in the middle of the day, providing ample access to reporters without spending too much time on America's TV screens. Bush abandoned any attempt to strike a daily pose, set a weekly theme, or even win spot news coverage from the print and broadcast reporters who cover the White House. Television coverage was banned when Bush met privately with police officers, Amish families, victims of drug crimes, business leaders, and various constituency groups. Bush traveled frequently with no purpose other than to meet and speak to an out-of-town group. He even attempted to travel around the Washington, D.C., area without reporters in tow—and occasionally succeeded.

At the same time, the White House made sure that news stories, which in the Reagan era emanated from the West Wing, trickled out of cabinet agencies. In a speech to the National Press Club in March 1989, Fitzwater said, "There are not enough stories out of the White House to keep one honest person doing an honest day's work. What's happened is this: An exaggerated preoccupation with the White House has forced stories to come from the president that should be coming from the secretary of state, the secretary of defense, or any one of the other cabinet officials who help run the government. And so, one of my pieces of advice to those who really want to improve the quality of White House journalism is back off! Let real people do real work.''

It often seemed that some presidential scholar somewhere was releasing new findings each month showing that Bush was getting less network airtime than previous presidents. The numbers were dramatic: in his first twenty-two months in office Bush made the evening news a third as often as his predecessor. One survey by the Center for Media and Public Affairs announced that his dog, Millie, grabbed ''more airtime than three cabinet secretaries.'' National news coverage ceased to matter—a sentiment that drove network TV producers berserk. The problem was no less acute for print reporters, who found themselves no longer leading the newspapers every day but instead chasing quotes and doing legwork for their colleagues. *The Washington Post*'s David Hoffman, the reporter whom Bush was said to fear most, hung a mock book cover over his desk early in the term that read ''Sidebar to History: I came. I saw. I inserted.'' David Lauter, a *Los Angeles Times* correspondent, mulled the creation of ''the Poppy,'' to be awarded to the print reporter who generated the fewest column inches for the most miles traveled with Bush.

There were advantages for Bush in this approach. He believed that too much time on television would only raise public expectations about what he could accomplish. Reagan, after all, was on television all the time. The constant exposure contributed to the sense many Americans have that a president could address, and solve, almost any problem. ''It's not honest,'' Fitzwater said. ''The president of the United States cannot solve every problem from warts to AIDS.'' David Demarest, Bush communications director, put it this way: ''This president does not see himself at the center of national attention.'' Bush had reason to worry that if he became too commonplace in America's living rooms, the public would tire of him prematurely. Bob Teeter had poll data that suggested the public actually resents a president who is on the news every night. Teeter regularly surveyed Americans for their sentiments about Bush and discovered that, as he once put it, ''they don't like having to come home every night and turn on the television to learn what he did today.'' A president, as

Bush put it, could get "overexposed," just like the stars of sitcoms and television talk shows who burn brightly but then flame and fade out. "People get tired of seeing anybody on television," explained Fitzwater.

In this environment, rhetoric was judged to be of little use. When their White House mess privileges were revoked early in 1989, Bush's speech writers realized their work would be less important to the forty-first president than it had been to his predecessor. Bush regarded speeches primarily as yet another way to work in small groups. His writers complained privately that the only portions of speech draft that the boss seemed to care about were the "acknowledgments"— the several paragraphs of names and perfunctory thank-yous that led nearly every Bush speech, in which he recognized by name the friends, political allies, and routine famous people in every audience. Bush insisted that researchers call ahead and discover the names of VIPs who would be attending and then include polite hellos to them; if Bush saw someone he knew who was not mentioned in the text— and he nearly always did—he would break away in the middle of his comments to recognize the luminary and often sent a stiff note to the errant researcher afterward. It was, several speech writers explained, the only thing Bush ever complained about. "The acknowledgments are the bane of our existence," said one. But, to Bush, they were often the heart of the speech.

As with television, rhetoric's reduced role matched a Bush handicap. Plainspoken by nature, Bush was uncomfortable with dramatic language and hyperbole. He often deleted the most memorable passages from his speeches as he delivered them. He skipped over emotional lines about patriotism and national service, both before the Gulf War and after. (Radio reporters, who relied more than most reporters on strong words from a president for good stories, routinely let loose howls of frustration when Bush omitted the best lines from prepared texts.) The president didn't really believe that ideas could change people's minds. That, he figured, required careful, one-on-one negotiation—the kind of personal hard pitch that works best after a personal acknowledgment in a presidential speech. Bush pleaded in February 1990 that he didn't fully grasp the extent of his power to influence. "I think sometimes that I as a person—as the president— perhaps underestimate the bully pulpit aspect of the presidency. Or perhaps the fact that the presidency has a very special and thus specific role in exhorting or encouraging people to do whatever it is."

47

Pundits, presidential scholars, and numerous reporters lamented that this was no way to lead; that Bush would eventually need the trust and familiarity of Americans in a crisis. Michael Deaver, Reagan's image maker, said, "Control of the evening news and the headlines is one of the few tools a president has."

That analysis was correct but, for Bush, irrelevant. Leadership at home was never a goal of George Bush. By keeping a low profile and asking little of Americans, Bush was simply tuning himself to the national mood. Voters had grown tired of an omnipresent, ubiquitous commander in chief. After the ugly campaign of 1988, they had hung a "Do Not Disturb" sign on their front doors, preferring to be left alone by Washington except in case of emergency. He never mentioned his approach in public, beyond a few hedged comments about "being overexposed." Probed directly in a January 1990 interview, he offered a Delphic reply. "I think," he said, smiling broadly, "that is an interesting theory."

As a long-term strategy, diminished expectations would produce, in effect, a kind of double indemnity in case things turned up—or turned bad. By stressing little more than his energy, charm, and normalcy in the first few months, Bush erected a low-slung backdrop against which even modest proposals would stand tall.

But he was also laying a predicate for possible failure. If there was to be a disaster on his watch, Bush wasn't keen to take the blame. And big storms could not be ruled out: Bush had taken the helm as the nation finished its seventh year of uninterrupted economic growth —a boom that could not last forever. Many economists had long predicted recession in 1989; by August 1990 it had begun. How long it would continue, or how deep a gash it might carve in Bush's fortunes, was anyone's guess. Bush and his advisers hoped that the lull would run its course and sputter into recovery well before 1992 and thus the president decided to take no action to quell the recession's effect. By lowering expectations, and keeping his head down, Bush was subtly telling Americans not to look to Washington, and particularly the White House, for answers.

Food, Folks, and Fun

By the middle of 1989 Bush was routinely inserting into most of his speeches a self-evident stock phrase: "In case you hadn't noticed, I really love my job." This disarming confession was certainly welcome news: by trying hard, by working eagerly at a task almost universally believed to be impossible, the man once vilified as a wimp was winning newfound respect and affection. "I really love my job" never failed to meet with a rousing cheer. Bush was subtly signaling to Americans that everything was fine. It was as if to say "I know I have the hardest job in the world. But I like it, so there's no need to worry. The problems facing the nation are under control."

As straightforward confessions go, "I really love my job" was also a vast understatement. After taking the oath of office, Bush resembled nothing so much as a medieval boy king who woke up one morning, found himself atop the throne, and began tugging at the bell ropes for servants, ordering up royal carriages, and scheduling banquets and tournaments. Though Bush had worked at the White House for eight years, and had been in the presidential orbit for another four or five, he often acted like a wide-eyed political novice who had slipped away from a White House tour. As he said in late 1991, "I still get the same emotional feeling when I walk into the Oval Office as I did when I first maybe peeked my head in as a tourist to the White House."

Bush's ebullience seemed limitless—as hundreds of local congressmen and political officials who attempted to buttonhole him during a presidential visit to their states would discover. Most solons try to put to good use the brief ride from the local airport into town, making a pitch for help with a local project or a hand in solving a snarled political problem. Bush, however, often preempted such appeals with an adult car game called "Light 'em up." In the back of his armored Cadillac limousine, Bush faced forward with his guest on the jump seat facing aft. As the limo moved through the streets, Bush would pick out someone from the crowd, usually an attractive woman or child, point, and wait until—pow!—eye contact and the victim realizes, He's looking at me! That's when the target "lit up." Because the limo was moving forward, it fell to the guest facing aft to report to the president when he asked, "Did I get her? Did I light her up?" And then the game would begin again. The anticipated tête-à-tête about the local water project never came off. The bewildered politician's

49

disappointment, not to mention the spectacle of another local dignitary forced to play the silly game, never failed to amuse the president's staff, or the president.

Aides noted privately during the first few months of Bush's term that nothing seemed to spur the boss's imagination quite like party planning. A delighted Bush singlehandedly organized an all–White House horseshoe pitching contest, drawing up some of the ladders himself. (His aides would deny this, fearing allegations of micromanagement that helped sink Carter, who was notorious for overseeing the White House tennis court schedule.) Planning a quiet Rose Garden dinner for cabinet members and their spouses one perfect evening in June 1989, Bush called in David Valdez, his photographer, swore him to secrecy, and asked him to dig up incriminating photographs of his future guests, which Bush eventually signed, annotated, and had framed as door prizes. (The Brent Scowcroft Award for best sleeping on the job went to the national security adviser himself, a workaholic who often spent the night on his office couch and whose idea of relaxation was jogging when he got home after midnight.) Though Bush had been vice president for two terms, aides reported that Ronald Reagan had never once invited him upstairs to the private residence. When Bush finally saw the suite of rooms during the transition, his first words were characteristic: "I can have forty people in here."

When Bush heard that America's best Little League team was coming by one afternoon, he rounded up such old-timers as Mickey Mantle and Ted Kluszewski to mix and mingle at a dinner afterward. With no warning to anyone, he once invited more than two hundred guests at an East Room Black History Month event upstairs to see the Lincoln Bedroom, where the Emancipation Proclamation was signed. (It was a rare group of black visitors to the White House that didn't get the Lincoln Bedroom treatment.) On one five-night stretch in Washington while his wife was in Kennebunkport, Bush had some friends over for tennis, took a second group out to a Mexican restaurant in nearby Bethesda (washing down his fajitas with three beers), invited a third group of friends in for drinks and dinner, attended a congressional barbecue, and caught a Texas Rangers game in Baltimore. On many occasions Bush threw soirees not even his staff knew about. Joe Hagin, who had served Bush for years and was his scheduler through 1990, recalls running into University of Michigan basketball coach Steve Fisher at the White House the day after Bush had congratulated his championship team in a Rose Garden photo opportunity. "Back again?" asked Hagin, thinking Fisher was simply taking in the sights. "Well, no, actually," replied the coach. "The president invited us to sleep over last night."

Bush had always preferred the personal touch to the grand gesture. But as commander in chief, he would work his will step by step, voter by voter, phone call by phone call, and note by note, painting his presidency in the tiny brush strokes of a pointillist. Few White House insiders missed the symbolism when Bush commandeered a small office in the West Wing, once the office of Reagan image master Michael Deaver, for his own use as a private dining room. There, Bush would have lunch with the vice president, cabinet officials, lawmakers, reporters, former officials, old friends, and family members. Where picture-perfect backdrops and tear-jerking images for mass consumption were once conceived would now become the working office of the master of the one-on-one meeting.

A self-described "creature of Congress," Bush courted no group as he would lawmakers. Fred McClure, Bush's chief congressional lobbyist, was allotted time each week to bring members of Congress— and five carefully chosen constituents of each—into the Oval Office for pictures and brief conversation. Bush reserved neither access nor generosity for members of his own party. When he visited Kennebunkport, Bush offered Senate Majority Leader George Mitchell plane rides home to Maine. During a Clean Air Act ceremony in 1989, Bush looked out into the Rose Garden and noticed that Speaker of the House Tom Foley was sitting in the second row. Bush immediately ordered aides to squeeze Foley in up front. He invited Senator Don Nickles to go golfing along with Lee Trevino. He visited Capitol Hill frequently, playing racquetball with Sonny Montgomery and lunching with John Hammerschmidt, two colleagues of Bush's in the House Class of 1966; Bush even kept a locker in the House gymnasium.

The courtship paid off. By the end of May 1992 Bush had vetoed 28 pieces of legislation and had never been overridden. Many of these votes were close; in several cases Bush personally made the difference. The closest call came on the veto override vote on a bill permitting some expatriate Chinese students to remain in the United States, rather than return home in the aftermath of the Tiananmen massacre. Many conservative Republicans had considered the measure a free vote in the name of democracy, only to watch Bush oppose and eventually veto it. As the override vote approached, Bush decided to make it a test of GOP strength and brought GOP lawmakers to the White

House for an arm twister over breakfast in the State Dining Room. "Stand with me on this test," Bush pleaded, later working the phones, meeting with senators individually, and deputizing former president Richard Nixon to call GOP members. When he heard that she opposed his veto, Bush even telephoned the wife of Senator Charles Grassley to make his case to her: "I want to answer your concerns," he said. "I don't want any problems in your family."

Bush most enjoyed the personal give and take among equals—foreign leaders with whom he'd been hobnobbing since the early 1970s, when he served as Richard Nixon's ambassador to the United Nations. He enjoyed close relations with Canada's Brian Mulroney; the two men ironed out an acid rain agreement early in 1989 and kept in touch, attending the All Star game together in 1991. Early in the first term Bush quickly became close to Helmut Kohl, the burly and gregarious German leader on whom he relied heavily for advice about the fast-paced change in the Soviet Union and Eastern Europe. While Nelson Mandela was still imprisoned, Bush quietly corresponded regularly with South Africa's F. W. De Klerk in lieu of inviting him to Washington. Bush was careful to refer to former Japanese prime minister Toshiki Kaifu by first name—an important gesture to the Japanese. He took Egypt's president Hosni Mubarak to an Orioles game. He treated King Hussein of Jordan to a Potomac cruise. He played tennis with the emperor of Japan. And after several failed attempts, he lured Mikhail Gorbachev into a horseshoe toss.

As taken as Bush's advisers were by the president's energetic personal diplomacy, they were simply astounded by his apparently limitless patience with the most trying of international personages. A case in point was François Mitterrand, the French president. The two men are as dissimilar as meat loaf and Meursault: one is a socialist intellectual, the other an anti-intellectual social animal. One likes to pilot powerboats over eight-foot swells; the other likes to talk about books (his own). During preparations for Mitterrand's first American visit with Bush, his aides realized that what their boss had envisioned as a quiet and private weekend by the sea in Kennebunkport, Mitterrand saw as a grandiose state visit with flags, honor guards, and martial music. They were appalled to learn that the French president wanted a bidet and a special bed installed in a Bush family cottage. "He wants us to do what?" asked an incredulous American official when he heard of the special considerations. But Bush swept aside such questions, directing his subordinates to do exactly as Mitterrand requested. And when the French president, who suffered from seasickness, demurred at Bush's suggestion of an afternoon on the boat, the two men went for a walk in the woods.

Privacy was a big part of the Bush's courtship. He liked to get his quarry alone—in a cozy room, in the woods, on the telephone, or on some secluded island. But the personal touch had its limits. Bush never got on particularly well with Margaret Thatcher, who had been Ronald Reagan's chief overseas ally and was distinctly to Bush's right politically. Bush's relationship with Gorbachev, who was close to Thatcher, also progressed slowly. It took several years, repeated meetings, and a coup attempt to fully cement their shared concerns, and by then Gorbachev had been eclipsed by Boris Yeltsin. But the coldest shoulder in the club belonged to Israel's Yitzhak Shamir, both in the early days of the administration, when bilateral relations were good, and later on, when they soured over Israel's insistence on continued West Bank settlements. Bush's attempt to bond with Shamir backfired continually, and alienation rather than intimacy resulted. "How can I get through to this guy?" Bush asked aides repeatedly. He pressed assistants for information about Shamir's hobbies and favorite sports but was told that Shamir had no real interests outside his work and family. Bush tried to bridge the gap by taking Shamir to see a movie at the Air and Space Museum in Washington.

Because Bush sees diplomacy through a prism of personality, he tends to see evil people, not evil systems or governments. Bush repeatedly referred to Saddam Hussein as the sole villain of the Iraqi power structure, and to Manuel Noriega as the only bad pineapple in Panama. During the Gulf War and afterward, Bush stated repeatedly that "my problem is not with the people of Iraq, but with their leader." Of course, it was the politics and cultures of Baghdad and Panama City that had elevated Saddam and Noriega to power; it was unlikely that either leader's replacement would offer much improvement. Conversely, Bush put more faith than was warranted in Chinese leaders he considered to be "good men" and was reluctant to impose sanctions on them following the Tiananmen massacre. A year later even Bush would be forced to admit that personal diplomacy had failed to nudge Beijing any closer to democracy or respect for individual rights.

Despite its drawbacks, Bush's Rolodex diplomacy quickly became something of an international fad. Within months many of the leaders whom Bush had wooed on the phone were picking up on the idea, calling him—and each other—like old chums. Bush quietly asked White House communications officers to install direct secure telephone lines to London, Bonn, and Paris and upgraded the "hot line" to Moscow from a noisy Teletype to a direct high-speed data link. He investigated ways to install similar private links to ex-presidents Richard Nixon, Gerald Ford, Jimmy Carter, and Ronald Reagan. Brent Scowcroft once explained that Bush's personal diplomacy "can't change national relationships. But it can facilitate negotiations."

On many evenings between 8 and 10 P.M., Bush retires to his private study on the second floor of the White House, to do what he has done since he was a young oilman in Texas: write 20 to 40 personal notes—notes of thanks, notes of sympathy, notes for kicks. After his successful NATO summit trip in May 1989, Bush completed 40 thank-you notes to aides between his departure from London and his arrival back in Washington. Bush wrote to a Washington-area woman whose husband, a pizza truck delivery man, had been shot while he was working. When pop singer Gloria Estefan was injured in a car crash, Bush called her several times.

Bush indulged Maureen Dowd of *The New York Times* with a lengthy note about the real Marlin Fitzwater. ("Marlin," wrote Bush, "is a hat man.") He even wrote notes about notes: after journalist Chris Matthews wrote an article explaining that the president had won the Gulf War because of his relentless personal diplomacy and note writing, Bush wrote Matthews back, congratulating him for recognizing that his lifelong habit helped him "keep in touch" and then close a deal or make thing happen in an emergency. Note writing, wrote Bush, "has a purpose" and wasn't "just Ivy League politesse."

The president's mother, Dorothy Walker Bush, was his first guest in the Oval Office, and he called her nearly every day afterward. Ann McDaniel of *Newsweek* recalls a stop during the 1988 campaign at which Bush was photographed eating liver and onions at a cafeteria in Ft. Lauderdale, Florida. McDaniel mentioned to the president that her mom was in the room, Bush sprinted over to say hello, noted how proud she must be of her daughter, and posed for a picture. Later in the day, in West Palm Beach, Bush grabbed McDaniel and pointed to another woman waiting on the tarmac: "See that woman over there? Well, that's my mother. I said nice things about you to your mother. Now you go over there and say nice things about me to my mother."

Bush directed his press office to compile lists of reporters and their favorite hobbies—jogging, horseshoes, movies—so he could invite favorites to join in the nonstop recreational fun. Some journalists naturally purchased special togs and shoes for this assignment, arriving at the White House in spandex and then jogging alongside the president as they carried on breathless, and off the record, conversations. Reporters were invited to the White House for lunch, upstairs to the private residence for drinks, out to dinner for Chinese food, to the White House at night for buttered popcorn and movies. During his August vacations in Kennebunkport, Bush took reporters golfing and had the entire press corps over to his seaside mansion for hot dogs and hamburgers—and spent hours shaking hands and posing cheerfully for pictures with the families of people he saw several times each day. As with everything, this courtship was not without calculation. A guest approached the president at the Kennebunkport lawn party for reporters in 1989 and said, "Hasn't anyone told you you're the president of the United States? You don't have to do this anymore." To which Bush replied with a smile, "How do you think I got here?"

To Bush's way of thinking, there is simply no event that can't be improved by the addition of more people. Barbara Bush used to complain that she often returned home in Houston with "dinner for twelve" to discover her husband at home with twenty guests. Once he became president, this only got worse: after a formal press conference in the garden of the American ambassador in Paris, Bush turned to several dozen reporters and invited them inside to look around. (Barbara Bush, horrified by this bit of free-lance hospitality, ordered reporters to wipe their feet.) One cabinet officer recalls that Bush invited him and his wife to Camp David for the weekend, where they would have the run of the navy installation's impressive sports facilities. The official's wife begged off, preferring a quiet weekend at home with the kids. Since one rarely says no to a presidential invitation, an alibi was hatched: out-of-town guests made the invitation regretfully unacceptable. "Folks from out of town?" Bush asked, then brightened. "Bring 'em along!"

When more people can't be found, they can be telephoned. Fitzgerald Bemiss, a childhood friend of Bush's from Maine, recalls speaking with the president at a private White House dinner party about their youthful high jinks 60 years before. As they reminisced about their old gang, Bemiss recalls, Bush got an impulsive hankering to track them all down. "Let's give 'em a call!" he said.

So, right in the middle of dinner, Bush grabbed a nearby telephone and began dialing.

3

"WATCH WHAT WE SAY . . ."

The new president's style, amiable and aimless, sat well with the public for most of his first year in office, but it was only a matter of weeks before it began to worry many of his aides. They knew that Bush still smarted from news stories during the fall campaign that portrayed him as the puppet of savvy "handlers" like his old friend Jim Baker. They knew that was why as president he stubbornly resisted staff attempts to harness his energies to a long-range strategy, instead following his instincts, which were to strike out merrily in every direction at once, like a one-man covey of Texas quail. Yet several senior White House officials fretted that Bush's fear of looking "handled" had made him lurch too far in the other direction.

Bush, they complained, was flitting around from St. Louis to South Korea to South Carolina without communicating any clear sense of his purpose or priorities to the country or even to his staff and his party. After campaigning as "Ready to Be a Great President from Day One," he attracted ridicule by refusing substantive comment on major developments abroad, pending delivery of a set of make-work "policy reviews" that he had ordered from the federal bureaucracy. Meanwhile, all of Washington could smell the president's coming defeat in his first clash with the Democrats in Congress, who would reject his appointment of John Tower as secretary of defense. Only seven weeks into his term, Bush felt obliged to call a press conference to deny that his administration suffered from "drift" or "malaise." But if Bush and Sununu had charted a political course, its heading was a mystery to their crew in the White House.

In fact, Bush did have a strategy, and Sununu revealed its essence during a fractious staff session in his big corner office on the evening of March 6, 1989. That meeting, unusual amid the informal, walk-in-anytime atmosphere of the Bush-Sununu White House, was called at the urging of a group of senior and midlevel officials, who for weeks had been telling each other, in whispered asides and computer-mail messages, that the president was being badly served by his scattershot scheduling and planning. Most of these officials knew Bush well and knew that there was, at bottom, very little that he wanted to accomplish in domestic policy. Still, they had expected that he would lay out his basic governing and political priorities at home and abroad, if not in public, at least for their private guidance. They also had assumed that however complacent Bush might privately feel about the state of the American economy and society, he would seize control of the public agenda by manipulating symbols via television, as his campaign team had done so effectively in defeating Michael Dukakis. But as the weeks rolled by, neither expectation had been fulfilled.

Several senior aides recommended that the White House plot its recovery from the Tower mess by agreeing on a set of legislative priorities and political messages and pursuing them single-mindedly over the next several months: coordinating Bush's travel, speeches, meetings, and—especially—TV news coverage, in a theme-of-the-week, line-of-the-day routine. During the transition, Bob Teeter had prepared a thematic plan for Bush's first one hundred days, arguing that the president "has enormous power to lead simply by focusing public attention on certain things." But Teeter was no longer around, having declined to work with the abrasive Sununu. So several officials at the March 6 meeting suggested that the message and schedule be coordinated by a group including Communications director Demarest, Budget director Darman, Sununu's deputy, Andrew Card, and Stephen Studdert, who staged Bush's public appearances.

Hearing this, Sununu erupted: "No! No! Government doesn't work that way!" What he meant was that George Bush wouldn't work that way. Weekly themes, Sununu insisted, were "too confining, too cumbersome" to suit Bush's peripatetic personality or the political constraints that he had inherited. Bush, unlike Reagan, did not have a Republican-controlled Senate, effective control of the House, or a clear mandate from the voters to accomplish any specific, big-ticket reforms. Bush stood at the head of a government more divided than any in memory. No new president had faced a House and Senate so dominated by the opposition party, nor had any new president won election with such short coattails that he failed to reduce the opposition's majority in Congress. And few presidents held so little influence as Bush over the activist ideologues in his own party in the Congress.

Also, as Sununu's lieutenants well understood, Bush lacked Reagan's rhetorical talent and appetite for taking his case to the public over the lawmakers' heads. Harry Truman, faced with a House and Senate controlled by the opposition party in 1948, had responded by sending it a stream of popular legislation, selling his program aggressively to the public, labeling his Republican opponents the "do nothing Congress" and using that pitch not only to win reelection for himself, but to recapture Democratic control of Capitol Hill. But George Bush was no Harry Truman. He had judged that an attempt to confront a Democratic Congress with a distinctly Republican program would only insure four years of stalemate, undermine the bipartisan cooperation that he would need to score the foreign policy successes that he craved, and risk reducing him to a failed, one-term president. None of these were risks Bush wished to take.

Instead, Sununu explained, Bush would negotiate compromises with the Democrats as opportunities arose for incremental progress on a wide range of issues: to lay aside the long divisive issue of the Nicaraguan contra rebels, discourage the smuggling and use of illegal drugs, stabilize the shaky banks and S&L's, whittle down the budget deficit. Bush, Sununu declared, would "rather be sharing the credit for solving a problem than sitting around arguing about why a problem wasn't solved."

Bush would coopt the Democrats through compromise, to neutralize any big domestic issue on which they might gain partisan advantage: the environment, education, civilian research. Bush also, of course, would develop wedge issues, including crime and racial hiring quotas, to distinguish himself and other Republicans from the Democrats. And all along he would work to distinguish himself in the field where his strongest interest and expertise lay and where he enjoyed the greatest latitude for individual initiative: foreign policy.

Sununu then provided his aides what they needed: not a set of domestic priorities so much as a political strategy and a way of understanding what Bush was up to. Trained as an engineer, Sununu had a

habit of working through political and policy questions very methodi-
cally, even ploddingly, questioning assumptions and reasoning back
to first principles. Thus he asked: What was the single overriding goal
of the Bush administration? Answer: A "successful presidency" that
would bring reelection in 1992. Next question: How can the Bush
administration best assure that the voters judge it a success? Sununu's
answer: By putting together a solid record of accomplishment on
which to campaign in 1992; a checklist of bills passed that major
constituencies would applaud, of bills vetoed that other constituencies
—particularly conservatives—had despised; and a tally of presidential actions taken, crises handled, opportunities seized.

Here, finally, was "the vision thing": the image Bush saw when he
imagined a better future for America was . . . himself in the Oval
Office through January 1997! Silly as it might sound, this revelation
proved useful as "an organizing principle," in the recollection of one
senior official present at the meeting, and "gave us a quiet, internal
coherence" that had been missing until then. Bill Kristol, the chief of
staff to Vice President Quayle, later explained that Sununu "had us
think of the record that we'd like the president to run on in 1992 and
work backward from there." Ed Rogers, by then Sununu's assistant,
added that "everything works backward from 1992. What we planned
was a successful presidency. We wanted there to be deeds."

Sununu referred to this presidential platform in the making as "talking points": a bit of political slang that referred commonly to a set of
arguments on an issue, agreed by the White House and Republican
leaders and faxed or phoned to operatives around Washington and
across the country, so that spokesmen for the party could sing from
the same sheet of music. The first batch of talking points to be pursued
by the Bush administration, Sununu explained, would flow naturally
from the 1988 campaign, as the president sought to deliver on, or at
least to address, the promises he had made and the themes he had
stressed. These would include new legislation on clean air, child care,
crime control, banking reform, and civil rights for the disabled.

Where Bush was not able or willing to fulfill a campaign promise,
he would at least make what Sununu and other officials referred to as
little "down payments." Bush would, for example, propose relatively
minor, symbolic spending cuts in programs with small constituencies
but would not suggest nearly enough savings to meet his own deficit-
cutting targets without new taxes. Similarly, he would propose record
new money for the Head Start early-childhood education program,

even though he would not "fully fund" it as he had promised during his campaign. He would instruct the appropriate departments to prepare much ballyhooed "strategies": for the "war" against illegal drugs, for energy policy, and for transportation. Independently Bush would promote a "kinder and gentler" civic culture and would seek to restore public confidence in the ethics and efficiency of the executive branch.

Working from a list of campaign pledges and themes assembled by James Pinkerton, a former campaign aide who moved over to the White House, the Bush administration would dispose of the talking points one by one, checking them off like items on a "to do" list. Bush approached this list much as he did his résumé, which emphasized the impressive-sounding jobs he had held—UN ambassador, Republican party chairman, CIA director—and glossed over both his brief tenure at each post and his dearth of substantive accomplishments. Still, by 1992 Bush would be able to revive an overarching theme he had employed effectively in 1988: that his life, from bomber pilot to Yale first baseman to Texas oilman to senior government official, was one of "missions assigned, missions accomplished." Or, as Sununu put it in defending Bush's domestic attainments in late 1991, "That's not just an agenda proposed; that's an agenda accomplished."

Rather than concentrate their firepower on a couple of big crusades, as Reagan did in his exertions for income tax cuts and new defense spending, the Bush administration would creep forward on dozens of fronts simultaneously, if incrementally, so that by the start of the 1992 campaign it could impress the voters with the variety of its achievements, if not with their heft. David Bates, 37, the White House cabinet secretary and longtime Bush aide and tennis partner, observed that "it took a while to sink in. Some people on the staff were looking for a thematic approach, or tried to build events around issues. What we got instead was an approach that was reflective of the president's character: he moves in a lot of directions at once, content to keep his head down and make progress over time." Or, as Sununu told his senior staff, "If it looks like the president and the government are juggling thirty small balls, that's because they are."

This approach offered another advantage, which Sununu described as "tactical flexibility"—a nimbleness, unencumbered by sticky specific goals or principles, that would allow Bush to quickly seize political opportunities as they arose. During the 1988 campaign, Bush committed himself to as few specific policies as possible, believing that such undertakings would confine him after the election and would especially inhibit one of his favorite pursuits: claiming victory out of compromise. After Bush took office, his reluctance to commit himself only grew stronger and gained an additional rationale: laying out to the public a clearly defined agenda would make it more difficult for Bush to shift his attention to unexpected crises and opportunities, at home and abroad, that offered bigger political payoffs. Darman made this point to his colleagues at the March 6 meeting, in words that nicely prefigured the next three years: "Remember, much of how a president is going to be evaluated is how he handles surprises, not necessarily how he handles his own agenda."

Bush and Sununu privately believed that President Reagan had been excessively concerned with maintaining the appearance of vigorous action and accomplishment, along with his public approval ratings, *throughout* his two terms. Bush told his aides, and hinted to the public, that a president need only show a record of accomplishment by the time he enters his reelection campaign. Bush insisted that his staff "not just worry about what's going to happen to us in the press or in the polls in the short term," according to Sununu. "The agenda, in terms of issues and timing, is a four-year agenda." Bush "is less concerned with how it looks than the results. . . . This may not be as flashy, as well presented, to the outside as the last administration, but it is a style that will allow this nation to get some of its tough problems examined."

It followed that Bush need not react to every criticism or demand for action by the Democrats or the press, and particularly not within the same news cycle, as the Reagan administration and the Bush campaign usually had. "You don't get extra credit for doing things early," Bush often told his aides. Sununu would parrot that line, but more often, characteristically, he would exaggerate it into something that sounded like an immutable law of physics: "You can decide as late as you want if you're the executive." Sununu took this proverb from his six years as governor of New Hampshire, and what he meant was that a governor or president has the power to set the agenda, to change the subject, to put forward his own proposal—above all, to command far more attention from the press and public than any of his rivals whenever he finally decides to move.

Bush explained his approach this way: "I don't think about my schedule in terms of image. I think of it in terms of substance: doing things that need to be done." He added, "In this kind of work more is going on that meets the eye, or makes the headlines. The proof will come when we look back from the year 2000." Darman observed of Bush, "In the campaign, he was saying, 'Look at my character.' Now he's saying, 'Look at my performance.' . . . And what matters in the end is performance. I think he is making a bet with himself that he and his team will deliver under a lot of the headings, and that will be more important than the vision." By 1992, added Darman, "he will be able to say, 'We did this, we did this, and we did this.' "

"I'll Leave It Right There"

On its face, there was nothing uncommon or unseemly about a president and his staff thinking ahead to the record on which they would like to campaign for reelection. What was remarkable about the Bush White House, however, was the rigor, clear-eyed cynicism, and political self-interest that drove their domestic policy. Bush's high-flown claim that contemporary mortals could not judge his record —that it could be assessed only by looking back from the next millennium—was considered laughable by much of his staff. Bush, Sununu, and their aides were consciously and tough-mindedly looking out no further than 1992. All of domestic policy was subordinated to the goal of Bush's reelection, and almost everything that didn't fit was thrown overboard.

The clear implication of the 1992 focus was that the Bush administration would spend little political capital on domestic projects that might require serious arm-twisting and calling in of chits by the president or might drag down his ratings in the polls. Political capital was to be scrounged and hoarded at home and spent where it mattered to Bush, where he would prove his greatness: in foreign adventures. Bush would thunder righteously, for example, that "government is too big and it spends too much," but he would not propose significant spending cuts except through his aides, and even then only in closed-door meetings with lawmakers where no one could be held accountable.

Bush occasionally would concede that the central reason for the runaway federal deficit was the explosion of welfare spending on the upper and middle classes—he used the preferred euphemisms "entitlements" or "mandatory programs"—but he would not think of leading a call for reform of, say, Social Security subsidies for the well-to-do. In fact, in the wake of his weak showing in the New Hampshire primary in February 1992, Bush audaciously positioned himself as the defender of government largess for well-off retirees: he attacked both his Republican challenger, Pat Buchanan, and the Democrats in Congress for proposing middle-class tax cuts that he claimed would force cuts in federal spending on subsidies to recipients of Medicare and Social Security.

Bush would not take seriously either of the major currents of his rhetoric during the campaign and his presidency. There would be no charges up Capitol Hill to shrink the size and reach, the spending and taxing, of Big Government; no gutting of the bloated bureaucracies that line the Mall. Instead, despite his barking against federal taxes and spending and regulation, Bush by 1992 would establish himself as the biggest taxer, the biggest spender, and one of the most expensive regulators in American presidential history.

Nor would there be any sustained crusade in a "kinder and gentler" direction. Bush, to his credit and in contrast with Reagan, would set a compassionate tone by posing for photos with crack babies and homeless children, and his proposals would more than double funding for AIDS research, to $4.9 billion a year. But when faced with persistent social problems that had defied conventional bureaucratic approaches and cried out for boldness, Bush would shirk. He would refuse to lobby aggressively for the conservative, antibureaucratic, poverty-fighting agendas championed by Kemp, drug czar William Bennett, Quayle chief of staff Kristol, and White House idea man Pinkerton, among others. Bush would not battle Congress to win significant funding for Kemp's proposal to turn public-housing tenants into owners. Nor would Bush press for the competing and no less iconoclastic ideas, flowing from the budget office and elsewhere, for breaking the cycles of poverty, illness, ignorance, unemployment, and criminality.

For George Bush, the size of government and the condition of America's economy and society were like the baby bear's porridge in the story of Goldilocks. They were just about right the way Bush found them: not too hot and not too cold; not too big and not too small. Indeed, in his curiously self-revealing argot, Bush often would observe of a contentious situation: "I'll leave it right there" or "Better to let it sit there."

"Repackage Our Philosophy"

Bush's rejection of an activist presidency reflected his political and social philosophy: a deeply conservative worldview that he seldom discussed openly, but one that can be seen clearly in his statements and actions over the years, particularly during his time in the White House.

Bush is generally viewed as a relative "moderate" in national political terms, especially when compared with Ronald Reagan. In his actions if not in his rhetoric, Bush is less averse to higher taxes and government spending. Before 1980 he was pro-choice on abortion. And he had a record of at least mixed support for civil rights. Yet in his fundamental attitudes toward change, progress, established institutions, and hierarchies, and the proper role of government, Bush is far more conservative than Reagan and more in the mold of Warren Harding. Reagan was, in his way, a revolutionary and a crusader, as was Barry Goldwater. Both men sought ardently to change American society by debating their ideas and by vigorously exercising the power of government, even if one of their stated goals was to make the government smaller. Both men launched serious and sustained attacks on established institutions: the Democratic party, labor unions, the civil rights movement, and popular middle-class programs like Medicare and Social Security.

The contrast with Bush could not be more stark. He fears change and distrusts crusades. He is profoundly comfortable with the status quo. He is, in the words of one of his closest advisers, "not the kind of politician who engages in frontal attacks on established institutions" and authorities, including teachers unions and the Democratic leaders of Congress, and is reluctant to confront them in any systematic way or even to criticize them more than is necessary to get through the occasional political campaign.

When Bush says he considers himself a conservative, he sees his role as a *conservator:* one entrusted with an inheritance and concerned less with expanding it than with guarding it. His is an old-fashioned "order" conservatism, which seeks to impose no new vision of society but rather to defend the status quo and to avoid mistakes of commission—in sharp contrast with the charismatic, risk-taking, china-breaking conservatism of Reagan and Goldwater. Nelson Polsby, a Berkeley politics professor, labels Bush "an American Tory," adding that conservatives of this stripe "care about the society and the government that is handed to them; they want to keep the boat afloat."

Bush often volunteers, in contrast with the rhetoric of Reagan, that he does not "hate government," which makes sense, "government" being, after all, the sort of established institution that Bush respects instinctively. Bush is, however, deeply skeptical of attempts by government to force the pace of human progress. Such efforts, Bush believes, are the height of hubris and folly and often bring unintended consequences. He believes that progress comes, when it comes, through glacial changes in attitudes. And he believes that elected officials should follow their constituents in such matters, rather than lead them. When Bush ran for the U.S. Senate from Texas in 1964, for example, he made opposition to civil rights legislation the centerpiece of his campaign. He argued that the rights of minorities should not be guaranteed by law, but rather should be won gradually, through moral persuasion of the white majority. "I believe that the solution to this grave problem lies in the hearts and goodwill of all people," Bush said in a 1964 campaign brochure, "and that sweeping federal legislation like the Civil Rights Act can never fully succeed."

Out of this skepticism of government grows a deep caution and fear of mistakes that Bush often expresses, especially in the midst of crisis, as an overriding concern to "first, do not harm" and to "not make things worse." Bush exhibits what management gurus decry as a "bias for inaction"; he is looking always for a reason not to act, particularly in domestic policy. When he does move it usually is in reaction to someone else's initiative—and there he excels. His reflexes, instincts, and tactical skills are first-rate.

The common criticisms that Bush "lacks conviction" or "doesn't believe anything" are not quite right. To be sure, Bush often doesn't believe what he *says* he believes: "voodoo economics," "no new taxes," for and then against abortion choice, against and then for Star Wars, and so on. But if one looks instead at what he does—and does not do—a core of solid convictions emerges.

65

Bush believes in the goodness and justice of the status quo, meaning the established social and economic order at home and American leadership abroad. He believes the established order can always use some tinkering around the edges ("at the margins of practicable change," as Darman cleverly put it in his January 1991 budget message.) But Bush believes that radical change is both unnecessary and dangerous, and that the status quo deserves and requires a vigorous defense against such misguided efforts. He believes in himself as the rightful leader of that defense. And he believes in winning, by almost any means.

He believes that in foreign policy, the rightful role of the United States is as the world's preeminent power, and he will defend that role ferociously against all comers at home and abroad. He believes, as his hero Teddy Roosevelt put it, that "trade follows the flag": that America cannot be strong economically unless it is engaged politically and militarily around the world. He believes that he has a singular gift for advancing America's interests through personal relationships with other world leaders. He believes that what those leaders do to their people is none of America's business.

Bush believes that in economic policy what is good for wealthy investors and business executives is good for America. He believes that taxes must be kept low on capital gains and on top marginal incomes, so that members of the educated and monied elite—which he sees as *the* creative force in the economy—will have an incentive to risk their capital in the building of new factories and other enterprises, rather than simply collect interest on government bonds. He believes, implicitly, that taxes need not be low on the wages or savings accounts of ordinary Americans, who are not a creative force in the economy and who anyway have no choice but to work and scrimp.

These beliefs have guided Bush whenever he has governed and explain his custodial approach not only as president, but also in other high-level posts that he has held. These beliefs have proven a distinct liability, however, in the realm of electoral politics. If presented in an unvarnished manner, Bush's cramped, status-quo brand of conservatism would seem unattractive to most Americans, who (at least until recently) assumed that ever-expanding opportunity and prosperity were part of their birthright. So Bush, more than most politicians, has had to disguise his core beliefs and distract attention from them. This helps explain his long-standing attitude that what he says in a campaign has little connection with what he will do in office; that electoral politics is a squalid moat he is required to swim across every few years in order to regain his rightful place in the castle of governance.

Election defeats in 1964, 1970, and 1980 moved Bush to molt from conservative to moderate and back. Yet these political makeovers came easier to Bush than to most candidates because there was little that he believed needed changing and no specific agenda that he wished to accomplish. He simply craved the adventure and honor of holding office and would embrace whatever policy positioning and media imagery he deemed necessary to win. He learned to rely heavily upon his inherently cheerful, optimistic, and energetic personality. And he developed a complementary and often underestimated penchant for slashing, sometimes demagogic, attacks on his opponents, especially during the final weeks of a close race.

During his first campaign, the 1964 U.S. Senate race in Texas, Bush ran as a Goldwater conservative: against civil rights laws, against the "welfare state," against the nuclear test ban treaty, against union shops, and, of course, against crime and the Communists in Vietnam. Bush ran ahead of Goldwater in Texas, but the negativity of Bush's platform could not be overcome even by his ingratiating personality, and he lost to the Democratic incumbent, Ralph Yarborough, by a margin of 43 percent to 56.

Bush concluded that he, like Goldwater, had erred by attacking liberal welfare programs that were proving popular with middle-class recipients. "We should repackage our philosophy," Bush told a post-election symposium, convened by the conservative *National Review*. "Emphasize the positive, eliminate the negative, warn of the dangers from the left, but do so without always questioning the patriotism of those who hold liberal views. . . . Bush took his own advice, telling a University of Texas audience the following June: "I generally favor the goals as outlined in the Great Society—a better life for all, elimination of poverty and disease, fair play in civil rights. . . ." He told his Episcopal minister, John Stevens, "You know, John, I took some of the far Right positions to get elected. I hope I never do it again. I regret it."

Bush was quickly, and profitably, becoming one of those spend-but-don't-tax Republicans lampooned by Franklin Roosevelt, who warned in September 1936 against "the smooth evasion which says 'Of course . . . we believe in Social Security; we believe in work for the unemployed; we believe in saving homes. . . . We believe in all these things. . . . We will do more of them. We will do them better.

And most important of all, the doing of them will not cost anybody anything!' ''

In his next four races Bush radiated an aura of sunny, kinetic blandness. A campaign photo for his 1966 race for Congress showed him smiling brightly, sleeves rolled up and suit jacket slung jauntily over his shoulder. "Vote for the man who really cares about the things that are worrying you these days," blathered one of his newspaper ads. "Elect George Bush to Congress and watch the action!" There's a saying in Texas politics that the only things in the middle of the road are yellow stripes and dead armadillos. But Bush thrived there, too. The billboards in his 1966 campaign failed to mention any party affiliation. And when he ran for reelection in 1968, no Democrat opposed him. When asked why, the chairman of the local Democratic party replied, "George Bush has proved himself a better Democrat than Republican."

Bush continued to emphasize "the man, not the party" when he ran again for the U.S. Senate in 1970, expecting that the relatively liberal incumbent, Yarborough, would be vulnerable amid that year's backlash against antiwar and civil rights protesters. But instead of Yarborough, Bush had to face conservative Democrat Lloyd Bentsen, and he lost.

A moderate image remained with Bush until his defeat by Reagan in the Republican primaries of 1980. Then, as the price of joining Reagan's ticket, Bush once again had to repackage his philosophy to purge it of inconvenient positions. He embraced Star Wars, a constitutional amendment to ban abortion, and the borrow-and-spend fiscal program that he had recently denounced as "a free lunch approach" and "voodoo economics." (Reminded by a reporter of the last comment, Bush replied, "God, I wish I'd never said that." Later he denied having said it, until TV videotape proved him wrong.)

When in 1988 he launched his second campaign for president, Bush calculated that he had a better chance to win by hewing to Reagan's views rather than returning to the views on which Reagan had beaten him in 1980. Congressman Bill Green, a liberal New York Republican, urged Bush not to forsake his moderate image, but he recalled that Bush felt that Reagan "had gotten this enormous mandate in 1980 and 1984" and Bush "thought that he was the inheritor of it and he had only to continue the basic positions Reagan had taken to keep the same mandate." Bush calculated correctly, as his "no new taxes" pledge and negative campaigning on conservative "values" issues helped him come from behind in both the primaries and the general election.

"Bunt 'Em Over"

From the transition through his first three years as president, Bush made clear his view that Ronald Reagan had accomplished all the change and renewal that American society would need for a good long while. In his inaugural address Bush set his task and America's as "stewardship" of the Reagan legacy. That speech repeatedly praised "continuity," "continuance," and "continuum." Bush mused that "there are times when the future seems thick as a fog; you sit and wait; hoping the mists will lift and reveal the right path." Then, in closing, he implicitly contrasted the Reagan revolution with the Bush approach of day-by-day reactiveness: "Some see leadership as high drama and the sound of trumpets calling, and sometimes it is that. But I see history as a book with many pages, and each day we fill a page with acts of hopefulness and meaning. The new breeze blows, a page turns, the story unfolds."

The inaugural's tone of bovine contentment reflected the first victory of the forces of quiet continuity, in skirmishing that periodically would divide the administration, particularly during political crises, over the next four years. The fault lines split the Bush team into three shifting and overlapping camps. The dominant faction—call them the Passivists—was led by Sununu, Treasury secretary Nicholas Brady, and Budget director Richard Darman. The Passivists normally favored cautious, incremental approaches to policy and accommodation wherever possible with Democrats in Congress. Pressing for a more aggressive and confrontational approach—to "hit the ground running"—were the Activists, led by Housing secretary Kemp and drug czar Bennett, often joined by Vice President Quayle and his chief of staff, Bill Kristol, along with policy planner Pinkerton, a libertarian iconoclast, and several other younger, conservative staffers. Atwater was an occasional ally, as was Rogers.

Floating in the middle was a group that might have been labeled the Stylistics, led by pollster and strategist Teeter, the transition co-director who sketched the short-lived "Hundred Days Plan," and joined by Studdert, an avuncular leftover Reaganite. This faction took a moderate line on policy but cared less about its substance than that it be marketed aggressively through careful attention to message and media, symbols and scheduling. Teeter understood Bush better than most and differed with him mainly on the need to mask his domestic irresolution with activist imagery. "The problem is the president," said one of Teeter's allies in the White House, who added with some exaggeration: "He refuses to be managed. He refuses to do theatrical things. He refuses the bigger-than-life mode. If he gets a hint of it, he resists it."

What the Activists wanted was more of the Reagan revolution, with the emphasis on "more." What Bush intended, however, was to act as custodian of the Reagan movement, while reining in what he considered its unsightly excesses. What Bush represented was more of the same, but less. Less open acceptance of bigotry. Less braying insensitivity to the less fortunate. Less grasping and petty corruption. Less celebration of greed and gaucherie. Less indolence and inattention in the Oval Office. Less of a "lone cowboy" style in world affairs. Yet Bush was clear that he considered these matters of style rather than substance. "There's a general thrust, and President Reagan set that," Bush said in January 1989. "They asked me the other day about 'the one hundred days.' I said, 'we don't have to put it in terms of one hundred days. We're not coming in to correct the ills of the past, we're coming in to build on a proud record that has already been established.' "

Craig Fuller, the transition's co-director and Bush's vice presidential chief of staff, elaborated: "What he really came to do is to take eight years of Republican government and make it more efficiently managed. He had more challenges thrown at him than we expected. But he didn't come with this long litany of things to do. The American people knew that when they voted for him." Sununu added, "We're building on the previous administration. We're not moving in a new direction. We don't have any plans for radical change. And we don't need to hurry."

The first duty of a president, Bush believed, was "prudence," a quality he esteemed above all others. Bush further defined this duty in terms of the teachings of Hippocrates, the ancient Greek known as the father of medicine, who counseled young physicians, In trying to heal, first take care to do no harm. Though masked by the president's sunny disposition and boundless energy, the phrase "do no harm" became a pessimistic leitmotiv for the Bush administration.

Where John Kennedy won the presidency in 1960 on the slogan "We can do better," Bush's byword, uttered often by him and to him in private strategy sessions, was "We could do worse." His temperamental model could be British general Sir Edmund Allenby, like Bush an aristocrat of military daring and domestic complacency. Having captured Damascus in 1918, Allenby took little interest in the city's governance and was depicted, in the epic film *Lawrence of Arabia,* practicing casts with an imaginary fly rod while just beyond the balcony of his office suite fires smolder uncontrolled across the city. When Arabs protest outside Allenby's office, an aide suggests, "Look, sir, we can't just do nothing." Allenby drawls with well-bred aplomb, "Why not? It's usually best."

From his first weeks in office, when he came under criticism for not moving more swiftly to encourage the trend toward pluralism and market economics in Eastern Europe and the Soviet Union, Bush expressed both an Allenby-esque refusal to be stampeded and a determination to avoid mistakes of commission. "I don't want to make any early term mistakes like Kennedy and the Bay of Pigs," Bush told his advisers. Then he went public, repeatedly, with the generic formulation his aides had been hearing for years in private: "I don't want to do anything dumb." Bush could always see the pitfalls he wished to avoid more clearly than any affirmative goals he might have in mind. Defending his restrained response to the Soviet crackdown on Lithuania in early 1990, Bush quoted one of his favorite philosophers, Yogi Berra, saying, "I don't want to make the wrong mistake." At a press conference during the short-lived Soviet coup in August 1991, Bush spoke the phrase "I don't want to" five times in less than a minute.

When he was pressed in the fall of 1991 to fight the double-dip recession with a middle-class tax cut and extended unemployment benefits, Bush replied, "What I don't want to do" was to swell the budget deficit, drive up interest rates, and "make the situation worse." In November 1991 Bush endorsed the laissez-faire view that recessions can be beneficial in helping businesses to become "leaner" and "more competitive," adding, "My goal is to see that government doesn't get in the way." Bush also argued that recessions are largely self-correcting, saying, "That is an argument for not doing anything

71

dumb, not doing anything stupid that's going to make it worse." In early 1992, when Bush unveiled proposed legislation to combat the stubborn economic slump, he often talked less about what his plan would do than about the pitfalls it would avoid. "Just as important is what it doesn't do," Bush told a campaign rally. "It doesn't increase the deficit. It doesn't cloud the real issues with feel-good political gimmicks. And it doesn't raise tax rates on the American people."

Bush studies history not so much for insights into opportunities— how earlier presidents and other leaders found and forged and took advantage of them: how Truman sold the 1947 Marshall Aid Plan to a reluctant Congress and public; how Carter knocked heads to make peace between Egypt and Israel—but rather for mistakes to avoid. Speaking without the benefit of staff experts at press conferences, in interviews, or during social gatherings, Bush usually impresses his interlocutors with a sure and easy grasp of the current political scene at home and abroad, yet his references to history are few, strained, and narrow, generally centering on perceived mistakes.

He doesn't want to see the U.S. military demobilize too quickly after the Cold War as it did after the last two world wars. He doesn't want to engage in protectionism like "the Smoot-Hawley days," a reference to the U.S. tariffs imposed in 1930 that deepened the Great Depression. He doesn't want to appease Saddam Hussein the way Chamberlain did Hitler in Munich . . . or to make U.S. soldiers "fight with one hand tied behind their backs" as Johnson did in Vietnam . . . or to risk humiliation in some paramilitary rescue mission as Carter did in the failed Desert One mission in Iran.

For sports fans, Bush left no doubt of his defensive, risk-averse temperament in a 1989 interview about his baseball career at Yale, where he served as team captain and first baseman, despite having one of the worst batting averages on the squad: "I wasn't a really good baseball player because of my hitting. . . . As a fielder, I really felt good about it. I could contribute to the team. Cover the bunt pretty well. My arm was fair—not great by a long shot, but I could catch the ball. They could make bad throws, and I was pretty dependable." Asked what kind of manager he would be, Bush replied, "Probably fairly cautious. I'd play by the averages, probably get people on, be cautious about too much stealing, and bunt 'em over. . . . I think just steady is what I'd say."

Turtle Excluders

Such fear of mistakes and skepticism about the ability of government to lead society are not often found in a man of Bush's obvious vigor, optimism, and love of work. The result has been a president who substitutes frenetic movement for lasting action; whose idea of long-range planning is choosing the menu for tomorrow's lunch; who governs by reaction to whatever his staff and events put in front of him. Bush is more than half-serious when he says, paraphrasing Woody Allen, that "90 percent of life is just showing up."

For all his proximity to the Oval Office under Reagan, Bush faced a difficult transition from the vice presidency, where he had few pressing duties and plenty of time for the ceremony and small talk that he enjoyed, to leader of the Free World, with the planet's thickest stack of phone messages and mail. "His instinct is to return as many of his phone calls as possible, to drop in on his buddies in Congress, to initiate a lot of calls, even in the middle of meetings, to anybody he thinks can shed light on a subject he's interested in," Craig Fuller said. "He's also prone to overcommit himself when any of his six thousand best friends ask him to do things"—to make a visit or give a speech or consider an arcane policy change that would enhance their fortunes.

Since Bush declined to organize his schedule around any specific domestic agenda, he found himself with plenty of time, at least early on, to kibitz and meddle, to indulge his restless curiosity. Senior officials' "In" boxes began to fill with paperwork churned out by Bush: reports they had sent him, returned with extensive editing, questions, additions in the margins and notes hanging out with more presidential scribbling on them; letters from various First Friends asking favors—the creation of a new national park near Los Angeles; reversal of various business regulations—with a presidential note attached asking, "Is this legit?" or "Would you check this out?"

Bush's chief assistant for domestic and economic policy, Roger Porter, set up a system of six "In" boxes in descending order of urgency, with the first two filled mainly with messages from Bush. Brent Scowcroft, the president's national security adviser and the White House aide closest to him both personally and professionally, worked regularly until 10 P.M. to clear his desk, only to despair the next morning when he found that Bush had sent him a new sheaf of

73

notes based on his readings of intelligence cables and memos and press clippings the previous evening. If the president would not set priorities, every errand he assigned had to be treated as urgent, at least until obvious crises came along and swept aside everything else. In the meantime Bush was having a fine old time trying out all the new bells and buttons in the Oval Office. His staff was overworked, even by the macho standards of the White House, and with precious little to show for it for the first several months.

The nadir of Bush micromanagement, White House officials concur, came in September 1989 during a day trip to New Orleans, when the president wandered into the middle of a ferocious but small-bore flap over a new federal requirement that shrimpers install on their nets devices called "turtle excluders" to allow endangered sea turtles to escape. The shrimpers complained that the devices also allowed countless bushels of shrimp to slip through, and Bush promised to seek a compromise. The controversy eventually occupied the time of several White House officials, up to the president. From that day forward, whenever anyone at a White House staff session would suggest presidential involvement in some nitty controversy, he could be shut down if a colleague inquired, deadpan, "Are we talking turtle excluders here?"

If his aides' desks and credenzas groaned under piles of reactive make-work, it was because Bush was a slave to his own "In" box. Bill Bennett, who served Bush as drug czar, worked closely with him in the Reagan administration, and remains one of his most ardent admirers among Republican conservatives, relates, "When I have an extra day to catch up on the paperwork in the office, I'm glad to get it out of the way, but that's not *doing* something, to me. That's the stuff you have to do to make time to get out and *do* something . . . giving a speech, debating Republican ideas and values against the Democrats." Thus, when Bush asked Bennett to move to the RNC, the president said, "This is great. You can go out and give all the speeches. You like to speak; you're good at it. Go to it." For Bush, unlike Bennett and Reagan, public argument and persuasion "weren't the real work of the president," Bennett says. "The real work of the president was reading the paperwork and making decisions"—in other words, tending the "In" box.

A favorite aphorism of harried, crisis-driven managers goes, "When you're up to your ass in alligators, it's easy to forget that you came to drain the swamp." That was never a problem for George

Bush. He came precisely to wrestle all the reptiles and wildcats anybody could throw at him, confident that he was good at it and savoring
the contest. In part for that reason, Bush's reactivity cost him little
during his first two and a half years and often allowed him to take
advantage of the "tactical flexibility" that Sununu had prescribed. As
political analyst William Schneider observed, there developed a "pe-
culiar rhythm" to the Bush presidency: "A crisis suddenly emerges
and dominates the public agenda—an oil spill in Alaska, a new Soviet
proposal on arms control . . . a stolen election in Panama. The press
attacks the administration for weakness and indecision. Commentators accuse Bush of having no policy to deal with the situation. The
administration responds that it is being prudent. Critics say it is being
timid. Suddenly the president steps in and makes a dramatic gesture.
There is a burst of activity . . . and a compromise results. The crisis
ends, even though the problem may be unresolved. . . . The press
pronounces Bush's intervention a success. The president's popularity
goes up. And public attention shifts to something else."

Contrary to their public rhetoric, Bush and his top aides were
keenly sensitive to opinion surveys and news coverage from their
earliest days in the White House. During press conferences, Bush
would aver with a dismissive wave that he never paid attention to
polls but would—sometimes in the same sentence—remind reporters
that 68 or 73 or 81 percent of Americans supported his position on the
issue of the moment. "I have told you that I don't live and die by the
polls," Bush told reporters in November 1991. "Thus, I will refrain
from pointing out that we're not doing too bad in those polls." Refer-
ring to opinion surveys that showed him beating all likely Democratic
opponents, Bush added, "I've seen these head-on-heads, and I feel
pretty good about it." In private lobbying sessions, Bush would sometimes brandish poll data broken down by state and congressional district to demonstrate that a particular constituency agreed with the
president—and not with the luckless lawmaker—on gun control or
some other issue.

Bush and Sununu frequently consulted a chart entitled "Comparative Presidential Job Approval," which showed Bush's poll ratings
month by month on a line, alongside lines that tracked the ratings of
Presidents Reagan, Carter, Ford, and Nixon, and they grew concerned that Bush might suffer a first-year "August slump" like those
experienced by several of his predecessors. Sununu therefore mailed
the polling chart to members of "the List," a collection of three dozen

75

Bush relatives, friends, and GOP political operatives whom the chief of staff frequently canvassed, this time inviting advice on "how we can beat the August slump." Some members of the advisory group urged that Bush become more activist: for example, that he move beyond restrained applause for the collapse of communism and push a new Marshall Plan that would help build free-market economies in the emerging democracies of Central Europe, Latin America, and Asia.

During the same period, pollster/strategist Teeter and RNC chairman Atwater came to very different conclusions after poring through cross-tabulations from recent polls and peering through one-way mirrors in airport hotels around the country while "focus groups" of voters discussed their perceptions of the president and the state of the nation. (It was a similar focus group in Paramus, New Jersey, in May 1988 that revealed to Atwater and Teeter the potency of the Willie Horton, Pledge of Allegiance, and Boston Harbor "issues" in Bush's campaign against Dukakis.) What the two concluded this time was that Americans were generally well disposed toward Bush, as long as he stayed out of their faces and didn't try to lead them on any expensive or risky crusades.

This was good news indeed to Bush, for it buttressed his natural inclination to say the right thing while doing as little as possible. He ignored his more activist advisers and embarked on a July tour of Eastern Europe. He offered little in the way of financial help but staged some evocative TV pictures of himself embracing democratic reformers and helped to overcome the unpopularity of his support only one month earlier for the Chinese rulers who ordered the Tiananmen massacre. Bush beat the dreaded August slump: his popularity, rather than slipping, actually swelled. Through the fall of 1989 and into 1990 he posted record-setting 70 percent approval ratings.

Bush is also keenly attentive to press coverage. Most mornings between 6 and 7 A.M., he scans five newspapers—the *Washington Post, New York Times, Wall Street Journal, Washington Times,* and *New York Post*—which shape the agenda for his questioning of aides in his three regular morning briefings: by intelligence officers, his national security advisers, and the chief of staff. He scans the newsweeklies soon after they hit his desk on Monday morning. During trips on *Air Force One,* he can be seen grazing through bound packets of clippings from the *Los Angeles Times,* various Texas dailies, and other regional papers; through TV news transcripts and copies of *The New Republic, The Economist,* and other political journals, many of them bristling with notes marking articles recommended by advisers in and out of government.

Like President Kennedy, Bush closely follows news reports to keep track of what his government is up to—and to keep his advisers honest. "He reads and scans a lot of news stories as a check on the bureaucracy," Scowcroft observed, "and to see how his policies are being understood and interpreted." Bush is constantly popping into Press Secretary Fitzwater's office after a major presidential speech or action or (more likely) reaction to ask, "How are the overnights, Marlin?"—meaning, How is it playing? If the answer is negative, Bush, having little commitment to any domestic policy, is apt to change it or else push it onto a back burner.

Red Lines

The "talking points" strategy implemented by Sununu included not only compromise on legislation, but also confrontation, which was no less important to Bush's reelection. Critical as it was to demonstrate what Sununu would call a "record of performance" by 1992, Bush would also devote substantial time and energy to thwarting the Democratic agenda. Just as he would seek marginal changes in domestic policy, he would work to protect his political base from changes that went beyond those margins. Among his top domestic attainments at the end of 1990, Bush cited his use of the veto to insure that "we didn't get any new programs jammed down our throat by the majority party."

The veto was a particularly handy tool for Bush because it enabled him to take clear and simple stands that his accommodating politics did not otherwise allow. Although he took fire from his right flank for compromising with Congress on a host of issues, the veto permitted him occasionally to stand resolute as Horatio against the "liberal" horde. Bush was outnumbered by unprecedented margins in both houses of Congress, yet he was not without leverage. House Speaker Tom Foley needed 218 of 262 Democrats to pass a bill in the House;

George Mitchell needed 51 of 57 in the Senate. But Bush needed only 34 of 43 Republican votes—retaining one more than one-third of a full Senate—to sustain a veto.

Bush used the veto skillfully, even creatively. In three and a half years he built a perfect record of vetoes: 10 in 1989, rising to 21 by the end of 1990 and to 28 by the end of May 1992. None of Congress's override attempts succeeded. By the end of Bush's third year, Democrats had begun to wonder if a Bush veto could be beaten. "We have fallen into the trap," said Representative Vic Fazio of California, "of thinking that if we don't have a two-thirds vote, we should do nothing."

White House domestic policy chief Roger Porter, while teaching at Harvard and authoring a book about White House policy management, had extensively studied the history of presidential vetoes and emphasized to Bush that the veto should not be seen as a purely negative tool. It could and should be used as merely one step in a process of negotiation between the president and Congress. With the help of Sununu, C. Boyden Gray, Darman, Porter, and other aides, Bush would normally lay out markers when he sent bills to Congress or when Congress looked likely to pass legislation to which Bush took exception. Where Reagan would adopt an extreme public position, then compromise with Congress at the last minute, Bush would enunciate—sometimes publicly, sometimes only in private sessions with leading lawmakers—the general, minimal principles that he sought in a bill and the "red lines" that would move him to veto it.

During the Reagan years, vetoes were threatened all the time by various officials but only rarely deployed. Bush put a halt to this, authorizing a series of carefully calibrated veto threats. If legislation moving through committee on Capitol Hill had begun to traverse a red line, lobbyists or cabinet officers were deputized to state in private or in public that they would "recommend" a veto if the controversial language was not removed. If the Democrats didn't get the hint, Press Secretary Marlin Fitzwater would be authorized to say that "the president's senior advisers" recommended that he veto. This middle step, always coordinated with Bush, heightened the pressure while preserving the president's options. If that threat didn't force the Democrats to compromise, Bush himself would go public with a veto threat. In August 1991, for example, he told the National Governors Association via satellite hookup from Kennebunkport that he would veto the transportation bill, then wending through Congress, if it included a new tax on gasoline. By the time the measure reached his desk in late October, the offending levy had been excised.

When the Democrats ignored Bush's threats, the White House pulled out all the stops to avoid Democratic attempts to assemble a two-thirds vote to override. Bush made every such vote a test of GOP solidarity. Nor was he afraid to push all his chips to the middle of the table. During last minute negotiations between the White House and Capitol Hill in 1990 over child care, Sununu convinced Bush to threaten a veto of the entire budget agreement one morning at 2 A.M. unless his principles of parental choice and federal aid for church-based child care were included in the law. The Democrats agreed to compromise, and both chambers passed the measure with the White House amendments written by hand into the bill's margins.

Drawing a line in the sand on such issues helped Bush with several important Republican constituencies who otherwise regarded him with suspicion. Six of Bush's vetoes—a quarter of those through his first three years—were cast to restrict access to abortion, an issue of strong interest to many conservative Republican voters. Another seven vetoes helped Bush win favor with various business interests, including those who opposed mandatory family leave and restrictions on railroad takeovers. Bush was particularly keen to veto Democratic proposals for "mandated benefits," meaning federal requirement that businesses provide health care, child care, or other benefits to their employees. Never mind that the Clean Air Act and the Americans with Disabilities Act, both supported enthusiastically by Bush, were two of the biggest regulatory nightmares for American business in years. Indeed, those measures made it all the more important for Bush to rail against "federal mandates."

For all its success, Bush's veto strategy also carried the danger that it would come to symbolize the negativity and marginality of his domestic policy. After two and a half years Democrats in Congress began to hammer that theme. "If he intends to veto everything, we ought to put out things that demonstrate the differences between him and us," said Senator John Kerry of Massachusetts. Thus, in October 1991, when Bush vetoed a bill that would extend benefits for unemployed workers, Congress passed the measure again, with relatively minor changes. The next time Bush signed it.

House majority leader Richard Gephardt, doubtless driven to distraction by Bush's perfect veto record, complained, "If you're looking for George Bush's domestic program, and many people are, this is it: the veto pen. The president's veto pen is more powerful than the votes of 66 senators and 289 representatives. He has used it to thwart the will of the American people, to defend the status quo of a declining economy, to preserve the privileges of the powerful, and to deny the positive role of government as an agent of renewal and change." Gephardt went on to quote John F. Kennedy, who said of Eisenhower, "We cannot afford a chief executive who is praised primarily for what he did not do—the disasters he prevented, the bills he vetoed." Senator George Mitchell, the Democratic leader in the Senate, went further. Bush used the veto, he said, to "prevent others from dealing with the nation's problems, even though he himself offers no solutions to those problems."

By the end of 1990 the legislative scorecard kept by Sununu and Bush was filling up nicely with campaign talking points. The president had won quick passage of a bill to strengthen the rights of disabled Americans. His support broke a decade-long legislative stalemate on reauthorization of the Clean Air Act. He could claim credit for modest steps to restrain the growth of subsidy payments to well-to-do farmers. He had significantly increased spending on Head Start, AIDS research, and civilian research and development. Congress had passed most of his drug-control "strategy," and even though use of illegal drugs had begun to decline before Bush addressed the problem, he was able to declare that victories were being won in that war.

On the other hand, the economy had turned south in August, triggered by Saddam Hussein's invasion of Kuwait and the accompanying spike in oil prices. And during the summer and fall, Bush had surrendered his "no new taxes" pledge and twenty points in his approval ratings in exchange for a budget deal that promised to trim the Treasury's borrowing by nearly $500 billion over the next five years.

But those little negatives were transitory, according to calculations that Bush and Sununu made in late 1990. On the whole, things were going their way. With caps on federal discretionary spending, interest rates would fall and the economy would right itself in the first half of 1991. Then the naysayers would see the wisdom of the budget deal. Meanwhile the United States and its allies would score a major victory in the Gulf crisis. Bush would continue to "manage"—and take credit for—the collapse of communism in Europe. And Bush would coast to reelection. He had set out to accomplish a handful of initiatives at home, prevent a host of Democratic measures from becoming law, and distinguish himself in foreign policy. And he had succeeded beyond his imagining.

In large measure the Bush–Sununu strategy was complete. "Our talking points were in order," recalled Ed Rogers, Sununu's assistant until September 1991. "Bush was already a successful president in late 1990. He had successful pieces of legislation. He was going to have a successful war or a huge capitulation by Saddam's army." After that, in the 1991 session of Congress, "we were going to have some successes . . . maybe a highway bill, maybe a crime bill, maybe get some nominees through. Fine. We'll do a lot of foreign travel. We always get good visuals and good press from that. We'll come back in December and do domestic travel, tamp things down, and tide everybody over. By then they'll be writing that we really came out of the recession in June, and we'll pick up at the State of the Union address. We'll have a campaign by then, and we'll really be rolling." Bush's campaign for reelection, his advisers chortled, would rest on three issues: Kuwait, crime, and quotas.

Heartened by this rosy scenario, Sununu in November 1990 marched confidently into a lion's den: a roomful of surly fellow conservatives at a Holiday Inn banquet room in downtown Washington. Bitterly blamed by many on the Republican Right for President Bush's abandonment of his "no new taxes" pledge, Sununu had accepted an invitation to explain himself and his boss over dinner during the annual Conservative Leadership Conference. Sununu's tone, as usual, was unrepentant, his argument audacious. Far from a debacle, Sununu claimed, the recent budget deal represented an underappreciated and far-reaching triumph over the forces of Big Government.

Yes, Bush had broken his single most memorable commitment to the voters who had elected him, but the alternative, Sununu said, was "chaos": a budget crisis, government shutdown, and likely panic by the bond and stock markets during a fragile period when the economy was weakening and the largest American expeditionary force since Vietnam was faced off against Iraq. And Bush had given in, Sununu emphasized, only after winning from the Congress unprecedented controls on future federal spending. The cycle of annual budget showdowns and the weedlike growth of new spending programs finally had been halted. What was more, Sununu said, the Congress now had given Bush everything he needed to build a successful record for reelection. Bush now could stop being Mister Nice Guy and shift into a stance more to the taste of Sununu's audience, in which the president escalated his use of the veto and "the battles we fight focus on preventing things from taking place.

"Let me suggest the following," Sununu said. "There's not another single piece of legislation that needs to be passed in the next two years for this president. In fact, if Congress wants to come together, adjourn, and leave, it's all right with us. We don't need them."

At this, the lions of American conservatism, ready to devour Sununu only moments earlier, applauded.

4
"... NOT WHAT WE DO"

Had he been willing to sell it with the bluster of John Sununu—or the sangfroid of Ronald Reagan, who approved a dozen tax hikes starting in 1982—Bush might not have suffered lasting damage from his surrender on taxes. Instead he continued to lurch back and forth over whether the budget deal was a good idea, even after he agreed to it. He would praise the deal: "It is balanced, it is fair, and in my view, it is what the United States of America needs." Then he would say the new budget made him "gag." He ended up with the worst of both worlds: he got all the blame for raising taxes and little of the credit for new controls on federal spending. He also subtly undermined his "talking points" strategy for domestic politics and policy. Before, Bush was criticized for not sufficiently embracing his conservative critics' agenda or his liberal critics' agenda. Now it was clear to ally and adversary alike that Bush brought little commitment, persistence, or follow-through to the cardinal promises of his own agenda.

This irresolution was evident on almost every domestic issue that Bush chose to emphasize: education, the environment, civil rights, gun control, the war on drugs. But it was most vividly demonstrated in the center ring of the Washington circus—on taxing and spending.

For most of 1990, White House activists pleaded with Bush and Sununu that they should stop merely whining about the Democrats' hold on Congress and do something about it. Pinkerton, the policy planning director, urged the course taken by a Democratic president, Harry Truman, who in 1948 campaigned effectively against the Republican-controlled "do nothing" Congress. Pinkerton was so taken with this approach that he studied the memo to Truman in which Clark Clifford, then a Truman aide and now an influence-peddling Washington lawyer, laid out the 1948 campaign strategy, and he invited Clifford over for lunch in the White House mess.

The "blame Congress" strategy appealed to Bush in theory, but he had a few practical problems with it. One was that even after abandoning his "no tax" promise, he remained entangled in bitter closed-door budget negotiations with Congress and expected to remain there through much of the fall campaign. Another was that Bush had many personal friends among Democrats in Congress and was loath to bash them. Another was that Saddam Hussein had invaded Kuwait in August; Bush had vowed to liberate the oil sheikdom and had dispatched the largest U.S. expeditionary force since Vietnam. He would find it far more difficult to deliver on his promise without congressional support or at least acquiescence.

Bush ordered up a tough, Congress-bashing speech, based on Pinkerton's ideas, and said that he planned eventually to deliver it while campaigning for Republican candidates for Congress. But as the budget talks dragged on, the speech had to wait. And wait. Eventually the thing had hung around so long and gone through so many updatings that it became known as the "Dead Cat" speech. As Halloween approached, White House staffers adorned their pin-striped lapels with black-cat stickers. Those whose call was "unleash the cat" wore their stickers right side up. Those who would rather "bury the cat" wore theirs upside-down.

Before the election, as often happens with Bush, each side got part of what it wanted. The president delivered screeching, armflapping versions of the partisan speech early in the last week of October but undercut its combative thrust by also praising Democratic support for his policy toward Iraq and for compromises on clean air and other legislation. By Thursday, when several news stories ridiculed his straddle, Bush buried the cat.

The results of the 1990 elections should have come as no surprise but still were disappointing to Republicans and especially to Bush. Though he targeted his personal campaigning on 62 races he thought were closest, 35 of those candidates lost. Bush would enter the 1992 campaign with fewer Republicans in office than when Reagan was elected in 1980: 10 fewer senators, 25 fewer house members, two fewer governors, and majorities in 13 fewer legislative chambers. Bush told aides that he seemed fated to serve out his full term with both houses of Congress controlled by the opposition. If so, he would be only the second president so hamstrung. The first: his mentor Richard Nixon.

Torn between confrontation and accommodation, Bush veered between bemoaning "the great frustration of having to deal with a Democratic congress" to predicting that the same Congress will pass "a good, sound education program" and to praising it for cooperating with him during the Gulf crisis, as well as on clean air, child care, the Americans with Disabilities Act and other legislation. When traveling the country, he begged voters to "send me more Republicans" in Congress. Then he heaped praise on local Democratic incumbents with whom he needed to cut deals (saying of House Veterans Affairs Committee chairman Sonny Montgomery, A Mississippi Democrat, "I wish we had more like him in Congress") or whom he embraced to deter partisan fire at his symbolic approach to domestic issues (praising Governor Roy Romer of Colorado for his work on education reform.)

Former president Nixon observed to reporters in early 1992 that Bush's pride as a member of the club, from his own two terms in Congress, combined with his strong need to be liked, prevented him from rewarding lawmakers who supported him or punishing those who did not. Often it worked the other way around, with those who supported Bush's initial position on legislation getting their political legs cut off when Bush struck a compromise. As columnist George Will wrote, "Congress likes Bush, but does not respect him because it doesn't have to, which is why it likes him." Robert Bartley, the conservative editor of *The Wall Street Journal,* aptly labeled Bush and his administration as inheritors of the Mugwump tradition in American politics, circa 1884: "The heart of Mugwumpery was distrust of the brutish instincts of the common voter, an urge for government by 'the best men' "—including, of course, established powers in the Democratic party. The "open, optimistic, and populist" politics of Reagan contrasted with those of the Bush administration: "elitist, pessimistic, and crabbed," Bartley wrote. "President Bush offers competence and experience. But an agent of change he definitely is not."

. . .

Though most critics castigate Bush for lacking a domestic agenda, Bush in fact has set forth a formidable array of promises, concerns, and guiding principles. He is, instead, vulnerable for the irresolution that has accompanied his fulsome rhetoric—a contrast that has only grown more glaring since the Gulf War, where he showed what he can do when he is motivated. The conviction, persistence, and ingenuity that Bush demonstrated in driving Saddam Hussein from Kuwait, including the assembling and constant reinforcement of an unwieldy international coalition, have been starkly absent from his conduct of domestic policy. "It's not that he doesn't believe anything," said one senior White House official who has pressed for a more aggressive domestic policy. "It's that he doesn't see much connection between expressing beliefs and acting on them in a serious way."

Complaints that Bush has devoted no time to domestic policy and accomplished nothing there also miss the point. Bush in fact spends the lion's share of his working hours—totted up from his appointment books by Sununu and announced as 75 percent—on domestic policy and has accumulated a list of genuine legislative accomplishments, led by the Clean Air Act and protections for Americans with physical and mental disabilities. Bush also has won congressional passage of elements of his much ballyhooed "strategies" to deal with transportation and illegal drug use. That he has done *something* at home is not in dispute.

But in emphasizing the quantity of the president's input into domestic policy, Bush and Sununu, and his successor as chief of staff, Samuel Skinner, only reveal their eagerness to divert attention from the output. And when they do discuss domestic attainments, the president and his spokesmen often try to discourage inquiry through the sheer volume of their covering fire: a numbingly repeated litany of bills passed and vetoed and personnel appointed and presidential visits made. At the end of 1990, for example, the White House compiled an eight-page, 140-item laundry list of domestic accomplishments for that year alone, ranging from the budget deal (not an item anyone other than Sununu and Darman cared to emphasize much thereafter) to such overlooked accomplishments as:

- Sold $7.7 billion in U.S. Savings Bonds.
- Conducted a census.

• Negotiated arrangements with Canada to permit freer movement of meat and poultry shipments.

• Completed compliance reviews of alleged bias against Asian-Americans in the admissions processes at Harvard (no violations found) and UCLA (one violation found).

• Issued revised Dietary Guidelines.

• Launched workforce initiative to develop national competency guidelines for work readiness [translation into English not provided].

Similarly, in an interview in December 1990, Bush griped that he had not gotten credit for "the travel I have done on drugs and education and the points of light." He doesn't think or talk at home, as he does abroad, in terms of the hard work of putting together coalitions and creative new approaches for getting things done. Instead he thinks and talk about how many places he has just shown up. In this and other defenses of its domestic record, the Bush administration emphasizes quantity over quality or salience, much in the manner of those pre-*glasnost* Soviet newscasts that trumpeted the latest glorious production records at factories whose shoes and appliances were laughingstocks even (or especially) to the factories' employees.

The central question is not whether it is a good thing to have passed a Clean Air Act (even though, for all its laudable features, the act's net value is not beyond dispute, including challenges by several of the president's economic advisers, who object to its $25-billion-plus annual cost). The question, rather, is whether marginally cleaner air, marginally enhanced rights for the disabled, and marginal aid for child care constituted the nation's top domestic priorities during Bush's first three years as president, sufficient to stand as the centerpiece of the administration's domestic attainments.

The answer, of course, is no, particularly considering Bush's neglect for his first 18 months of the domestic subject of overarching concern to his countrymen—the economy—and the wrenching damage Bush then did once he *stopped* neglecting it, during the 1990 budget negotiations, when he raised taxes in the teeth of a recession. Instead of addressing the structural weakness of the economy head on, Bush consciously chose marginalism.

A second question is whether the Clean Air Act, the Americans with Disabilities Act, the Child Care Act, the transportation bill, the drug strategy, or the other domestic accomplishments that Bush touts resulted from his initiative. Again, in most cases, the answer is no.

Bush and his lieutenants participated vigorously and, for the most part, intelligently and cooperatively in complex negotiations over these bills, forcefully employing the threat of a presidential veto to shape the final products to their liking and often improving them considerably, as in the case of the Clean Air Act. But each of the bills cited above originated in the Congress, among Democrats. Even Bush's drug strategy, the occasion for his first prime-time television address to the nation from the Oval Office, was in response to a congressional requirement.

"I Want to Be Positioned"

This emphasis on reacting to the initiatives of Congress flowed naturally from the strategy adopted early in 1989 by Bush and Sununu to avoid aggressive promotion of their own initiatives and instead to maintain the "tactical flexibility" to take credit for improving—or for vetoing—the initiatives of Congress. To be sure, Bush sent Congress several initiatives that it declined to pass (at least as of this writing in late May 1992), including a comprehensive crime bill, a measure to cut the capital gains tax, and a banking reform bill. Only the capital gains measure, however, received persistent backing by Bush and his top officials. The crime bill fell victim to Bush's preference for preserving the crime-cum-race issue for the 1992 campaign, rather than compromise on such matters as gun control and the death penalty. The banking bill, well crafted by the Bush administration and badly needed to modernize the antiquated and shaky financial system, was beaten back in part by smaller banks, which feared increased competition and were delighted to see that their lobbying blitz was answered only in tardy and lackluster fashion by Treasury secretary Brady.

John Mitchell, attorney general in the Nixon administration, used to advise reporters to "watch what we do, not what we say." It was his way of helping outsiders pick, from among the jumble of administration initiatives, which ones mattered and which were for show. Bush, however, has struggled to turn Mitchell's axiom on its head. In most of his domestic exertions, Bush has preferred earnest expressions of right-mindedness over sustained and resourceful action.

Lip service, in fact, was an integral part of administration strategy.

Teeter's polling and focus groups suggested to him and to Bush that while many Americans worried about the burden of the national debt on future generations, about drug abuse, sorry schools, pollution, child care, and a dozen other issues, most neither expected nor trusted big fixes by Washington. Many feared that any serious medicine might be worse than their nagging aches and pains—at least until the recession entered its second year. What they did expect from the beginning was a president who, in contrast with Reagan, would speak with compassion on social and economic issues. "They like that the president says the right things about the environment and education and those other issues," Teeter observed in 1989, "and they don't mind that he doesn't want to spend much on them . . . so long as he doesn't raise their taxes." What the public wanted in domestic policy through mid-1991, in other words, was the preaching of Christian charity without the passing of the plate.

In part for that reason, Bush constantly emphasizes "how strongly I feel" and "what I feel in my heart" about people who have lost their jobs or homes or health insurance, and even about the *Exxon Valdez* oil spill. Bush also emphasizes how important he considers the very fact of his public professions of emotion. "Gotta let people know how strongly I feel," he intones repeatedly, as if from a Leo Buscaglia tape.

With disarming transparency, Bush often talks not about his convictions on difficult issues, but about how he wants to be "positioned." In December 1989, after he was exposed as having secretly violated his own announced sanctions against China over the Tiananmen massacre, Bush emphasized that "I think we were positioned in the forefront of human rights." Shortly before the Louisiana governor's election in November 1991, Bush said, "I want to be positioned" as opposing Republican candidate David Duke, the former Klu Klux Klan leader and neo-Nazi, while declining to endorse his Democratic opponent, Edwin Edwards, who ultimately won. In March 1992 Bush explained why he was campaigning so frantically, bouncing from state to state before the Super Tuesday primaries in the South: "What I want to do is look like we're not taking anything for granted."

Bush makes similar use of the phrase "where I want to be" or "beyond where I want to be" to resist attempts to elicit specifics to back up his political rhetoric. During a campaign press conference in October 1988, for example, Bush was leading Dukakis handily in the polls and refused to discuss which spending programs he would cut to balance the budget without new taxes. Such questions, Bush said, were "putting me beyond where I want to be. . . . I don't want to be dragged beyond that because things seem to be going well now."

When things stopped going well and the recession deepened in the latter half of 1991, Bush responded by talking sympathetically while blocking—first in August, then in October, the fifteenth month of the recession—bills to extend unemployment benefits that had expired for hundreds of thousands of jobless workers. These congressional acts of compassion, unlike Bush's rhetoric, would have cost money: $6.4 billion. Bush judged the cost was too high—until he saw that the cost in his plunging approval ratings was even higher. Then he reversed field and approved $5.4 billion in extended unemployment benefits.

Bush could argue, of course, that unemployment and the overall economic outlook grew worse between his October veto and his November approval. Another part of the explanation, though, was that Bush, not trusting that his core, status quo conservative beliefs were politically salable, found himself highly dependent upon polls and positioning, press notices and what he perceived to be the "lessons" of election results.

Once, as a Texas congressman, Bush directly and knowingly took a stand contrary to the sentiment of his constituents: voting, in April 1968, for President Johnson's open housing bill, which forbade discrimination in real estate transactions. Bush had opposed the bill during his 1966 campaign, but in the wake of Martin Luther King's assassination on April 4, 1968, and with several major cities erupting in race riots and arson, he was urged by moderate Republican colleagues to support the bill. Typically, Bush straddled. He voted to kill the bill on a procedural vote, then turned around moments later and supported the bill on the vote for final passage. Many of his white constituents deluged Bush with angry mail and phone calls, and he offered to face them at a packed and tense community forum at Houston's Memorial High School. Bush explained that the previous year he had visited South Vietnam, where he saw black soldiers fighting and dying for their country, side by side with whites. "The idea that our young people could come back from fighting in Vietnam and our government would tell them where they could or could not live . . . I would never be able to do that in my whole life. I would die first."

When Bush finished, he won a standing ovation. Two decades later he recalled, "Nothing I've experienced in public life, before or since, has measured up to the feeling I had when I went home that night." Emboldened, Bush began sending critics of his vote on the open housing bill a passage by the British statesman Edmund Burke, whose thinking shaped the paternalistic, we-know-best conservatism to which Bush subscribed:

> It ought to be the happiness and glory of a representative to live in the strictest union, the closest correspondence and the most unreserved communication with his constituents. Their wishes ought to have great weight with him; their opinions his highest respect. . . . But his unbiased opinion, his mature judgment, his enlightened conscience—these he ought never sacrifice to you. . . . Your representative owes you not only his industry, but his judgment; and he betrays, instead of serving you, if he sacrifices it to your opinion.

"The Buck Stops *There*"

Bush often tries to portray his dearth of principles and his irresolution as virtues. His concessions to political rivals become, in Bush's retelling, a gutsy willingness to break with his political allies. Responding to criticism of the 1990 budget deal, he said, "Nobody thinks you can be popular by standing up and having to take a compromise, ingredients that you wouldn't necessarily want." Similarly Bush presented his reversal on abortion rights, when he embraced Ronald Reagan's staunch pro-life stance, as the product of his fearless intellect. Asked by an Iowa student to defend the flip-flop, Bush replied, "Have you ever changed your mind? That's one thing about intellectual honesty."

At other points, however, Bush has defended his abortion switch by pointing out that the number of abortions had grown enormously and convinced him that the practice should be curtailed by law. This line of argument is common with Bush, and telling. Few particular practices, whether abortion or S&L shysters forking out billions in taxpayer-insured deposits to their cronies in commercial real estate, are abhorrent to Bush inherently, but only when taken to excess. Thus, after reading *Den of Thieves,* the James Stewart tale of Wall Street market rigging and self-dealing, Bush pronounced himself disturbed by the "greed" involved but drew no larger conclusions about deregulation of taxpayer-insured financial industries. Thus, the moral question at the heart of the abortion debate—the rights of a fetus versus those of its mother—are of less interest to Bush than the *number* of fetuses involved. As Aaron Wildavsky writes, "It is easy to lose track of the times President Bush has changed his mind without even necessarily being aware that he is doing so . . . perhaps because he thinks general rules cannot cover specific circumstances."

Teeter naturally saw little wrong with Bush's attention to public opinion and his reluctance to foreclose options. Teeter, like Bush, often quotes former RNC chairman Ray Bliss, who advised that in politics one should always wait a few days before taking an important position or making a major decision, because "by then, you might not have to decide at all." With the Democrats in control of both houses of Congress and with Bush disinclined to wage partisan jihad, compromise seemed the president's only hope of accomplishment. Still, even Teeter warned Bush to guard against the impression that he was some sort of national real estate broker whose only goal was to close a deal, any deal. Teeter and other close advisers urged Bush to "tell people what you would do if you were a dictator, if you didn't have to deal with Congress."

Bush seldom followed that advice. Whenever he was asked why he wasn't leading on some controversial issue—say, the need to reduce the burden of regressive Social Security taxes on middle-income wage earners—Bush would spread his arms, shrug, and reply, "Why don't Republicans and Democrats [in Congress] rise up and do something about it?" Bush fully expected the Democrats in Congress to take the lead in domestic policy and told them so repeatedly in private sessions. While Ronald Reagan had staffers dig out Harry Truman's old placard "The Buck Stops Here" and place it on his desk, Bush as president sent the thing back into storage. As House majority leader Dick Gephardt observed, "Again and again, President Bush points to the Capitol dome and says, 'The buck stops *there.*' " Many of Bush's aides pointed out that the inherently quarrelsome Congress was never designed to lead the country. Bill Diefenderfer, the deputy budget director for Bush and former staff director of the Senate Budget Committee, observed that "the Congress will never do it. If tough decisions are going to be taken, the President has to lead the way."

Foreign policy was, of course, another matter. There, the message to Congress from the Bush administration was "Leave the driving to us." That was also the message from Bush to his staff. He didn't hesitate to knock heads among the Departments of State and Defense and the National Security Council over foreign policy matters. Closer to home, however, Bush made clear that he expected cabinet secretaries and other senior advisers to work out disagreements among themselves in all but the thorniest, high-stakes disputes. When consensus could not be reached, the likeliest outcome was inaction. Bush gave effective veto power to each of his top domestic advisers on all but the most politically potent issues. He thus built into his White House a strong bias for doing nothing at home.

In mid-1990, for example, the White House Domestic Policy Council painstakingly examined a long list of conservative ideas for attacking poverty but could not agree on any of them and got no leadership from Bush, so all of them were dropped. In the fall of 1991, after corporate executives and other big campaign contributors urged him to take the initiative to stimulate the economy out of recession, Bush convened frequent sessions of his Economic Policy Council. Those advisers, too, failed to agree on a program, and though Bush flared in anger at them at least twice, he declined until January 1992 to choose one faction's program over another's (which was, in itself, a choice to continue doing nothing, as favored by Treasury secretary Brady and Chief of Staff Sununu).

Bush took to blaming the public for not spending more confidently and not electing more Republicans to Congress so he could get the economy moving by cutting capital gains taxes on the rich. In response to questions in January 1992 about his broken "no new taxes" pledge, for example, Bush said, "What I need a pledge about is to get more Republican congressmen and senators . . . and then we would be able to see that we get those tax improvements I've been asking for. So that's the pledge I want. It's the pledge for the people to give us more Republicans." Sununu expanded the blame to corporate executives who, he harrumphed, had given the president inconsistent economic advice.

In both instances Bush was frozen not only by conflicting advice, but by his fear of Congress. He worried aloud during White House strategy sessions that any legislation he initiated would only get mucked up by Congress. It would spend too much money and create new bureaucracies. Then his only options would be to accept a bill that would make things worse or to veto it and take political heat. Better, Bush thought, to do nothing; to at least do no harm. That way, when the Democrats became willing to negotiate a deal in private, Bush would be unencumbered by previous positions and could claim whatever compromise emerged as a victory for his principles.

This approach, however, consistently got Bush into trouble with members of his party in the House, who begged him to "give us something we can be *for!*" During late November of 1991 House Republicans complained that they couldn't go home for the holidays and tell scared and angry constituents that their president and party would be studying their response to the recession over the next two months between golf matches, quail hunting expeditions, and foreign trips.

Bush was hearing another version of Teeter's advice: We can't effectively blame the Democrats unless we tell the voters how we would do it differently. The cross-pressures from Democrats and Republicans in Congress brought out the worst in Bush: he flip-flopped almost as desperately as he had a year earlier, one day rejecting the highly regressive and gimmicky tax-cutting plan pressed by House Republican whip Newt Gingrich, then, in the face of a revolt by Gingrich's troops, calling in reporters to tell them bald-facedly to "put me down as enthusiastically for" the Gingrich plan. Which then, of course, was dropped.

It is not uncommon in politics, of course, to see shifts of position and even naked reversals, broken pledges and failures to follow through. But Bush has shed so many stated beliefs over the years—moving up politically at every turn—that he has elevated irresolution to an art form and invented new ways of disconnecting political rhetoric from performance.

Bush's most blatant contradictions have come at the core of what government does: taxing, spending, and regulation. Since his earliest days in politics, Bush has portrayed himself as the enemy of Big Government: a position that is respectable and generally popular—as long, Bush knows, as one does not question the parts of Big Government that benefit large industries, other influential special interests, and upper-income voters. During his 1979–80 campaign for president, Bush promised a politics of "new candor," of "tough choices," in contrast with the "free lunch approach" and "voodoo economics" of Ronald Reagan. But Bush has yet, as candidate or president, to specify enough program cuts to reach his budget-balancing goals. Rudy

Penner, a former director of the Congressional Budget Office, observed that Bush took the attitude that the White House is in charge of tax cuts and spending hikes in popular programs like education, Head Start, and law enforcement, while the Congress is in charge of spending cuts. Stan Collender, director of federal budget policy at Price Waterhouse, added that the White House "hyped all the good things they want to do without saying how they'd pay for it." Jim Cicconi, a senior aide to Bush until late 1990, agreed: "Spending cuts are the job of the Congress, and the public knows it."

Not surprisingly, without presidential leadership to cut federal spending, the budget has soared to its highest level in U.S. history: $1.5 *trillion* in the budget Bush submitted in February 1992. Federal spending under Bush rose from 22 percent of GNP in 1989 to 25 percent in 1992, the highest proportion since World War II. The average annual growth in domestic spending under Bush was $29 billion: five times the rate under Reagan. On the tax issue, similarly, Bush not only abandoned his campaign pledge, but allowed total federal taxes to rise to an average of 19.6 percent of GNP from 1989 to 1992, higher than any previous four-year period in U.S. history. Federal regulation, too, has increased sharply under Bush. Total regulatory spending in 1991 was more than 20 percent higher, after accounting for inflation, than when Carter left office. The *Federal Register* ran 68,000 pages of new regulations in 1991, the most since Carter was president and up by a fourth from the 1990 total.

Starting with his inaugural address and its plaint that "we have more will than wallet," Bush has argued, sensibly enough in many cases, that increased funding should not be the litmus test of seriousness about addressing a national concern. "We cannot permit the measure of concern on any issue—drugs or education or environment —to be determined simply by how much federal money goes after the problem," Bush told reporters during his first week in office.

Yet when it suits his purpose, Bush frequently cites spending increases to prove his commitment. In the days just before and after the 1992 New Hampshire primary, for example, Bush bragged about his increased spending for the war on drugs, general law enforcement, math and science education (up to $2 billion, "a 120 percent increase," he claimed), Head Start (up "exponentially"), environmental protection, AIDS research, and "a record investment in research and development of $76 billion" in fiscal 1993. As Robert J. Shapiro, an adviser to Democratic presidential candidate Bill Clinton, wrote in

March 1992, Bush's economic policy amounts to "a poll-driven mélange of tax breaks and spending increases that represents a compromise between two failed ideologies of the 1980s—supply-side
Reaganism and big-spending liberalism."

Bush has undermined his stature by contradicting himself on a half
dozen issues, from trade to the environment. Though the president
considers himself a free trader, and he is by comparison with most of
his political rivals, James Bovard, author of *The Fair Trade Fraud,*
demonstrates that he "has been closing off American markets almost
since his first week of office" by "ceding to the demands of one
domestic lobby after another." Bush extended import quotas on steel,
railroad axles, oil pipes, semiconductors, textiles, machine tools, and
other products. After collecting the endorsement of the maritime
union during his 1988 campaign, Bush failed to negotiate to open U.S.
coastal shipping to foreign competitors, a protectionist system that
costs U.S. businesses and consumers about $10 billion a year.

During his 1988 campaign, Bush appealed for farm votes on the
promise that he would never engage in any "Jimmy Carter grain embargoes"—a reference to Carter's bitterly unpopular cutoff of U.S.
grain exports to the Soviet Union after its 1979 invasion of Afghanistan. Yet when Iraq invaded Kuwait, Bush responded with an embargo of grain and other food exports to both countries: two
significant markets for U.S. farmers.

Another set of Bush's campaign promises were intended to coopt
the environmental concerns of suburban swing voters. He vowed, for
example, to insure "no net loss" of wetlands, the marshes and estu-
aries vital for flood control, water purification, and breeding of many
birds and mammals. Once elected, however, Bush encouraged Vice
President Quayle and his Council on Competitiveness to restrict radi-
cally the definition of "wetland" so as to exclude nearly half the
acreage formally protected. "There's not going to be a net loss of
wetlands," Bush said in January 1991. "There's going to be some
redefinition."

Bush advised one audience during his 1988 campaign to "step back
from the trees for a minute and look at the forest." He should have
taken his own advice. At the urging of idea man Pinkerton, Bush early
in his term made a big show of planting trees on his travels around the
country, encouraging his countrymen to do the same and promising in
his 1990 State of the Union address "the money to plant a billion trees
a year"—on top of the 2.2 billion already planted annually in 1989. At

the same time, however, he did little to curtail federal subsidies to the timber industry, which cost about $200 million annually and encourage the destruction of 70,000 acres of mature forest each year, including old-growth forests that are essential to many species of wildlife, including the endangered northern spotted owl. In fact, in his budget for fiscal 1991, Bush proposed an extra $67 million for Alaska's Tongass rain forest, a 20 percent increase over the previous year, about a third of which would be used to subsidize the felling of seventeen thousand acres of four-hundred-year-old Sitka spruce. Bush's policy, then, amounted to planting symbolic baby trees to distract from the federally subsidized destruction of big, mature ones. When asked why Washington should finance such logging, Bush replied breezily, "I don't think the federal government should subsidize much of anything," and claimed ignorance of the details of the program.

Bush claims to be a staunch proponent of federalism: of removing Washington, wherever possible, from government functions better handled, or traditionally handled, by the states. He cited his devotion to federalism in backing his Justice Department in August 1991 when it sided with antiabortion protesters and against a federal judge in Wichita, Kansas, who ordered them not to block access to clinics. But when he wished to demonstrate his toughness against crime, Bush did not hesitate to expand the jurisdiction of federal law, law enforcement personnel, and courts into state crimes such as murder. In the process he has contributed mightily to the congestion of federal courts and prisons and drawn complaints from Republican-appointed conservative jurists right up to Chief Justice William Rehnquist.

No Follow-Through

Bush often reveals his lack of interest and cynicism toward a domestic issue by raising it for a transitory political purpose, then failing to follow through. The biggest example is his hyperbolic campaign promise to create thirty million new jobs. (During the eight years of the Reagan administration, a period of relatively rapid economic growth when many women entered the workforce for the first time, "only" eighteen million jobs were created.) The point is not that Bush should bear all the blame for the 1990–92 recession; rather, it's that

97

he took no initiative to accelerate economic growth, beyond pushing his all-purpose remedy of cutting capital gains taxes on the rich. Conservative and liberal economists alike agree that the tax Bush would have cut, had job creation been a priority, is the one that most directly discourages employers from hiring and unemployed people from taking low-wage jobs: the Social Security tax.

In another area of economic policy, Bush and Treasury secretary Brady have decried the rapid growth in corporate debt and the tax advantages conferred on companies that finance themselves with loans as opposed to issuance of stock. But his Treasury Department stalled for more than a year in releasing a study on exactly that topic, and Bush has failed to follow through on its recommendations to reduce the inequities in tax treatment of debt and equity financing.

Bush in his 1990 State of the Union address vowed that "I am committed to bring the staggering cost of health care under control." But he and Sununu privately considered the issue a political "poison pill," in the chief of staff's words, and planned to postpone action on health care until after the 1992 election. "All we have to do," one senior White House official smugly explained in August 1991, "is to say that the Democrats are for socialized medicine and we're not." That plan, however, was changed abruptly after health care became a cutting issue in the surprise defeat of Dick Thornburgh in the 1991 Pennsylvania Senate race. The morning after that election Bush had his own surprise for his health and human services secretary, Dr. Louis Sullivan, and most of the rest of his aides, when he promised to unveil a health-care initiative twelve weeks hence in his State of the Union address. There, Bush enunciated a sensible, market-oriented framework—but he left the framework hollow. He refused the key reform that the conservative Heritage Foundation had urged: to slash the $43 billion federal tax subsidy for big companies that buy expensive health insurance for their employees and to use the savings to make private insurance more affordable for individuals, who then would have more incentive to hold down the cost of their health care. He left it to Congress to find the money to pay for the expansion of health insurance that he proposed. And he still had not submitted detailed health care legislation four months later, in late May.

Bush would not even bother to follow through completely on his most specific campaign commitment in the kinder and gentler department: to fully fund the Head Start early education and nutrition program, which is praised for its efficiency by Republicans and

Democrats alike. To be sure, Bush proposed record increases in funding for the program, but his 1993 budget request still would fail to serve at least two hundred thousand, or one-fifth, of the disadvantaged four-year-olds who qualified for it. And a much larger number of three-year-olds would continue to be turned away for lack of funding.

When he does follow through on a domestic issue, Bush often adopts a carefully worked-out straddle: a favorite position on issues serious and silly. During his first campaign for president, in 1980, Bush declined to describe himself as either "conservative" or "moderate," leaping to accept a reporter's offer of "moderate conservative." Bush struggled to avoid angering either supporters or opponents of organized labor during a tour of a North Carolina furniture mill, where he said: "I'm for unions; I'm for nonunions." He tried to please those who like their turkeys on the plate and on the hoof during Thanksgiving of 1991: he humanely assured the nation that the live gobbler he was presented by turkey growers would be donated to a local petting zoo but also took delivery of another bird that had been butchered out of sight of TV cameras. When faced with a choice of mashed potatoes or fries, he once asked what everyone else was having, then, finding no consensus, ordered both.

During his speech commemorating the fiftieth anniversary of the Japanese attack on Pearl Harbor, Bush quoted the patrician Henry Stimson, who, as Franklin Roosevelt's secretary of war, spoke to Bush's graduating class at Phillips Andover Academy in June of 1942, shortly before Bush signed on and became the navy's youngest pilot. Bush cited Stimson's admonition that a soldier should be "brave without being brutal, self-confident without boasting, part of an irresistible might, but without losing faith in individual liberty." Bush thinks and talks that way himself: balancing every sentiment lest it offend someone; heading first in one direction, then hedging from the fear that he might go too far, and finally tacking back in the other direction.

On policy matters Bush's straddle-happy approach resulted in a splitting of the difference on the 1989 increase in the minimum wage: the wage was $3.35 an hour, the Democrats wanted $4.65, and the president, according to one top adviser, "just picked a number" at $4.25, portraying his position as a profile in political toughness: "A penny more," growled Sununu, "is vetoland."

Bush also split the difference on many disputed sections of the Clean Air Act to make the legislation more cost-effective and sensitive to business interests—but not nearly as sensitive as those interests, and some of Bush's top economic advisers, thought necessary. Corporate executives and small-business owners complain that the administration has saddled them with heavy costs in scores of other major regulatory laws, including the Americans with Disabilities Act's requirement that almost all apartments and businesses be accessible to wheelchairs, estimated to cost nearly $2 billion a year. They could only marvel at Bush's audacity when he decried the costs of federal regulatory "mandates."

Again, on gun control, Bush tried to have it both ways. After a gunman armed with a semiautomatic assault rifle massacred seventeen schoolchildren in Stockton, California, in January 1989, Bush went along with drug czar Bill Bennett—and most of the nation's police chiefs—in calling for controls on the weapons. Then, when the National Rifle Association and a few conservative groups complained, Bush reneged. He had the White House operators track down Heritage Foundation president Ed Feulner on his car phone and asked the conservative leader to draft a compromise to get him out of the gun control mess. Feulner wrote Bush four pages of recommendations intended to "retain the support of your gun-owning constituency." He suggested that the NRA would probably not accept controls except on semiautomatics with more than ten bullets in their ammunition clips—and then only on imported models. (The NRA relies on domestic gun manufacturers for much of its financing.) More important, Feulner recommended that Bush change the subject from the political mine field of gun control to a more broadly appealing "tough on crime" pitch. "The focus of government action," he wrote, "should be to prevent crime, not to ban guns." Bush implemented Feulner's suggestions almost verbatim.

The biggest straddle, by far, of his presidency has come on civil rights. Early on, Bush said he supported a new civil rights bill to redress a recent Supreme Court decision that made it very difficult for women and members of racial minorities to prove discrimination in the workplace. But, he added, the bill must avoid imposition of racial hiring "quotas" on employers. In October 1990, under fire for abandoning his "no new taxes" pledge, with Republican congressmen facing midterm elections, and with polls showing racial hiring quotas to be a potent issue among working-class whites, Bush vetoed the civil rights legislation passed by Congress, calling it a "quota bill." Thirteen months later, however, Bush was under pressure from a different direction. Former Ku Klux Klan leader and neo-Nazi David Duke had outpolled Buddy Roemer, the incumbent Republican, for a spot in the runoff for governor of Louisiana. Bush was accused of failing to do enough to defeat Duke, and news stories compared Duke's emphasis on quotas with Bush's. The president's advisers feared that Bush would be tainted in the eyes of young, well-educated voters who are highly sensitive to charges of racism. So this time Bush signed the civil rights bill, which sustained only cosmetic changes.

There was never a whit of consistency in Bush's position, for all along he had supported federal "set aside" rules that guaranteed preference to minorities and women in the awarding of federal contracts, favoring them over white males of equal or higher qualifications. One explanation for Bush's support for set-asides—a creation of President Nixon—is that they are received by many black businessmen who are active as financial contributors to Republican campaigns and who give the party more diversity than it would have otherwise. When Bush invited black publishers and printers for a private meeting in the Oval Office in February 1990, for example, his visitors took the opportunity to appeal for more federal contracts. Bush also has accepted the Republican party's ghetto-ization of its black members by relegating them to nonvoting special-interest seats for racially or ethnically exclusive "auxiliaries." The 165-member Republican National Committee in 1992 had exactly three black members, all of whom represented the U.S. Virgin Islands.

One telltale sign of Bush's unprincipled approach to the civil rights debate was that he kept shifting his reasons for opposing the bill. The final dodge came after his objections to so-called quota provisions had been overcome. Then Bush protested that the bill would inhibit his efforts to improve American education, for example, by prohibiting an employer from requiring a high school diploma from applicants for a janitor's job. Senator John Danforth of Missouri, the chief Republican backer of the civil rights bill (who simultaneously was shepherding Bush's nomination of Clarence Thomas to the Supreme Court), expressed anger at these flip-flops and suspicion of White House intentions. Bush backed down.

Another sign was that Bush in 1990 campaigned harder for North Carolina senator Jesse Helms, the Republican extremist, than for almost any other GOP candidate, helping him to win reelection in a tight race against Harvey Gantt, the black mayor of Charlotte. Bush waved away complaints against the thinly veiled racial appeals contained in

Helms's television ads and against widespread reports that Helms's campaign was engaged in intimidation of black voters. But in 1992 the U.S. Justice Department filed a complaint, along with a consent decree signed by the Helms campaign, charging the Helms campaign with intimidation of black voters in violation of the Civil Rights Act and the Voting Rights Act. The department found that the Helms campaign had improperly mailed 125,000 postcards to registered voters in eighty-six predominantly black precincts, warning those voters that they might not be eligible to vote and adding that they could be prosecuted for fraud and sent to prison if they showed up at the polls. The Justice Department did not fine Helms or anyone involved in his campaign.

Bush again sided with Helms in opposing Health and Human Services secretary Sullivan's push to remove AIDS from the immigration exclusion list, where it had been kept through the efforts of the North Carolina senator. Sullivan had made the case that AIDS was not an "infectious" disease, except for those who shared needles or unsafe sex. But the White House feared an outcry from the Right if it removed the disease from the exclusion list, so it fell back onto a new argument. Now, immigrants with AIDS were called a threat to the public purse because they might need expensive taxpayer-subsidized medical treatment. Never mind that immigrants with heart disease and a dozen other ailments that posed a far greater risk to the public purse were never asked about, much less tested for, these conditions.

Silly Pulpit

Bush often protests that liberal Democrats criticize his domestic policies simply because he resists "throwing money" at problems. Leaving aside for a moment the reality of Bush's record level of spending, he has a point. As Bill Bennett, one of the most aggressive and conservative members of Bush's cabinet, observed, "You don't have to spend a lot of money on government programs to be an activist president." What you do have to do in that case, however, is to lead through the effective use of rhetoric: to educate and persuade; to clearly and provocatively frame real choices. And it is there—not in failing to spend enough money—that Bush most vividly demonstrated his irresolution in domestic policy.

From his first days in the Oval Office, Bush spoke of using the "bully pulpit" as an alternative to spending money on social ills. Yet Bush demonstrated little historical or practical sense of what the "bully" party means. For example, in what was meant to be a red-meat campaign speech in October 1990, Bush started out in a bully mood: "Harry Truman reminded us that only a president represents all the people; can stand for the national interest and stand against the special interests." But in the very next sentence Bush said, "In this spirit—I think you'll remember this—I did extend my hand. I worked for a bipartisan solution to this horrible budget mess."

The most effective presidential preachers, from Bush's hero Teddy Roosevelt to Bush's predecessor Ronald Reagan, used their speeches to inspire support for their programs, to attack special interests who placed their greed and inertia above the public weal, and generally to knock heads and get things done. President Truman took on the "do-nothing Congress." President Eisenhower, finally, took on segregationists in Little Rock. President Kennedy took on the price-boosting steel companies. All of them made enemies, but all also won respect from most Americans, who like their presidents, at least occasionally, to "kick ass" (as Bush once said in another context). Under Bush, however, the bully pulpit has been gelded into a platform for right-minded, mushy sentiments—for better schools, against illegal drugs —while taking care not to say anything disagreeable.

One example came during Bush's trip in February 1990 to the anti-drug summit in Cartagena, Colombia, where he met with presidents of the Andean drug-producing countries. In their private sessions with Bush, the Andean leaders emphasized that much as they feared their countries' drug lords, they feared economic catastrophe more. The United States was asking them to shut down an industry that employed hundreds of thousands of peasants and urban service workers and provided the foreign exchange their countries needed to serve heavy debts to U.S. banks. Yet the United States offered little help in reducing demand for drugs or encouraging alternative exports. Modest aid to help deliver legal crops from the countryside to air and sea ports, via roads and refrigeration facilities, would go a long way. So would slashing U.S. trade barriers to Andean exports of flowers, citrus, sugar, and other legitimate exports.

103

Bush replied that he could do little to loosen U.S. trade barriers. In fact, to move the well-financed U.S. agribusiness interests that benefit from tariffs on Andean food and flowers, Bush needed only to point out forcefully—privately and then, if necessary, from the bully pulpit —that they were impeding the war against illegal drugs. "When your president wouldn't even take on your cut-flower lobby," said a top adviser to Colombia's president Virgilio Barco, "we knew he wasn't serious about a 'war' on drugs." To his credit, Bush eventually signed a bill that eased U.S. tariffs on some imports from the Andean countries, but that was at the end of his third year in office, and several of the countries' major exports continue to face high duties.

Shortly after he took office, Bush told reporters that he knew, from his leadership of Reagan's antidrug effort, that education, treatment, and other demand-side solutions were more important than interdiction of drug shipments and other supply-side solutions. "The elimination of drugs is going to stem from vigorous change in the society's approach to narcotics," Bush said. "It's going to be successful only if our education is successful. The answer to the problem of drugs lies more on solving the demand side of the equation than it does on the supply side—than it does on interdiction or sealing the borders." Treasury secretary Brady, who supervises the Customs Service, concluded privately in an early drug-strategy meeting that efforts at attacking supply were doomed as long as a high demand for drugs continued. But by the time Bush announced his drug control strategy, in his first prime-time TV address from the Oval Office in September 1989, that strategy had shifted strongly toward a crackdown on drug shipments and other drug crime—in part at the insistence of Sununu, who had noted polls that showed most Americans favored get-tough measures over the softer, more expensive, education and treatment options.

During his televised drug speech, Bush, who often decries "show biz" methods of promoting public policy, held up a clear plastic bag containing crack cocaine, which, he informed his nationwide audience, had been purchased by plainclothes lawmen in Lafayette Park, directly across the street from the White House. Bush was narrowly correct. But, as *The Washington Post* reported two weeks later, federal drug agents had lured a well-known dealer out of his usual turf to the park for the purpose of providing the president with a dramatic prop. Confronted with this embarrassment, Bush became as testy as

104

at any time in his first three years, barking at reporters: "Has somebody got some advocates here for this drug guy?"

The White House argued, with some justification, that all was well that ended well on the drug issue: drug use declined, especially among casual, middle-class users, from 1989 to 1992. But the results were not so heartening on another of Bush's priority domestic issues: education. Test scores of U.S. students remained abysmal, particularly when compared with those of America's major international competitors in Europe and Asia. Jeanne Allen, an educational specialist at the conservative Heritage Foundation, cited several bully-pulpit appeals by which Bush could do much to improve U.S. schools. He could, for example, argue that U.S. students are not inherently less capable of learning than their German or Japanese counterparts, but they don't attend academic classes or do homework for as many hours each day or as many days each year—and they should, by a date soon and certain. Bush could propose to increase federal aid to school districts that adopt such reforms, financed by cutting aid to those that don't. Instead Bush offered empty cheerleading that U.S. students will—he doesn't say how—be "number one" in the world in math and science by the year 2000.

Bush and his advisers believe that the education system should move toward "vouchers" tenable at any public or private school that meets minimum standards and is open to all races and creeds. But he has not really gone to bat for that approach. If he had, he could have cited the bloated administrator-to-student ratios of many big-city public school systems, as compared with those cities' Catholic systems, which take in similar students and educate them better. (New York City's public schools have an administrator at headquarters for every 243 students, versus one for every 3,330 students in that city's Catholic system.) Bush could have cited the cost per pupil in the same big-city systems, which approach the tuition for some of the best private academies. (New York public schools spend $7,100 per student, with a 38 percent graduation rate, while that city's Catholic schools spend $1,700 per student and graduate 99 percent.)

When Senator Ted Kennedy led the opposition to a modest school-choice plan that Bush proposed, the president declined staff suggestions that he point out that Kennedy was withholding from the poor the choices he and his brothers and his children had enjoyed as students of private schools. "The president wants to avoid having education become a partisan issue,'' said one senior official, ''so he ends up not being willing to fight for anything.''

Asked in December 1990, and again in April 1991, what one accomplishment he would most like to have in the second half of his term, Bush replied without hesitation, ''Our education goals''—conveniently choosing an area in which 90 percent of the funding and almost all the heavy lifting must be provided at the state and local level and where he sees the president's role mainly as ''encouraging people to do things.'' Pressed by a New Hampshire voter, shortly before that state's presidential primary election in February 1992, to name something specific that he had done for education besides talk about it, Bush replied that ''I got my wife to demonstrate her concern by reading to children. . . . Barbara's out there, and I'm trying to help as best I can, saying you've got to hold the family together, you've got to participate, you've got to read.''

Bush takes the position that there's little more he can do, given the American tradition of local control of schools. But many educators disagree, pointing to study after study that shows that a major reason students fail to achieve in school, particularly in high school, is that they cannot see it making much difference in their lives after school. Many will not be able to afford college or get sufficient financial aid to attend. These same educators point to strong anecdotal evidence that when public school students are promised money for college if they make good grades, they buckle down and perform much like kids at private academies. Here, then, is a way for the federal government to encourage better public school performance: by fulfilling Washington's traditional, but in recent years neglected, role of expanding college aid. Late in his 1988 campaign Bush declared, ''All the kids in America should have the chance to go to college if their ability and their desire carry them there.'' But he failed to follow through with the tough budgetary choices needed to deliver on that promise.

Among frustrated White House activists and many other Washingtonians, one of the favorite parlor games is spinning speeches or passages that George Bush *should* deliver. During the Gulf crisis Bush could have called for a gasoline tax—preferably rebated through cuts in payroll taxes—to reduce the nation's reliance on oil imports and its vulnerability to Middle East flare-ups. During the 1990 budget talks, several of his aides suggested, Bush could have forced Congress to reduce the deficit through spending cuts rather than taxes, while also undercutting the Democrats on the ''fairness'' issue, if only he had taken his case to the public and asked, "Would you rather have taxes go up on everybody, or have federal subsidies reduced for those who make over $100,000 a year?" But either appeal would have required a willingness to anger certain constituencies. Bush has little record of taking such risks.

Several White House officials have tried to take advantage of Bush's interest in public opinion polls, to present him opportunities for rhetorical leadership. They have sent the president surveys that ask respondents not only what they think, but how much they know and don't know, and whether new information and arguments might change their opinions. For example, a July–August 1990 poll by Teeter's old firm, Market Opinion Research, asked 1,000 registered voters whether the government spends "too much, not enough, or just the right amount on federal farm subsidies." Most of the respondents, thinking of aid to small farmers in need of drought assistance and such, answered "not enough" (43 percent) or "the right amount" (12 percent). Then the respondents were told, "In 1988, 43 percent of federal farm subsidies went to farm operators whose average net income was $96,000 per year." With this new information, 55 percent of those polled said that "the federal program should be changed [and] we should only help small farms." This offered an obvious opening for Bush to shift public opinion and policy against the farm subsidies for the wealthy that he said he opposed. But he failed to follow through in any bold way.

With his mangled syntax, his preppy locutions, and his "call waiting" manner of piling up non sequiturs, Bush has turned the presidential platform into something of a silly pulpit. His speeches often adopt a tone of "We know best" and "Do it because I say so." He avoids vivid, specific, persuasive detail and examples. The language he chooses is often that of a corporate executive or federal bureaucrat, larded with "the prevailing clichés of the time, the prevailing jargon," says University of Pittsburgh professor Theodore O. Windt, a former political speech writer and expert in presidential rhetoric. Windt sees in Bush "the administrator for whom speeches are something that need to be done but are not essential to the doing of the job. That's what comes across to me."

But those who think Bush is incapable of using the bully pulpit effectively are wrong. He proved otherwise during the one incident in his first three years as president when he did use it masterfully and successfully. The occasion, not surprisingly, was a major foreign policy dispute: Israel's demand for $10 billion in U.S. loan guarantees to build housing for Soviet Jewish immigrants. The president, along with Secretary Baker and General Scowcroft, knew that Israel would use the money, directly or indirectly, to build settlements in the occupied West Bank, Gaza Strip, and Golan Heights. Bush and his team feared that such settlements, built with U.S. backing, would discredit the United States as an honest broker in peace talks between Israel and the Arabs. Israel and its lobbyists at first assumed that they could push the loan guarantees through Congress whether Bush approved or not. They learned better.

When Bush took to the podium in the White House briefing room, in a hastily called press conference on September 12, 1991, he expertly employed all the persuasive techniques that he neglects for domestic speeches. He used persuasive evidence to back his arguments, citing the current level of U.S. aid—$1,000 a year for every Israeli citizen—and played effectively into strong, latent public opposition to all foreign aid. He also set himself up, in classic bully-pulpit fashion, as the lone defender of the public interest against a greedy special interest: "We're up against very strong and effective —sometimes—groups that go up to the Hill. I heard today there were something like a thousand lobbyists on the Hill working the other side of this question. We've got one lonely little guy down here doing it." That drew a laugh, after which Bush added, "However, I like this forum better." Bush carried the day. And his performance made his domestic advisers see what he could accomplish on their issues, if only he would.

5

COLOR ME BAD

People can tell just by looking at George Bush that he dislikes confrontation. His genuinely easy and outgoing manner is not common in a man who accepts discord and strife. Conflict simply isn't in his nature. It is what has made him so easy to like and so successful as a politician. It is also what has made his occasional attempts at flinty-eyed confrontation look petty, petulant, and unpresidential. As a matter of style, the role of antagonist warred with what former aide Fred Khodouri called "the image that he wished to convey as a high-minded and public-spirited person."

Vic Gold, Bush's biographer and former speech writer, recalls that during the 1984 campaign, he and onetime press secretary Pete Teeley would have to "pour gasoline on Bush and light a match to him and say, 'You should hear what those Democrats are saying about you' " in order to get him to counterattack. During the 1988 New Hampshire primary campaign, Bush had to be cornered into allowing John Sununu, Roger Ailes, and Lee Atwater to run television commercials that tagged Robert Dole as a senator who "straddles" such issues as arms control and taxes. Even after the controversial ad began to run, an aide recalled, "Bush didn't like it. He complained about it. Lee told him something reassuring and just kept it up there."

But Bush recognizes that politics often requires a brutish touch and is practical enough to keep around him the kinds of hardballers who

109

specialize in playing for keeps. Throughout his career, Bush has relied on a combination of bad boys (and girls) to do the unpleasant and unseemly chores that inevitably come with power politics: to crack heads, fire subordinates, turn down requests, deliver bad news, catch flak, and give the boss deniability. Bush always had various henchmen in his corner. As vice president Bush turned to executive assistant Jennifer Fitzgerald to be his doorkeeper. It was she who garnered the dislike of nearly everyone around the vice president for her brusque handling of her boss's political business. Various old-time Bush aides quit out of frustration with Bush's domineering scheduler. "I'm not saying she's Miss Popularity," he said in 1982. "She's doing what I want done. When you have to say 'no,' particularly to friends, there's bound to be some level of frustration."

As a presidential candidate, Bush turned to Lee Atwater to ride herd on conservatives and plan attacks on his rivals. He looked to Roger Ailes to help transform the public perception of him as a wimp into a fire-eating national figure. He counted on his eldest son, George W. Bush, as a kind of family enforcer who patrolled the corridors of the Bush campaign in search of traitors to the cause. As a top Republican official explained in early 1990, "Bush really needs a bad cop, and he knows he needs it." Bush once put it this way: "I'm a competitor, and I don't like, you know, being the javelin catcher."

If the bad boys were always changing over the years, the rules they played by did not. When aides had caught too many spears and had outlived their usefulness, Bush discarded them. Remarkably, this was an aspect of working for Bush that many of his top aides never seemed to grasp. He had a remarkable capacity to get the men and women around him to walk off cliffs on his behalf and assume all the while that he supported them every step of the way. Just as he worked constituents, Bush worked his various aides: conservatives among them were convinced he was a true believer; moderates emerged from meetings convinced he was a centrist. Many of the bad cops and sidekicks Bush kept around for years believed they were doing a perfectly acceptable job one day but found themselves out the door the next, used up. "It's called 'Think whatever you want,' " said one official. "Some people around here never figure it out."

Some have complained about having to wear the black hat, particularly because they found it hard to take off. Atwater often griped that once Bush cast someone in a certain role, it was almost impossible to overcome it. Bush, he said, divided his friends and advisers into neat

110

categories by expertise and experience. The president liked to joke
that he wouldn't play tennis with anyone whose game had not been
assessed in advance by an informal "ranking committee" made up of
family and friends who assessed a newcomer's play. But in more
important respects Bush also had an internal ranking committee: foreign policy aides weren't consulted on domestic affairs, and vice
versa. Commerce secretary Robert Mosbacher might be smart about
business but was weak on political strategy. Atwater might be an ace
political tactician but was not helpful about policy. "He compartmentalizes people," Atwater said. "And once he's made up his mind
about you, it doesn't change." Atwater lamented that the compart-
mentalization probably meant that his future under Bush was limited;
it was certainly ironic that one of the favorite recordings made by the
guitar-picking GOP boss was a rendition of "Bad Boy," an Eddie
Taylor song, which went, "I'm bad. I'm bad. I'm the worst you ever
had."

Because personal ties, rather than conviction, drove his political
success, Bush as president needed someone to manage the ever-
widening circle of allies who would place demands upon his time.
Bush was no manager—for the preceding ten years he had run a
nonstop campaign for the presidency, an effort for the most part managed by others. Apart from a year-long stint at the CIA, Bush had
never run a large public organization for an extended period of time.
"Bush's ability to sign people up one by one is what his political
success is largely based on," said one official. "He got elected because of all the people he knows. Because he was always saying yes,
he needed someone who could say no."

A man of unfailing manners, Bush often found it difficult to engage
people in argument and spark policy debates that often yield policy
breakthroughs. Aides would actually stage arguments, known as
"train wrecks," so Bush could watch people and their ideas collide.
"I don't want to say Bush is a wimp," said one veteran of the 1988
campaign, "but he has a tendency to agree with people and to leave
them all thinking he's going to do what they want. During the campaign, all kinds of people with all kinds of political views would talk
to George Bush, and all of them would come away thinking he was
their guy. Which is fine for a campaign but not so great when you're
president."

Bush's chief of staff would also need the heft to match the stature
of James Baker, Brent Scowcroft, Robert Mosbacher, Treasury sec-

retary Nicholas Brady, and others who would fill the top jobs. Each of these men had strong, independent relationships with Bush and already knew their own, and each other's, strengths and weaknesses. Additionally, Bush's other top advisers—Defense secretary Richard Cheney, Budget director Richard Darman, Agriculture secretary Clayton Yeutter, Trade representative Carla Hills—had also worked together, and with Bush, for more than fifteen years. (Bush, Baker, Cheney, Scowcroft, Darman, Yeutter, and Hills had all toiled for Gerald Ford, making the Bush cabinet look more like the Ford revival than the Reagan consolidation.) If the factionalized Reagan White House had seemed structured to spawn disagreements arbitrated by a passive president, the Bush White House seemed structured to spawn consensus. Bush realized that an absence of conflict could devolve into self-satisfaction without someone around to kick the administration out of its almost certain "we know best" complacency. "The group would have been too comfortable with itself," one of the long-time veterans said in 1990. "It needs a provocateur."

But the provocateur had to be devoted to Bush alone. Bush had watched his friend Baker, as Reagan's chief of staff, privately blame the commander in chief for much of what went wrong and take the credit for most of what went right, in the Reagan administration. Bush was determined to find a more selfless chief of staff. He wanted one who would take the heat, dish out covering and retaliatory fire, and make sure the president got all the credit. He wanted a chief of staff who would salute smartly at any request. He wanted someone who could take on his formidable cabinet if necessary, but who would not feel comfortable challenging the president. Someone who would, above all, be loyal.

"Thank You, New Hampshire"

John Sununu must be taking this hard, thought Steve Merrill as he made his way to see the New Hampshire governor on the cold bright morning after the 1988 Iowa caucuses. Sununu's candidate, Vice President George Bush, had been trounced in the Iowa contest by both Kansan Robert Dole and long-shot conservative televangelist Pat Robertson. Bush's lead in the Granite State seemed sure to shrink with the Republican primary just a week away. Merrill, at one time Sununu's counsel, figured his old boss might need some cheering up and found the governor with his back to the door, staring out his window onto the snow-covered statehouse lawn. "I heard the news from Iowa and thought you might like to talk about it," said Merrill.

Spinning on his heels and wearing a wolfish grin, Sununu replied, "Yeah, isn't it great?" Seeing Merrill's confusion, Sununu explained that the Iowa defeat had left Bush desperate for a win in New Hampshire. "Don't you see?" he asked. "Don't you see how much good I'm going to be able to do for the next president of the United States?"

Like Arnold Schwarzenegger and Danny DeVito, George Bush and John Sununu were about to become the stars of a real-life buddy film: one was tall, well built, and handsome; the other was short, pear-shaped, and homely. One was polite, graceful, and courteous, even when angry; the other was hostile, brash, and rude, even when perfectly happy. One dressed impeccably; the other couldn't keep his shirttail tucked in. One had been blessed with a fortune, a famous name, and a powerful father on a first-name basis with presidents, CEOs, and other power brokers. The other was born in Havana, the son of a foreign-film distributor, who bequeathed to his children a funny-sounding name and a polyglot Lebanese, Greek, and Salvadoran heritage. George Bush's brother nicknamed him "Have Half" for his habit of offering friends an equal portion of his candy bar. By comparison, the bullies in John Sununu's Queens, New York, neighborhood gave him the choice of getting beaten before class or after, which explained why a Band-Aid or tape usually adorned the bridge of his eyeglasses. Bush attended Phillips Andover, the prep school for the ruling class, and then joined the navy; Sununu became the top cadet at a military academy on Long Island, marching his contemporaries with a sword on his hip and entering MIT upon graduation. One played baseball and was scouted briefly by the pros; the other owned 50,000 baseball cards. One was known around the White House as "Mr. Smooth" and the other as "that fat little pirate."

Buddy film plots are always the same: two guys who seem to have nothing in common find themselves in a difficult spot, bail one another out against impossible odds, and somehow turn out to be the perfect team. In 1982, when Sununu's long-shot gubernatorial campaign was floundering and short of cash, Vice President Bush flew to New Hampshire, helped the long-shot challenger raise a war chest, and sent him on to victory. Six years later Sununu repaid the favor. When

Bush placed a disastrous third in Iowa, bringing Bush's political career to the brink of extinction, Sununu took complete control of Bush's New Hampshire campaign, convincing the candidate to drop his patrician pose, take off his jacket, and be seen driving a tractor-trailer at a truck stop. He spent fifteen hours a day with Bush, reassuring the vice president that his twenty-five-year-old political career was not yet over. Sununu turned his entire statewide organization over to Bush, chose the sites for events, cranked up the vice president's antitax rhetoric, and convinced the manager of the state's lone television station to air the straddle ad after the deadline for accepting spots had passed. Bush won the primary with 37 percent to Dole's 29 percent; in eight days—just as he had brashly predicted—John Sununu had converted the worst experience in Bush's political life to the best.

During those days together, Bush and Sununu discovered that they had more in common than either had expected. Both had big families. Sununu's home in Salem, New Hampshire, was less than an hour's drive from Bush's only real home, in Kennebunkport, Maine. Both were smart, well-trained politicians who had topped their classes and led their peers since high school. Both had a healthy sense of humor and loved to make jokes even in the most serious moments. Both were political transplants who got their start in politics by moving to a new, fast-growing state. Both had met political success by bringing together long feuding wings of their respective Republican state parties. Both men were restless to the point of hyperactivity and had a reputation among their friends for frenetic behavior. Both men were devoted to poll data. And both had been repeatedly underestimated throughout their political careers. David Carney, Sununu's longtime political aide who followed him to Washington to work in the White House, recalls how locals made fun of Sununu when he started in politics. "Nobody ever thought this fat little Lebanese guy could ever make it in New Hampshire politics," Carney explained. "People have consistently underestimated John Sununu's ability to adapt and change and learn, and that has been a big advantage to him. He's much like Bush in this way."

The bond forged in New Hampshire proved stronger than other, longer-standing, ties. Ten months later, as a just-elected Bush prepared to name a chief of staff, James Baker had backed a plan to put campaign chief of staff Craig Fuller, pollster Robert Teeter, and Su-

114

nunu in a kind of Reagan White House troika of presidential aides. But Bush ignored the suggestion and tapped the tenacious three-term governor instead. "When you go through a tough time like that," explained Charlie Black, a GOP consultant, "and sort of go through the valley of the shadow of political death, and then come back out of it and emerge victorious, the people who go through that together have a bond that is much different from just routine government business."

When Bush said, "Thank you, New Hampshire," after his victory in November, he was really thanking John Sununu.

"One Hundred Percent of the Negative"

In February 1990 eleven environmental groups sent a letter to George Bush, charging that the president's chief of staff was deliberately undermining his record on the environment. "Mr. President, you have articulated laudable environmental goals, but it appears your chief of staff is not committed to meeting them. Our organizations have promised to work with you to achieve the goals you set and to following through until they are met. But we cannot make good on our promise if Mr. Sununu takes it upon himself to implement policies that contradict the goals you have set." One Pat Oliphant cartoon pictured Bush sitting in a dentist's chair while Sununu, wearing a white coat, had lifted the "lid" off Bush's head and was reworking the machinery inside with large hand wrenches. The caption read "John Sununu, Environmental Attitudes Adjustment Engineer." Jay D. Hair, president of the National Wildlife Federation, said, "We believe George Bush is an environmentalist president. But what we have is an environmental nightmare in Chief of Staff John Sununu."

Bad press for Bush? Hardly. In fact, everything was going according to plan. While the president posed as the friend of the environment, his chief of staff worked behind the scenes on behalf of the interests of business. Those who felt double-crossed rarely blamed Bush. The problem, they thought, was Sununu. All Bush needed to do, his erstwhile supporters complained, was take his chief of staff to the woodshed. Such demands never failed to amuse the men in the

West Wing. "The perception was always worse than the reality. Sununu took all the arrows," explained a Sununu aide, "and Bush took all the credit. We were laughing all the way to the bank."

Sununu was hardly the only heavy Bush deployed to do his dirty work. Bush dispatched Deputy National Security Adviser Robert Gates to read the riot act to Pakistan prime minister Benazir Bhutto when her generals began making warlike noises toward India. He turned to longtime counsel C. Boyden Gray to take charge of the administration's foot-dragging negotiations with Congress in 1990 and 1991 on a new civil rights bill. (Gray was also a master of circumlocution. As one aide put it, "When a law degree was deployed, it was usually deployed to bollix something up, to come up with a convoluted reason for something we couldn't do. It was never a positive thing." But the effect was the same: to deflect flak from the right-minded president.) Bush took nearly two dozen American CEOs to Tokyo with him in 1992, hinting implicitly to his Japanese counterparts that they could play ball with him or take their chances with the more protectionist types from the corporate boardrooms—and their friends in Congress. In the 1992 primary campaign, Bush turned to "surrogates" Dan Quayle, Arnold Schwarzenegger, and retired Marine Corps commandant P. X. Kelley to take on Pat Buchanan. For weeks Bush refused to use Buchanan's name or entertain questions about his opponent's allegedly anti-Semitic views. "Let that," Bush said, "come from others." It did: asked six weeks later if Buchanan was an anti-Semite, Sununu's successor as chief of staff, Sam Skinner, replied, "I think the Jewish community believes he is. . . . They're the best ones to measure his record on that issue."

These stalking horses allowed Bush to play the self-described role he liked best: Mr. Smooth. If Ronald Reagan had employed conciliatory chiefs of staff such as Jim Baker, Howard Baker, and Ken Duberstein to cut deals with political allies and foes in Congress, Bush adopted that role himself and left the nut cutting to others. No one played the foil as effectively or as frequently as Sununu. Where Bush was pleasant and reasonable, the chief of staff was arrogant and insulting. While Bush was warm to aides and friendly in meetings with outsiders, Sununu ran the White House with an iron fist and regularly unloaded on lobbyists and lawmakers when they visited the White House. Bush might speak briefly to visitors on issues, but Sununu would pick up after Bush left and castigate the same group for undermining the president's position. "John has a great understanding of

George Bush," said one senior official. "He knows the guy does not like negatives. He does not like to say no. The kinder, gentler side is really the more dominant in Bush, so Sununu felt like, even more than with most presidents, he needed to be the guy to say no and take the flak. He set it up that way deliberately." Sununu's friends would worry about the arrangement from time to time, warning the chief of staff that he was getting too exposed as the in-house heavy. But Sununu dismissed such concerns with a wave and a favorite explanation. "I need to make sure I'm the guy saying no," he would say. "One hundred percent of the negative has to be here."

In fact, Bush deployed Sununu as a kind of double-sided human shield, whom liberals would blame for taking a moderate administration hostage and to whom conservatives would turn when the president abandoned their causes. Sununu ran interference when Bush needed to shuffle to the right on such issues as judicial appointments or abortion, absorbing the blame of Bush's latest pander to his party's extremist wing. But because his ties to conservatives were so strong, Sununu could mollify the powerful GOP faction when the president needed to veer back to the middle on taxes and fiscal questions.

Nowhere did this game work better than on environmental affairs. While Bush often likened himself to Izaak Walton, Sununu became a latter-day James Watt, parrying a seemingly endless string of proposed environmental protections with diluted versions that were more beneficial to business. It was Sununu who "personally" watered down a statement of administration policy on global warming in 1990 and, later in the same week, intervened to weaken a wetlands pact between the Environmental Protection Agency and the Army Corps of Engineers. Even in defeat Sununu reinforced the overall impression that he, not George Bush, was at the helm. Though it was Sununu who blocked a plan by Environmental Protection Agency director William Reilly to contribute $25 million to a fund that would have helped underdeveloped countries lessen their reliance on chemicals that deplete the ozone layer, it also fell to Sununu to announce a reversal of the plan five weeks later.

During most of the first two years, Sununu engaged in an unusually public war with Reilly, whose mainstream environmentalism was several notches to the left of Bush's and several more to the left of Sununu's. Though the feud had the effect of isolating Sununu as an enemy of ecology—and turning Reilly into a kind of environmental poster child—the chief of staff was in fact safely within the adminis-

117

tration mainstream. "The important thing to keep in mind is that Bush, [economic adviser Michael] Boskin, and Darman agree with John right down the line on this stuff," said a senior administration official. "He is not misrepresenting the president's position."

To his credit, Sununu often explained the game he was playing. "Look," he said in early 1990, "I have found that misperception of my sternness does not weaken my capacity to talk to people in the future. So you know, you all know, I'm a pussycat, the staff knows I'm a pussycat, but we try and keep that a secret and let all the misreporting about how firm I can be create a slightly tougher perspective than reality. And it's always good to have that reality give you the slightly tougher perspective, I mean, the perception being slightly tougher than reality . . . allows you to play a firm hand."

But nothing pleased Bush more than the way Sununu, as one family member later put it, "sliced and diced the Republican Right." Never fully certified as a conservative, Bush prized Sununu's ties to the party's extreme factions, not only because they trusted Sununu, but because Sununu seemed to know how to keep them in line. He often argued the conservative case in staff meetings, and like-minded activists counted on the chief of staff to be their voice at the table in difficult negotiations. Early on, too, Sununu had a hand in blocking a number of nominations that the Right opposed and nursing the appointment of key conservative favorites. The former New Hampshire governor was more conservative and more outspoken than the president on abortion, gun control, the environment, and taxes.

Sununu's marked conservatism made it easier for him to serve the president's interests. While Budget director Richard Darman recused himself from Clean Air Act negotiations on the grounds that its passage would place a $25 billion burden on private business at a time when the economy was turning sluggish, Sununu led the behind-the-scenes campaign to sell the costly agreement to conservatives. His approach with that segment of the Bush coalition was markedly different from the approach he took on the Sunday talk shows. "He was able to explain to the right what the president was trying to do and how that was what we all wanted, and they believed him," an aide later explained. "He told them, 'Hey, under this plan, you can pay someone to pollute.' What more could they ask for?" Similarly, it was difficult for the Right to complain about the outcome of either the child care bill or the disabled rights measure when both had been negotiated by the most outspoken conservative in the administration.

As one supporter explained it, "If anybody thinks he enjoyed negotiating with Teddy Kennedy on stuff like child care and disabled rights, they're mistaken. He was doing his job, not what he would have done."

Despite his self-made reputation, to the contrary, Sununu rarely exceeded his authority. He was often accused by more moderate Bush loyalists of leveraging his conservative backing against Bush in order to keep his job. But evidence of this is almost nonexistent. Even conservatives who pressed Sununu to nudge the administration to the right admitted, as did one in 1990, "I've never seen a crack of daylight between them in public or even in private meetings, which is a tribute to Sununu's discipline." Bill Bennett, another conservative, added, "I never saw him try to push his own agenda, even with a nod or a wink to say 'This is what the president wants, but I know better,' and that's not an easy discipline for someone with the strong convictions and intellect of John Sununu." In late April 1989, after Defense secretary Richard Cheney predicted that Gorbachev's reform efforts "would ultimately fail," Sununu angered conservatives when he took pains to say, "That is not the president's view."

With characteristic vigilance, Sununu led the charge to sell the 1990 budget deal, threatening Republican members of the House if they didn't get behind the president. At a White House meeting with Republican lawmakers, Sununu even suggested that Bush might campaign against members of his own party. When Bill Goodling, a Pennsylvania lawmaker, complained that the president would "never do anything like that," Sununu retorted, "George Bush is a much nicer guy than I am." Representative Jim Lightfoot wrote Bush a letter inviting him to visit Capitol Hill to discuss the budget but leave "the pit bulldogs at the White House." Democrats referred to Bush's three-man negotiating team as "Nick, Dick, and Prick." Sununu returned the disdain, reading newspapers and stamp catalogs while others talked. He exploded when a long awaited Democratic proposal yielded little in the way of specifics. By the end of the talks, even Republican leaders were dismissive of what Senator Dole referred to as the "chief of chaff." Democrat Robert Byrd of West Virginia took special umbrage. "I have had thirty years in the U.S. Senate, and I have participated in many such summits, and I have never in my life observed such outrageous conduct as that displayed by the representatives of the president. Your conduct is arrogant. It is rude. It is intolerant."

119

But the dutiful chief of staff insisted that this was what Bush wanted. "I think that I realized," he said after the budget pact was signed, "the president realized, we all realized, that in trying to get Congress to cast this difficult vote, a little china would he broken. There are people you encourage one way and folks you have to encourage another way. And that's part of my job."

Then, asked if he was being scapegoated, Sununu quickly ended his brief reverie, returned to his designated role, and replied, "No, no, I probably am as bad as they've all said I am."

"You Can't Learn How to Be Pigheaded"

"Jackie, could you get Lesher on the telephone?" Sununu politely asked his secretary one morning in January 1990. It was just after 7 A.M., and Sununu was going over the morning papers. Richard Lesher, the president of the U.S. Chamber of Commerce, had been named in the morning paper as a supporter of a proposal by Democratic senator Daniel Moynihan to cut the payroll tax for Social Security. Moynihan's proposal was dangerous to Bush because it appealed to both liberal Democrats and tax-cutting Republicans and thus threatened to increase a budget deficit that Bush had yet to address. Bush, who had vowed not to "mess with Social Security," was in danger of being outflanked by tax cutters on both sides. As Lesher came on the line, Sununu asked, "Where did I get you?" When Lesher explained that he was already at work, Sununu interrupted and, without mentioning the Moynihan gambit, said, "I'm going to chain-saw your balls off!"

And this was how the chief of staff treated the president's *allies*.

Before he got sick, Lee Atwater often warned Sununu that he had to make friends with several key groups in Washington if he was to survive as chief of staff. "I told him that a chief of staff, to be successful, has to have a base of support in the Congress, the news media, and the community of Republican consultants and party activists." Atwater advised him to court sympathetic members of these groups to whom he could turn in a crunch. Confident that his "tough love" approach was just something Washington would get used to, Sununu did not. "Washington is a *mañana* kinda town," he said,

120

proud of his manner. "People here spent a good deal of their time taking steps in order to look good in failure."

That would not be Sununu's epitaph. While Sununu seldom exceeded his brief from Bush in substantive terms, his style was gratuitously insulting. After Sununu hung up three times on Representative Mickey Edwards, an Oklahoma Republican, the chief of staff believed that a few minutes spent briefing some of Edwards's constituents weeks later would patch up the whole episode. He referred to Senator Trent Lott as "insignificant," prompting the Mississippi Republican to quip, "He just stuck the wrong pig," and print buttons for his colleagues that read "I'm Insignificant, Too." Using what had obviously become a preferred metaphor, Sununu once told EPA director Reilly, "I've got nothing against you personally, Bill, but there are some members of your staff that I'd like to castrate with a chain saw." Perhaps it was just coincidental that the National Wildlife Federation began publishing a regular newsletter entitled "Sununews," which pictured the chief of staff wielding a Homelite.

He made enemies neither he nor Bush needed to make. Sununu did not realize that most people in Washington are uncomfortable with antagonism as a negotiating style. But Sununu was largely oblivious of his habit; he did not see, or care, that he was making enemies for life. Nor did Sununu realize that by treating people maliciously he ceased to get the best out of them: most Republicans and White House aides, once burned by Sununu in staff meetings, just stopped saying anything or making suggestions. Over time, despite the few differences between Bush and Sununu, the chief of staff was becoming *the* issue. As Vic Gold once put it, "His line was, 'Well, I'm just taking the spears for the president.' But my feeling was, 'Well, John, there wouldn't be as many thrown at the president if it wasn't for you.' "

In late December 1990, a top administration official took the afternoon off and drove across town to see Paul Weyrich, a leading conservative who headed the Free Congress Foundation. The official pleaded with Weyrich to pay a call on Sununu and explain to him how isolated the chief of staff and the president had become. When Weyrich got to the White House on December 20, he greeted Sununu and proceeded to tick off the names of dozens of important political allies Sununu had insulted. "John," Weyrich said, "you're a brilliant fellow. As a matter of fact, you're probably one of the smartest guys ever to serve in this position. I want you to explain something to me. The liberals hate you. The media hates you. The Bushies [Weyrich's shorthand for Bush's moderate, longtime allies] hate you. And you have systematically alienated every conservative in town. I'm the closest thing you've got left to a friend, and even I can't defend half of what you do. So explain to me how you govern without a base?''

Sununu, as Weyrich later described it, looked "absolutely stunned.'' In his defense he explained that he was simply counter-punching, hitting back at people who had in some way or another criticized the president. "My job is taking hits, and I'm going to stand up for Bush and give it to anybody who is going to stand in the way,'' he said.

Weyrich interjected, "What you don't understand is that when you do this, you make it very difficult for these people to work with you again, because you do it in such a tough way. It's one thing to say 'You're wrong' or 'I disagree' or 'If you knew what I knew.' But you're calling them names.''

Edwin Feulner, president of the Heritage Foundation, recalls visiting Sununu a month later to patch up relations that had been tattered in the wake of the budget deal. Heritage had opposed the final package and a number of other Bush's compromises and found itself suddenly unable to get a hearing anywhere in the administration. Sununu used most of the 30 minutes allotted for the meeting to criticize Heritage about its role in negotiations earlier that year on a new child care bill. Feulner replied with a warning: "Look, Governor, Heritage has been in town for almost twenty years now. We're going to be in town for a long time. And there's going to come a point, somewhere in your career, when you're going to find that you need somebody broader and deeper in your corner than the one man in the Oval Office. There's going to be a time when people start ganging up on you for one reason or another where you're going to have to have somebody call the president and say, 'Hey, we really need this guy.' The logical people to do that are the people inside the conservative movement, but not if you're going to treat us like this.''

Feulner was so baffled by the session that he arranged a second meeting to patch things up once again. When he arrived, this time with Weyrich, Sununu asked the two men why they had come. Weyrich explained that Feulner was embittered by the previous encounter. Sununu interjected, "What do you mean, a bad meeting? I thought it was a good meeting.''

Feulner replied, "Sure, you thought it was a good meeting. You come and you drop this load of crap all over me and then you feel good, but you make everybody else feel bad. It might be a good meeting from your perspective, but it's not very good from mine.''

After the meeting, Feulner told Weyrich that the session was "the most bizarre" he'd attended in his twenty-five years in Washington. But it was not half so bizarre as the phone call Weyrich received ten minutes later at his office from Ed Rogers, who said Sununu wanted to know Feulner's *real* purpose for the meeting.

Sununu relished the role of bad cop in part because he played no other role as well. In the summer of 1991 Bush's allies on a slow-moving energy bill went to see Sununu to explain why the measure was about to die in committee. The two lawmakers, Wyoming Republican Malcolm Wallop and Louisiana Democrat Bennett Johnston, received a tongue-lashing for their trouble. Sununu attacked his Hill allies for giving up too easily and insisted that they stand by the bill, no matter how short of votes they were. After the inquisition ended, Ed Rogers, Sununu's aide, asked his boss why he took a hardball approach when they were all on the same side. "What did I miss here?" asked Rogers. "What don't I see?"

"You didn't miss anything," replied Sununu. "You can't learn to be pigheaded.''

"Your Choice, As Always"

If Bush didn't realize the damage Sununu had caused, it was partly because he had come to rely so heavily on Sununu for information. The president, who vowed never to isolate himself in his own White House, found himself by 1991 increasingly cut off from his far-flung network of friends and allies. To be sure, the Persian Gulf War had distracted Bush from his regular "call-arounds" to friends and family. But the war and the subsequent victory lulled the entire administration into the false assumption that they could coast through 1991 to victory in 1992. It was Sununu who had told conservatives that Congress could go home in 1990 and not come back to Washington until after 1992. By the middle of 1991 Sununu was simply shutting down any proposal or initiative well before it reached the Oval Office. "I don't think the president knew how much he was blocked,'' said one GOP official. "Not only did Sununu block options, they stopped coming forward."

Sununu's feeble attempt to hold weekly strategy meetings each Wednesday sputtered and died. One participant explained, "I stopped going to his political strategy meetings. There wasn't any point. He already had his mind made up when we came in the door. He did all the talking and no listening. If it wasn't his idea, it was the stupidest thing he ever heard. He was talking this way to people who had worked in three or four presidential campaigns.'' Cabinet officers refused to take his telephone calls. Inside the White House, top officials just tried to keep their heads down. When Communications director David Demarest asked Sununu for some long-term direction on upcoming speeches, Sununu snapped, "I'll give it to you speech by speech.'' Sununu's habit of running around the West Wing and accusing senior officials of speaking anonymously for newspaper and magazine stories did little to endear him to his subordinates. When he pressed Fitzwater for the identity of a "senior administration official" critical of Sununu, the veteran press secretary thought, Gee, it could only be any one of about a hundred and fifty people. As one official put it at the time, "On the foreign policy side, we have people, particularly Jim Baker, who have major league political and public relations savvy and who have independent access to the president. On the domestic side, though, Sununu is so secretive that nobody with that kind of savvy has any input. Sununu rules by fear, so nobody dares to tell the president anything that differs with Sununu.''

It wasn't until Sununu flew afoul of White House travel rules in May 1991 that Bush realized how few friends his chief of staff had. There was much about the six-week-long episode that, by itself, signaled Sununu's inevitable departure. The flights themselves were the least of it: Sununu had needlessly abused a White House privilege, taking taxpayer-financed air force Gulfstream jets on a variety of official, political and personal trips around the globe, including visits to his dentist in Boston and ski resorts in the West paid for, at least until they were made public, by a ski industry lobbying outfit. That he had taken friends and family along on some of the trips seemed almost beside the point; the sheer number of flights (99) seemed to itself defy justification.

Sununu might have saved himself from the worst of the backlash had he simply apologized, reimbursed the Treasury, and renounced all future travel. Instead he displayed his trademark arrogance and designated all but a handful of trips as official business, explaining that he needed to be in constant, secure voice contact with the White House. "My job is a seven-day-a-week, twenty-four-hour-a-day job," he said. "I have to be able to communicate, to work on sensitive papers, to coordinate the White House activities, even while I'm traveling." After a 21-page "internal review" by Boyden Gray cleared Sununu of wrongdoing but proscribed all future trips without prior consent, Sununu announced how gratified he was by the results. "Obviously, I am very pleased that the review . . . has concluded that 'these trips were properly classified.' "

It could not have been comforting for Bush to see old hands from around the country come out of the woodwork to tip off reporters to other Sununu missteps. Many of the people Sununu had insulted and alienated over the years joined in, barely able to hide their delight that the bad cop had finally gotten his comeuppance. Though *The Washington Post* had broken the story after months of work, speculation about the original leak had an Agatha Christie quality: so many people had a motive that it was hard to narrow down the list of likely suspects.

Bush, who had made ethics a personal cause since his earliest days in politics, was shaken deeply by the episode. He told friends that he was troubled both by the number of trips and by Sununu's utter lack of contrition. But he went out of his way to buttress Sununu's shaky position. After months of imploring aides to avoid even the appearance of impropriety, he reversed himself in Sununu's case. "You shouldn't be judged by appearance," announced Bush. "You ought to be judged by the fact." But Sununu rose to that challenge as well. Two weeks after he been forbidden from taking trips without prior consent, Sununu began soliciting and accepting flights on private corporate jets. Because the aircraft lacked secure communications equipment, Sununu undercut his claim that he needed to be in constant contact with the White House. Sununu not only misrepresented the owner of one plane—a businessman with interests pending before the administration—but had personally participated in arranging the flights himself. Then *Newsweek* reported that Sununu had used a government car to drive him to New York for the better part of a working Wednesday so he could attend an auction at Christie's and purchase nearly $5,000 in rare stamps. When an aide had suggested he take Amtrak's Metroliner instead, Sununu replied, "That would be a concession I should not make."

Sununu offered to resign following the frequent flyer episode, but Bush demurred, preferring to give his loyal aide the chance to leave on a high note. An opportunity seemed sure to present itself: Bush was flying high in the polls at midsummer, and the economy was growing for the first time in nearly a year. Given Bush's visit to Moscow in July, the abortive Soviet coup three weeks later, and preparations for the Middle East peace conference, most of the press focus shifted to foreign affairs. Sununu kept his head down throughout the summer, avoiding the press, keeping to himself on presidential trips, even driving himself around Kennebunkport in August (in a car with dealer plates). But by September he was telling reporters that he was back to stay—making it again difficult for Bush to move. Old Bush aides said the president had missed an opportunity. "I don't think Sununu's continued presence means that Bush wants somebody like that around," one said. "It just means that he has a hard time getting rid of somebody like that once he has him." Once again the vigil began. As one official explained, "Sununu is Sununu. It can't last."

It didn't. By autumn Bush was on the ropes politically. The economy had again stalled, and the White House, by Bush and Sununu's design, had no more arrows in its quiver. To buoy his sagging popularity in November, Bush flip-flopped on a host of last minute legislative items that he had vowed repeatedly to veto. After Sununu suggested to Bush that he might want to insert language into an otherwise inconsequential presidential speech that called on banks to lower the interest rate on credit cards—and Bush agreed—the Senate adopted an amendment forcing banks to do just that. Within days the stock market plunged 120 points. Ever the gallant, Bush covered for his chief of staff, telling aides to tell reporters that the idea was his, not Sununu's.

But Sununu couldn't help himself and began to self-destruct. As the president prepared to sign the civil rights bill in a Rose Garden ceremony, Sununu approached *The Washington Post*'s Ann Devroy and publicly screamed at her. "You're a liar!" said Sununu. "Your stories are all lies! Everything you write is a lie!" The next day Sununu committed what was seen to be a cardinal sin, explaining on a television show taped for release 24 hours later that "the president ad-libbed" the credit card comments. Bush had in fact given Sununu permission in advance to lay the blunder at the president's door. But to most of Washington, that was the last straw. "This guy just doesn't get it," said one Bush loyalist, echoing the prevailing mood. "He's like the guard dog who starts attacking the houseguests and has to be put to sleep."

Sununu's performance was little different from his behavior during the previous three years. But the spears were beginning to accumulate. Had Bush's popularity remained high, the missteps might have been insignificant. But as the lingering recession pulled down the president's approval ratings, Sununu's margin for error grew razor thin. "If George Bush were still at 75 percent in the polls," said Senator Warren Rudman of New Hampshire, "Sununu would have gotten through this rough patch just as he got through others. It's like when a baseball team is in a slump, the batters aren't hitting, the fielders are letting balls roll between their legs, you fire the manager."

But Sununu had misjudged his relationship with Bush, thinking he was a personal friend of the president's instead of just another disposable assistant. Bush had never brought Sununu into the first circle of his friends; never a golfing, tennis, or fishing buddy, Sununu could not make the leap from trusted aide to designated playmate, as Scowcroft and Baker had. The relationship was strictly business. Bush had compartmentalized Sununu as a bad cop, just as he had others before him. In one public attempt to demonstrate his close ties to Bush, Sununu and his wife and son greeted the president and his wife upon their return from Camp David in mid-November. Stepping from the helicopter, Barbara Bush hailed the embattled chief of staff with a kiss —widely read as a high-level endorsement. But the die was already cast. "They had no idea Sununu was going to be waiting for them on the lawn, much less with his wife and son," said a White House official. "But Mrs. Bush's attitude is that you don't wash your dirty linen in public. You keep up appearances. You make nice."

Bush began to nudge Sununu out just before Thanksgiving. He telephoned his friends, seemingly to talk about the campaign. After some small talk about that, he would get to his point: "Whaddya think about all this stuff about John?" he asked one adviser in mid-November. The old hand replied, "Mr. President, there are five guys I wouldn't want to piss off: Baker, Mosbacher, Brady, Teeter, and me. And he's pissed off every one of us." The president then asked, "He's pissed you off, too?"

Moving with characteristic indirection and stealth, Bush first dashed off an identical note to seven or eight longtime political allies asking for their "advice" about the upcoming campaign. He sealed the notes in White House envelopes and passed them to his eldest son, George W. Bush, who had served as the family's eyes and ears in the 1988 campaign (and had since gone on to make a name for himself in Dallas as the managing partner of the Texas Rangers). The younger Bush inserted the letters in larger plain brown envelopes bearing his return address in Dallas. He followed up with telephone calls, speaking individually with each of the outside advisers. The response to the secret letters was nearly unanimous: the recipients reported that they'd love to work in the 1992 campaign but could not imagine doing so if John Sununu would retain authority over the campaign as chief of staff. As one member of the high command put it later to another, "I'm not working for that little son of a bitch."

On the day before Thanksgiving, sounding more like a Dutch uncle than an executioner, the younger Bush tried to break it to Sununu gently during a session in the chief of staff's West Wing office. "You know, I've talked to a lot of people. They're down on you. It's going to be tough for you to work with these people. I've got to tell my father, and you've got to talk to him about it." George W. delivered his heave-ho but left the session doubtful that he had accomplished his mission. Indeed, Sununu concluded from the session that he still had some wiggle room left. He telephoned allies and advisers, such as Representative Newt Gingrich, Senator Warren Rudman, and Senate minority leader Robert Dole, to gauge his support. He suggested to his affable deputy, Andy Card, that he poll the White House staff to verify his support in the West Wing—only to be told that such a survey would backfire. Finally he went to see Bush, who told him to come to Camp David that Sunday.

When Sununu arrived he surprised Bush by fighting for his job. The president had expected Sununu to proffer his resignation and begin a speedy transition. But Sununu was unexpectedly unbowed: he had weathered rough patches before, and he could do it again. "I can survive this thing," he told Bush. "I can work through it." The commander in chief couldn't bring himself to cut the umbilical cord. Having relied on Sununu to do his dirty work, Bush discovered that there was no one around to ax the hatchet man. So Bush again demurred, postponing his next move for another day. "Let's think about it. Let's talk tomorrow."

On the morning of Monday, December 2, Sununu tentatively offered to resign, thinking Bush would reject it. Bush's response seemed vague: "Let me see what we ought to do," he said, "how we can handle it." Sununu didn't get it at first, but within an hour he realized that maybe meant "yes." Bush's ambivalent refusal to a half-serious offer of resignation was in fact a request for the real thing. "He didn't clear it up," Sununu later explained to friends. "He didn't clear it up."

In fact, he did, but in his own way. Both *The Washington Post* and *The New York Times* led their front pages the next day with stories about Sununu's pending departure—unmistakable leaks from the president's allies. As Bush flew to Florida the next morning for several political events, Marlin Fitzwater heard from reporters aboard *Air Force One* that network news organizations were cranking up Sununu stories for broadcast that evening. Fitzwater relayed the news to Sununu: "You're the lead. You're the story." Sununu immediately went to see Bush and told him that they had both suffered enough. "I don't want my family to go through another day of this," he said.

Within days the former governor had explained to friends that he was disappointed that Bush couldn't deliver the bad news himself but relied instead upon his son to do his dirty work. "What really bothers me," said one close Sununu ally from New Hampshire, "is that the president couldn't tell John to his face, that he sent his kid to do it. John deserved better than that, and I know it bothered John, too." Nancy Sununu, who White House officials believed was, if anything, more conservative than her husband, felt particularly aggrieved. "She felt bitter about it," explained another Republican with whom Sununu spoke afterward. "She had watched her husband, who had a pretty good reputation in New Hampshire, at least, get cut up and become a national symbol. She was willing to have this happen if the Bushes were in fact loyal to him. But she feels they weren't."

Weeks later, after Sununu was gone, many of the same officials who had received the secret letters from the president tried to impress upon reporters that George W.'s role had been vastly exaggerated. As one insisted, "I know for a fact that he hadn't been sent there by anyone." This was revisionism. Bush was just covering his tracks after the kill, perhaps embarrassed that he lacked the guts to fire his chief of staff himself.

Sununu's four-page letter of resignation, written aboard *Air Force One,* was full of praise for Bush and teemed with thanks for the trust Bush had shown him. It also explained why the relationship had worked so well, for so long. "As much as I will truly miss the opportunity to continue to work in the West Wing with you and my other friends there, I want you to know how strong and positive and upbeat I feel about doing this. I think you know that the responsibility and authority (contrary to legends out there) never meant as much to me as the chance to assist you to be (and to be recognized) a great president. I intend to continue that effort as an ordinary citizen, with all the benefits that accrue to man and family in the private sector of our magnificent system.

"I assure you that in pit bull mode or pussey [sic] cat mode (your choice, as always), I am ready to help."

6

SOMETHING TO
BELIEVE IN

During the heady days after his inauguration, Bush delighted in leading guests on private tours of the White House. He sometimes paused in the hideaway office beside his bedroom, before a favorite painting called *The Peacemakers,* which depicted Abraham Lincoln conferring with his generals during the Civil War. "He was tested by fire," Bush would remark, "and showed his greatness." And to at least one friend, Bush wondered aloud whether he, too, might be tested.

He got his answer on August 1, 1990. It was a Wednesday, about 7 P.M., Washington time, and Bush had retired to the White House residence for the evening when an aide phoned with an urgent bulletin from the Situation Room. Iraq had invaded Kuwait. National Security Adviser Brent Scowcroft, in a break from his workaholic routine, had gone out for a drink with a friend when his silent, vibrating pager summoned him. Back at his office, he and Richard Haass, his top assistant for Middle East affairs, examined the news reports and intelligence cables and talked through the situation for about thirty minutes, then walked over to the East Wing to brief the president. Chipping in by telephone was Robert Kimmitt, a top aide to Secretary of State James Baker, who was in Siberia for a meeting with Soviet foreign minister Eduard Shevardnadze. Kimmitt had already relayed the news to Baker, who was shocked, as was Shevardnadze. Only hours before he had assured Baker that although Saddam was a "thug," he was "not irrational."

Bush was aware, of course, that Saddam had been threatening Kuwait for weeks. He had mobilized an impressive army of one hundred thousand men, led by three crack armored divisions, along Iraq's southern border with the tiny oil sheikdom. At the same time Saddam had assured Egyptian president Hosni Mubarak, Jordan's King Hussein, and King Fahd of Saudi Arabia that he was merely rattling his tanks at Kuwait, as he had in the past, seeking to force concessions on long-standing disputes over oil production levels and rights to oil fields and ports along the Iraqi-Kuwaiti border. A few U.S. intelligence analysts warned of signs that Saddam meant to invade this time: he was moving more artillery, communications, and logistical support behind his troops. But the Arab leaders kept urging Bush not to issue any warnings that might provoke Saddam; in Mubarak's words, "Let us handle it within the Arab family." And Bush, in this case as in others, placed greater trust in what he heard in his frequent phone chats with fellow heads of state than in what he heard from U.S. intelligence analysts, who, he knew from his time as CIA director, sometimes predicted the worst just to cover their asses.

Among Bush's questions on the night of August 1 were "How far will Saddam go?" In search of answers, Scowcroft and Haass left the president about 8:30 P.M. and repaired to the Situation Room, where a secure audio-video link allowed them to confer with their counterparts sitting at the CIA, Pentagon, and State Department. With his deputy, Robert Gates, on vacation in Washington State, Scowcroft convened a teleconference of the Deputies Committee, a standing crisis-management team consisting of the number two officials at the National Security bureaucracies, which continued off and on until about 2 A.M.

Even after Iraq's army rolled across the border, many analysts believed Saddam would confine his thrust to the contested oil fields and ports. But within minutes after leaving the president, Scowcroft saw that Iraqi tanks were entering the Kuwaiti capital and forcing the royal family to flee. An officer of the Defense Intelligence Agency, who had been sent to the U.S. embassy in Kuwait City only days earlier, sent out vivid reports of Iraq's sacking of the capital. At 8:45 P.M. Scowcroft phoned the White House residence to tell the president, This is not a border thing—it's a full-blown takeover. What was more alarming, as the day turned into evening in Kuwait, and evening into morning in Washington, as the president and his aides followed the latest reports from the CIA and CNN, were satellite photos that showed that Saddam had sent into Kuwait a force far larger than was needed to subjugate the little country—a force capable of rolling down the coast to the main Saudi oil fields.

Two Augusts earlier Bush had given the speech of his career as he accepted the Republican nomination for president at the 1988 convention in New Orleans. After two terms as Ronald Reagan's obsequious second banana, widely derided as a "wimp" and a "lapdog," Bush projected a grace and force that few voters had seen from him. "For seven and a half years, I've worked for a great president. I've seen what crosses that big desk," Bush said, his voice firm and clear. "I've seen the unexpected crisis that arrives in a cable in a young aide's hand . . . so I know that what it all comes down to in this election, after all the shouting and the cheers, is the man at the desk. And who should sit at that desk. My friends, I am that man."

Before that speech, Bush had trailed Dukakis by seventeen points in the polls, but by November the voters agreed that the sober and seasoned Bush, rather than that silly-looking little man in the tank helmet, should be the one to sit at the Big Desk. Yet the voters had not, according to the polls, overcome their doubts about something that seemed missing in Bush. They had seen in the campaign that he would fight like a junkyard dog to get what he wanted. But what, beyond his ambition, did he believe in? And would he fight for that?

Those questions might have persisted if Iraq had not invaded Kuwait. Without the Gulf War, George Bush as president would be easier to dismiss. He might have been seen as an irresolute, do-nothing president whose answer to economic decline was to cut taxes further for the rich, who applauded from the sidelines as freedom swept across Eastern Europe, and who invaded Panama mainly to prove his manhood.

It seems clear in retrospect that Saddam Hussein, for one, viewed Bush in those terms, having watched with contempt as Bush tried for years, as vice president and president, to appease him with trade concessions, intelligence sharing, and an obsequious boys-will-be-boys attitude toward his use of chemical weapons and torture against his own people and his threats against Israel and Kuwait. Saddam also saw how Bush had tried to appease the rulers of China after the 1989 Tiananmen massacre, and Gorbachev after his March 1990 crackdown on Lithuania, and the right wing of the Republican party forever and always. Saddam was a hard man and reckoned he knew a patsy when he saw one. But Saddam learned better, and so did Bush's countrymen. In the opening words of his somber, televised address on August 8, 1990, announcing the initial dispatch of U.S. troops to Saudi Arabia, Bush could have been describing himself as easily as America: "In the life of a nation, we are called upon to define who we are and what we believe."

In the Gulf crisis, George Bush found something to believe in. He saw almost immediately that Iraq's invasion of Kuwait threatened vital U.S. interests and must be reversed—probably by force. And perhaps for the first time in his long political career, he never wavered. He defied the consensus of his aides on several crucial questions, including the decision to intervene in the first week of August and the move in early January to seek explicit backing from Congress before starting the air war. He encountered public resistance at a half dozen major turns in the crisis and overcame it, not with soaring rhetoric, but with bold and forcing actions, each of which shifted public opinion toward support of his policy. His vigorous personal diplomacy welded together an international coalition embracing such unlikely partners as Syria, Israel, and the Soviet Union.

Crucial to Bush's success in winning support at home and abroad was his well-practiced and ruthless use of deception. He repeatedly misled Saudi Arabia, the other coalition allies, the American public, and Congress by exaggerating the nature of the threat that Iraq posed to Saudi Arabia and by concealing a number of intentions: the massive size and duration of the military deployment he had in mind, his immediate determination not only to defend Saudi Arabia but to liberate Kuwait, and his private assessment from the early weeks of the crisis that all-out war was likely.

Through it all Bush radiated an eerie calm and sense of command. Gone was the shrill, arm-waving creature who repeatedly reversed himself on taxes, civil rights, and abortion. The qualities Bush displayed throughout the Gulf crisis—stubborn resolve and adherence to principle, resourcefulness, and foresight—were particularly striking in contrast with his feckless performance at home. The two arenas, however, were scarcely comparable by his lights. When he surveyed the home front, Bush was basically content. His relatives, friends, and campaign contributors were doing just fine. But as soon as Iraq invaded and occupied Kuwait, Bush saw implications that he could not accept. An aggressive, regional power was seizing effective control of half the world's oil supply and could dictate its price, was developing weapons of mass destruction, and, most important, was thumbing its nose at the United States and assuming that we lacked the will to defend our interests.

This was a threat to the established order and hierarchy for which Bush would go to war and for which he would summon all his personal resources. Less than 48 hours after the invasion of Kuwait, when asked by reporters what the United States could do about it, Bush replied: "I would simply say, the status quo is unacceptable." On December 20, 1990, only weeks before he launched the air war, Bush told *Time* magazine that "what is at stake in the Gulf" is the continuance of America's leading role in the post–Cold War world. "We have to do it just so the U.S. preserves its position."

In his speeches Bush evoked a "new world order" in which the United States, as the sole remaining superpower, would cooperate with the humbled Soviet Union and work through the UN to resolve international conflicts. This new order represented an appealing hope and vision, but Bush focused his war aims squarely on the restoration of the old order, which he and his aides strictly defined as the *status quo ante bellum*—the situation that existed before Iraq's invasion of Kuwait. In the Gulf crisis Bush performed with uncommon conviction and ingenuity, but he served as he did at home: as a warrior for the status quo.

The Gulf crisis was the moment for which, Bush told his closest advisers, he had been training all his life: as a combat pilot in World War II, an international oilman fascinated by the Middle East, a Texas congressman, UN ambassador, envoy to China, CIA director, and globe-hopping vice president; through all those phone chats and sports outings with foreign leaders and thank-you notes to their aides. "You have to remember that people like George Bush who play on the world stage don't think like the rest of us," one Bush confidante observed. "One part of him, frankly, welcomes the challenge. This is exactly the kind of high-stakes, history-making decision he hoped he would have the opportunity to make, and he has a quiet confidence that there is nobody better qualified to make it." For an ardent competitor like Bush, the Gulf War offered not only the chance but the imperative to play for the blue chips: the fate of nations, war and peace, a new world order, and a place in history, with the lives of thousands hanging in the balance.

In the movie *Patton,* the swashbuckling U.S. Army general of

World War II, played by George C. Scott, girds himself for his first armored clash with Germany's Afrika Corps and says, softly and intensely, to his valet: "All my life, I've wanted to lead a lot of men in a desperate battle." Bush's first public hint of a similar hunger had come during his "I am that man" speech. He spoke often to friends and advisers about the presidents he believed had faced withering trials and demonstrated "greatness." It was characteristic of Bush that he would think of greatness as something a president has thrust upon him, or does not. Bush was not inclined to strike out independently, as Ronald Reagan had with his massive, debt-financed tax cuts for the wealthy and his military buildup, or as Richard Nixon had done in his peace initiatives toward China and the Soviet Union, or as Lyndon Johnson had done with the 1964 Civil Rights act and his Great Society programs. Bush's reading of history was that the truly great presidents were the ones who were tested and victorious in war.

Lincoln and Eisenhower were Bush favorites, as was Teddy Roosevelt. Like Bush, TR was a hyperactive aristocrat, athlete, outdoorsman, war hero, and believer in "big stick" diplomacy. During his first year in the White House, Bush had read Edmund Morris's biography of TR and remarked that he had drawn parallels between many of his own experiences and those of the "hero of San Juan Hill," as TR was known after his youthful exploit in the Spanish-American War. Like Bush, TR was reared in a family of wealth and power and set out to prove himself in the American West. He used family connections to gain appointments to top federal offices and won the Republican party's nomination as vice president. As president, TR intervened militarily in the part of Colombia that today is Panama. He set new records for presidential travel abroad. He negotiated closer ties with China. And he was the only American president to win the Nobel Peace Prize for his diplomatic exertions. "Who knows," Bush commented in March 1989, "maybe I'll turn out to be a Teddy Roosevelt."

Bush revealed his priorities by naming one of the strongest foreign policy teams ever fielded in Washington: a group that cast a heavy shadow over the president's less impressive domestic advisers. His secretary of state, James Baker, had been his campaign manager and closest confidant. Much of the foreign policy establishment in Washington and New York grumbled that Baker lacked experience in the field, but as President Reagan's chief of staff and then as his Treasury secretary, Baker had hopped among the capitals of Europe, Asia, and

Latin America, splicing together complex monetary accords. Anyway, Bush fully intended to provide most of the foreign policy experience himself. What he wanted and got in Baker was one of Washington's ablest negotiators and political tacticians, with a gift for selling policies to foreign leaders, Congress, and the press.

After the Senate rejected John Tower as secretary of defense, Bush turned to Dick Cheney, a Yale dropout with a lopsided smile who had been elected to Congress from Wyoming and had served at age 34 as White House Chief of Staff for President Ford. Cheney lacked the defense expertise of Tower but commanded far more respect on Capitol Hill and was credited with stronger character, political judgment, and management ability.

For chairman of the Joint Chiefs of Staff, Bush chose Colin Powell, 51, a widely admired army general who had served as Reagan's national security adviser, rebuilt Volvo engines as a hobby, and ranked as the senior black in the Bush administration. For deputy national security adviser, Bush chose Robert Gates, 45, a career CIA analyst who had advanced rapidly from Soviet specialist to acting director. A boyish-looking Kansan of simple tastes (he loved roller coasters, hayrides, and hiking), Gates was deeply suspicious of Gorbachev and other Soviet reformers.

Rounding out this team was the man on whom Bush most relied in foreign and defense policy: Brent Scowcroft, 64, the retired air force lieutenant general, arms-control expert, and historian whose advice had been prized by three earlier Republican presidents. Like Baker, Scowcroft commanded such respect and trust from Bush that he could, in Baker's pungent phrase, "give it to him with the bark off" and disagree bluntly if he thought Bush was wrong. Both men also could tease Bush, deflate him occasionally, make jokes at his expense: all to keep him loose and performing at his best.

In contrast with Baker and Cheney, Scowcroft had spent his entire adult life in foreign and military policy. He was a pro: among the last of the Wise Old Men. Like Bush, Scowcroft served as a pilot (until he broke his back in a crash landing in 1948). Like Bush, he served as a diplomat: as military attaché in Yugoslavia, 1959–61. (Scowcroft and Deputy Secretary of State Lawrence Eagleburger, another veteran of the Belgrade embassy, annoyed their colleagues by bantering in Serbo-Croatian during White House meetings.) Unlike Bush, Scowcroft was a scholar, a voracious reader, thinker, and explainer. He held a doctorate in politics from Columbia and had learned to speak

Russian at Georgetown. He had taught at West Point. As President Nixon's military aide, he had carried the doomsday "football," the leather-covered, antenna-topped briefcase containing the codes to launch a nuclear attack. He had been national security adviser to President Ford fourteen years before Bush returned him to the post. Then, during the Carter interregnum, he socked away some money as a partner in the consulting firm of his old boss from the Nixon years, Henry Kissinger.

Scowcroft held another edge, beyond his expertise. As Bush explained admiringly to close friends, "Brent doesn't *want* anything." The younger men who remained in the Oval Office when the door closed during foreign crises—Baker, Cheney, Vice President Quayle, perhaps even Powell and (believe it or not) Chief of Staff Sununu— saw themselves as potential presidents and therefore were playing to larger constituencies in the GOP, the Congress, the press, and the public. Gates hungered to return to the CIA as its director, and for that he would need the Senate's support as well as Bush's. Such ambitions did not make any of these advisers disloyal. To the contrary, they constituted the most collegial and seasoned national security team of the postwar era: Bush, Baker, Cheney, and Scowcroft had collaborated in top administration jobs since the Ford presidency, and they had worked closely with Powell and Gates during the Reagan administration. Still, in weighing the advice of most of these men, Bush had to keep in the back of his mind that their interests were not always identical with his.

Scowcroft was the exception, the rare Washington creature who harbored no ambition beyond helping his president succeed and being part of the action when the wheels of history were squealing through some very sharp turns. Scowcroft, in fact, had little life outside serving Bush. He was devoted to his long ailing and reclusive wife and his daughter, a New York lawyer. He enjoyed a glass of chardonnay, a good broiled fish, a late night jog, an exchange of political gossip. But mostly he worked. Bush delighted in phoning Scowcroft at all hours —6 A.M., 10 P.M.—and finding him already, or still, at the office. That was why Scowcroft had become famous for nodding off—"cratering," in Bushspeak—during White House meetings that were not about his specialty. He sometimes even napped on his feet, like an old Clydesdale, during Bush's speeches and press conferences. Bush treated the general less like an aide than like a beloved older brother, valuing not only his counsel, but his easy companionship in the golf cart and the fishing boat. The president spent more of his waking hours with Scowcroft than with any other adviser, including Barbara Bush.

Scowcroft's worldview meshed easily with Bush's. Both men were unsentimental about power politics. Both believed in conducting diplomacy as quietly and secretly as possible, building trust with foreign leaders. Both viewed the use of military force as a legitimate tool of foreign policy: to be employed neither lightly nor reluctantly. Discussing his views on the use of force, Bush told one interviewer, "There are certain decisions that have to be made here. I've recognized that early on. Panama was a warm-up. And it just kind of came that there are certain things you have to do if you're going to lead the country."

"What If We Do Nothing?"

Within minutes of Iraq's occupation of Kuwait, on the evening of August 1, Washington time, Bush began moving to rally opposition. He issued a sharply worded statement that the United States "strongly condemns the Iraqi military invasion of Kuwait and calls for immediate and unconditional withdrawal of all Iraqi forces. . . . We deplore this blatant use of military aggression and violation of the UN charter." Bush had UN Ambassador Thomas Pickering rousted from a small dinner party at his home to convene an all-night session of the UN Security Council. At dawn on Thursday, August 2, the council passed the first resolution opposing the invasion of Kuwait.

When Bush awoke at 5 A.M., Scowcroft was standing at his bedroom door, seeking his signature on a pair of executive orders that would block Saddam from access to Iraqi and Kuwaiti assets in the United States and would prohibit U.S. business transactions with either country. Overnight, U.S. intelligence operatives had checked for recent movements of Iraqi financial assets out of foreign banks, which Saddam might have ordered in anticipation of Western sanctions. They were relieved to find no major withdrawals. It was one of Saddam's first missteps. Bush and Scowcroft talked through the latest developments, the best analyses, and their next moves: Get the allies to follow us on the asset freeze. Buck up the other Arabs to condemn Saddam. Get the Soviets on board. Work the UN. Go for Chapter VII economic sanctions. Offer the Saudis a squadron of F-15's—a down payment on the long-standing U.S. commitment to defend them.

Meanwhile the world was waiting to hear what the president might do to back up his tough initial condemnation of Iraq's aggression. About 8 A.M. on August 2, at the beginning of an emergency session of the National Security Council, Bush invited in a small press contingent for a brief exchange. "We're not discussing intervention," Bush told them. "I'm not contemplating such action." He stammered a bit, as he often does when he is tired or when he is lying. This time it was both. As Bush would later recall in an interview with *Time,* when he heard that Iraq had occupied all of Kuwait, he had made an "almost instantaneous" judgment that the United States must intervene. In fact, he already had asked for military options. As Bush denied that he was "contemplating" intervention, there sat an unfamiliar figure at the cabinet table: a barrel-bellied army commander who had hustled to conceal his top-secret maps and slides before the reporters entered. General Norman Schwarzkopf had been awakened at 2:30 A.M. to rush to Washington from his base in Tampa.

Once the reporters had been herded out and fresh coffee had been poured, the atmosphere was relaxed and matter-of-fact: disturbingly so to Bush and Scowcroft. One by one, Bush's top spy masters and diplomats, generals and energy experts, reeled off their analyses. The most troublesome facts were the simplest: Iraq was six thousand miles away and had the world's fourth-largest military, armed with sophisticated tanks, missiles, and chemical weapons. Among the military options were bombing Iraq's oil pipelines and refineries and embargoing its oil shipments. When Schwarzkopf unfurled his maps, the group even discussed a long-standing contingency response: "Operations Plan 90-1002" to dispatch 100,000 to 250,000 U.S. ground troops, airmen, and sailors to defend Saudi Arabia.

But each option was dropped in its turn, the last because the Saudis were considered unlikely, based on past performance, to allow an army of infidels on soil considered holy to Moslems worldwide. The consensus was that there wasn't much the United States could do. Treasury secretary Nick Brady, echoing Baker's line in phone conversations with Bush and Scowcroft before the NSC meeting, talked in terms of how the United States and the industrial world could "accommodate" and "adjust to" the new reality of Iraq in Kuwait. There was little sense that vital U.S. interests were at stake—until the president spoke. At this first NSC meeting, and more insistently in sessions over the following three days, Bush demanded to know, "What happens if we do nothing?"

Senior advisers had heard Bush ask that question a dozen ways on a score of domestic and foreign policy issues, usually when he wanted the case for action to be made more crisply or when he doubted the urgency. This time he doubted the complacency and wanted the consequences of inaction to be spelled out. Most of his aides, Bush complained to one confidant at the time, could not think beyond the difficulties of intervention. Bush accepted that those difficulties were formidable. But his method was first to insist that they consider whether the invasion's implications were acceptable. If they were not, *then* he would consider how best to reverse it.

After that first NSC meeting on August 2, Bush met privately with Scowcroft, and both men lamented that they seemed to be the only ones at the table who believed that the invasion must be reversed and could not be "accommodated." Bush was scheduled to fly to Colorado that day to speak on post–Cold War defense policy at a symposium of the Aspen Institute. Against the advice of several top aides, he decided to follow through with the trip, in part to avoid looking panicked. This was always a major concern for Bush in a crisis; he told aides he would never let himself be "held hostage" in the White House the way Jimmy Carter had been after Iranian militants seized the U.S. embassy in Tehran. Before he departed, Bush conferred with White House counsel Boyden Gray to make sure he had the legal authority to deploy military air power without congressional approval. En route to Aspen, Bush and Scowcroft talked through the implications of the invasion, particularly for U.S. leadership in the post–Cold War world. The president's resolve only hardened. His first response, as in other crises large and small, was to reach for the phone: in this case the secure radiophone on *Air Force One,* from which he began to line up allies against Saddam.

In *Doctor Slaughter,* a novella by Paul Theroux, a young scholar observes that China's population has recently reached one billion. "Wrong," interjects another guest at the dinner party, a prominent international banker. "There are two people in China. And I know both of them."

George Bush could make the same claim about almost any country one could name. The intimate knowledge of world leaders and world politics he had acquired over two decades of high-level diplomacy would serve him well in the Gulf crisis. From his days in the Texas oil

fields, Bush had shown a special interest in the Middle East and particularly in the Gulf. He had visited the region before he entered
politics, and his Zapata Offshore Company had drilled one of the first
wells off the coast of Kuwait. As ambassador to the UN and director
of the CIA, Bush had met both senior and up-and-coming royals,
diplomats, and spies from the region, including King Fahd, who was
crown prince when Bush was CIA director. As vice president, Bush
visited Saudi Arabia and bolstered his relationship with Fahd, who by
then was king and enjoyed after-dinner talks with Bush that sometimes lasted until the small hours. As president, Bush had assiduously
maintained that link, talking regularly with Fahd on the phone and
savoring bits of gossip about the internal wrangling among the several
thousand cousins and brothers who made up the royal family.

Saudi Arabia would necessarily become the initial focus of Bush's
diplomatic offensive in the Gulf crisis. As Cheney later observed, "It
was apparent when you looked at the map that unless you can get into
Saudi Arabia, there's very little you can do" to oust Iraq from Kuwait. Bush knew that King Fahd was reluctant to accept non-Moslem
ground troops whose presence might provoke protest among xeno-
phobic elements of the Saudi clergy and populace. Fahd also could
not afford to have Iraq's invasion of Kuwait portrayed as a conflict
that pitted Saddam Hussein and the have-not Arab masses against
wealthy Kuwait and Saudi Arabia and their Western imperialist de-
fenders. Therefore Bush saw his first task as providing the Saudis
with political cover. The UN already was helping in this regard, by
condemning Iraq's invasion of Kuwait. Initial indications were that
more help would come from the Soviet Union, where Gorbachev and
Shevardnadze already had been cooperating with Bush and Baker to
tamp down other Third World brushfires. Now, it was essential that
other Arab states be brought on board.

Still en route to Aspen, Bush contacted Egypt's Mubarak and Jordan's King Hussein, who then were meeting in Alexandria and apologized for leading Bush to believe Saddam's assurances that he would
not invade. The two Arab leaders passed the phone back and forth as
Bush encouraged them to denounce the invasion. They urged Bush
not to intervene just yet, lest he inadvertently spur the Arab world to
rally in support of Saddam against threats from the imperial West.
They urged Bush to give them time to work out an "Arab solution."
Bush replied that Saddam's takeover of Kuwait threatened vital interests of the United States and the world and was no longer a regional

dispute over borders and oil production quotas. Nonetheless Bush would hold down his rhetoric to give the Arab leaders a couple of days to persuade Saddam to withdraw. If he did not, Bush would expect the other Arabs to join the United States, the West, and the Soviet Union in further measures to force Saddam out.

In Aspen, Bush closeted himself with British prime minister Margaret Thatcher, who had led Britain to victory in the 1982 Falklands War and who privately doubted that Bush possessed the "bottom," or conviction, to become a strong leader. At a joint press conference after their talks, the Iron Lady predictably denounced the invasion of Kuwait in a ferocious tone and threatened strong action against Iraq. Bush emphasized his hopes for "a peaceful solution" and his willingness to show "restraint" for "a short period of time in which to have an Arab solution evolve." This scene gave rise to news analyses that Thatcher was struggling to stiffen Bush's spine. In fact, Bush already had decided to intervene militarily but was holding his tongue—an act of discipline less appreciated in public than among the Arab allies, where it mattered most at that crucial moment.

As Mubarak and King Hussein and other Arab leaders tried to talk sense to Saddam, and as they arranged an emergency summit meeting of the Arab League in Cairo, Bush worked every angle he could think of. He was on the phone every few hours with Secretary Baker, whose presence in the Soviet Union turned out to be another lucky break. Baker was positioned to win a quick agreement from Gorbachev and Shevardnadze for the U.S. and other foreign ministers to issue a joint, televised declaration from Moscow condemning the invasion of Kuwait and cutting off arms shipments to Iraq. This unprecedented superpower alliance, Bush exulted privately, was a three-bagger for the United States. It struck a crippling blow against Iraq, whose military had for decades relied on arms and training from the Soviet Union. The failure of Washington and Moscow automatically to take opposite sides in any major Third World conflict, as had been the pattern through the Cold War, would make it very difficult for Iraq to recruit allies. And Soviet support in the UN Security Council would make it easier to pass resolutions that would isolate Iraq and give its Arab neighbors international cover to join the U.S.-led coalition.

The last potential obstacle among the five permanent members of the Security Council was China, which might be eager to pick up Iraqi arms deals dropped by the Soviets. Almost as soon as the crisis broke,

Bush moved to cash in the favors Beijing owed him for his restrained response to the Tiananmen massacre. He had Scowcroft work the Chinese leadership by phone and assigned Richard Solomon, the assistant secretary of state for East Asian affairs, to peel away from Baker's entourage in the Soviet Union and fly to Beijing to press the U.S. case in person. It worked. The Chinese agreed to cooperate with the other members of the Perm Five: another development that Bush hoped would buck up the reluctant Saudis.

The final, essential piece of the puzzle remained: King Fahd himself. Bush spoke to him from Aspen and told him the United States feared that Iraq, grown hungrier by eating Kuwait, might move next for the Saudi oil fields, perhaps even the capital, Riyadh. The United States had satellite photos and other intelligence that indicated that Iraq was piling up tanks and other forces along Kuwait's border with Saudi Arabia. Saddam's invasion of Kuwait had proved that his intentions are malign, Bush emphasized; Saudi Arabia must assume that Saddam would take whatever he could. In fact, the best estimate of U.S. intelligence analysts and the president's top advisers was that Saddam would not likely attack Saudi Arabia, which unlike Kuwait had a long-standing and public security guarantee from the United States. Such a thrust would dangerously stretch the Iraqi army's supply lines and expose them to easier attack from carrier-based U.S. aircraft. As Powell liked to say, even Saddam Hussein knew, in the words of the Jim Croce song, "you don't tug on Superman's cape."

But Bush knew that the tight-fisted Kuwaiti royal family was not popular with the Saudis or the other Arabs, and that he was more likely to get Fahd to accept U.S. ground forces if he hyped the possibility of an attack on Saudi Arabia. Fahd expressed three concerns: If the United States sent troops to protect his kingdom, would the force remain until Iraq no longer posed a threat? Once the threat was removed, would the United States withdraw its troops immediately? Finally, would Bush take on the Israel lobby and sell Saudi Arabia the advanced warplanes and other weapons it would need to defend itself in the future? Bush replied: Yes, yes, and yes. The cautious king, however, remained noncommittal for three days after the invasion, so Bush worked another channel: the king's most trusted nephew, Prince Bandar, the Saudi ambassador to Washington.

Bush laid a little ambush for Bandar. He had Scowcroft invite the Saudi ambassador to his White House office and make the case, one on one, for U.S. ground troops to protect the kingdom. Bandar bitterly reminded Scowcroft that after the fall of the shah of Iran in 1979, President Carter convinced Fahd to accept a squadron of F-15 fighters as a symbol of the U.S. commitment to defend Saudi Arabia, but when the planes were en route, the United States announced that they were unarmed. The last thing Saudi Arabia needed, Bandar said, was for the United States to send some token force, then pull it back and leave the Iraqi leader and his army, angry and unchecked, on the Saudi border.

At about that point Bush strolled into Scowcroft's office. He teased Bandar about his recent assurances to Bush that Saddam would not do anything aggressive. Then he turned serious. The Kuwaitis had not asked for help until it was too late, he said, and the Saudis should not make the same mistake. Bandar reiterated his questions about U.S. resolve. Bush stiffened; he took Bandar's doubts as a personal affront. He said, firmly and evenly, that the Saudis had his "word of honor" that the United States would "see this through."

Bush then invited Bandar to visit the Pentagon to see top-secret satellite photos of the Iraqi buildup in Kuwait and the equally secret U.S. plans to thwart it. Hearing General Powell describe the array of air wings, army divisions, and warships that the United States wanted to send to Saudi Arabia, Bandar asked how many fighting men and women that added up to. Powell replied, "About one hundred thousand."

Bandar's head visibly rocked backward as if he had been slapped. "Well," he said, smiling, "at least it shows you are serious."

Bush was more serious than Powell let on; the deployment he had in mind was for 250,000, and that was just for the *defensive* phase.

Even after Bandar informed his uncle of these plans, Fahd resisted the dispatch of U.S. ground troops. So Bush kept the pressure on. He placed a call to the emir of Kuwait, Jabir al-Sabah, who was in exile in Saudi Arabia. Bush knew very well that the emir and his family were held in contempt by the Saudis and the rest of the Arab world, and he knew why: the Kuwaiti royals were, on the whole, arrogant, decadent, and cowardly. All but a handful had fled their country without a fight, taking as much cash and gold as they could carry, leaving behind their servants and, in some cases, their wives. Nonetheless, as Bush often told his aides, "you don't always get to pick your allies." And Bush needed the emir to reinforce to his host, King Fahd, the resolve of the American president. Speaking by phone to the emir on Saturday, before he had raised publicly the possibility that U.S. forces would be sent to the Gulf, Bush promised flatly that the United States would return his country to him.

On Sunday, August 5, to the surprise of most of his top advisers—and the consternation of some, including Powell—Bush made his vow in public. Stepping from his helicopter on the White House lawn, Bush found Haass waiting with a summary of the latest developments in the Gulf, including evidence that a withdrawal from Kuwait that Saddam had announced was a fraud. He strode over to waiting reporters and snapped, "Iraq lied once again." The Arab solution, he declared, "obviously has failed." In a message aimed squarely at Saudi Arabia, he said, "I view very seriously our determination to reverse out this aggression. . . . There are an awful lot of countries that are in total accord with what I've just said. . . . They are staunch friends and allies, and we will be working with them all for collective action. This will not stand. This will not stand, this aggression against Kuwait." The president had just committed the United States to its biggest military engagement since Vietnam.

Things moved quickly. On Monday King Fahd and his top advisers received a U.S. delegation led by Cheney and including Gates and Schwarzkopf. The Americans deliberately shied away from specific troop numbers and emphasized the defense of Saudi Arabia rather than the liberation of Kuwait. Fahd approved, and massive deployment began immediately. Iraq, meanwhile, began taking hostage hundreds of foreigners in Kuwait and Iraq—another lucky break for the United States. By taking hostages from almost every country, Saddam helped to turn almost every country against him.

On Tuesday, August 7, the leaders of Egypt and Morocco promised Bush that they would contribute troops to what now was known as Operation Desert Shield. Turkey and Saudi Arabia agreed to close their pipelines to oil exports from Iraq. Bush persuaded the leaders of Saudi Arabia, Venezuela, and other oil-producing countries to increase production to overcome the expected four-million-barrel daily shortfall. Before the invasion of Kuwait, oil prices had been quite low, with supplies plentiful and storage facilities filled to the brim worldwide. That was another of those lucky breaks, as was Saddam's announcement the next day that Iraq was annexing Kuwait, which henceforth would be known as Province 19 of Iraq. This came only three days after Saddam had promised that his army was withdrawing from Kuwait, and it helped to turn his Arab neighbors against him.

Also on Wednesday, August 8, Bush announced the deployment of

U.S. troops to Saudi Arabia in a televised address to the nation. It was followed by a press conference. His performance in both forums blended forceful and calibrated action with weak articulation and out-right deception. His speech was halting, and he smiled nervously at inappropriate moments, as he often did sitting alone in front of a camera. He was seldom comfortable articulating his foreign policy, feeling that the more he told the public, the more he constrained his options. In his speech Bush emphasized the defense of Saudi Arabia and said nothing about the possibility that Kuwait might be liberated by force. In his press conference he sought to mislead the public about his intentions, saying, "That is not the mission, to drive the Iraqis out of Kuwait." Questioned about how many troops the United States would send, Bush refused to own up to his plan's 250,000-man first phase or to specify any figure at all. (Chief of Staff Sununu handled the lying on that one, speaking as a "senior administration official" and telling reporters that the deployment would amount to only 50,000.) Asked how long the troops would stay, Bush declined to pass along his generals' estimate of four months to complete their defensive deployment. "I don't know," he replied. Two days later he was off to Maine.

From the waist up, where the TV cameras focused throughout his Kennebunkport press conference, the president was all business: gray tweed jacket, starched white shirt, and red rep tie. From the waist down, however, he was dressed in faded chinos and well-worn athletic shoes. As usual, George Bush was splitting the difference: half of him was at war, and half was on vacation.

Having dispatched U.S. troops to Saudi Arabia, he felt there was no reason to delay any longer the holiday at Walker's Point to which he had become accustomed every August (with the exception of his navy service). Several of his top aides canceled their vacation plans: Cheney, for one, dropped a scheduled two-week fishing excursion because of the lack of seriousness it would signal to the hundreds of thousands of troops he was sending to risk their lives and broil in the desert. But Bush rejected suggestions that he change his plans and stay in Washington, seeing any such move not as leadership, but as "show biz" and posturing. He was still mindful of Carter's imprisonment in the White House while Iran held U.S. hostages. That sort of amateurism, Bush told his aides, only granted leverage to America's enemies, while setting unrealistic public expectations that the president could resolve every crisis if only he blocked out everything else.

Besides, Bush had his own ideas about the symbolic signals he should send to his countrymen: he wanted to avoid alarming them about the Gulf crisis. His reading of the public mood, now as on the day he took office, was that Americans wanted to feel good about their country doing the right thing and standing up against aggression, at least as long as the sacrifices were left to the volunteer army and the reservists; as long as the average American was not asked to contribute through higher gasoline taxes or through a campaign for conservation and austerity.

A different president might have seen the Gulf crisis as an opportunity to exhort the participation of his countrymen; to galvanize the home front and build support for a sensible energy policy. But Bush, like most big-league politicians, knew his personal limitations. He knew he was not capable of sustained rhetorical leadership, so he wanted the least possible public involvement in his handling of the Gulf crisis. He was going to prosecute his campaign against Iraq by bold, unilateral actions, and if he was successful, public opinion would follow. As he put it, "I just am not one who flamboyantly believes in throwing a lot of words around. I'm more interested in action." Bush's instincts were reinforced by the fragile state of the U.S. economy, which already was tipping into recession when Iraq invaded Kuwait. And the subsequent spike in oil prices was not helping. Any contraction in consumer spending brought on by presidential calls for home-front participation in the war effort, Bush calculated, would only make things worse.

Therefore, as he stood in his jacket and tie and sneakers on August 22, and reporters pressed to know why he had not called upon Americans to conserve fuel, Bush replied in a flat and mocking voice, "I call upon Americans to conserve." Yet when asked whether he would make less use of *Fidelity*, his gas-guzzling speedboat, Bush shot back, "I'm going to keep using my boat. And I hope the rest of America will prudently recreate. I don't think we've reached the point where I want to call on everybody in the recreation industry to shut it down or everybody that's taking a vacation in America to shut it down."

Despite his casual dress at that press conference on August 22, Bush had urgent matters on his mind, including a brewing conflict at sea that might trigger an early war between the United States and Iraq. Ten days earlier he had declared that U.S. warships would enforce the UN embargo of Iraq by interdicting all shipping to and from Iraq —by force, if necessary. Saddam had challenged the new policy within days, sending an Iraqi tanker, the *Khaneqan,* steaming out of the Gulf toward Yemen, one of Iraq's few allies. An American frigate fired warning shots across the bow of the tanker, but it had failed to heave to. Saddam warned of "grave consequences" if further shots were fired. To complicate matters, the fully loaded tanker rode unusually low in the water, so it could not be stopped by the usual method of disabling its screw or rudder. The frigate instead would be forced to shoot out the cables leading from the bridge to the rudder or destroy the bridge and perhaps the pilot. Bush summoned his top national security advisers to Kennebunkport that day to consider whether to force the tanker to stop, at the risk of war, or let it pass and risk undermining U.S. credibility with allies and enemies alike.

As each adviser spoke his mind, the pattern of the early NSC meetings of the crisis recurred: Scowcroft favored the immediate use of force against the tanker lest the United States be discredited as a "paper tiger," while Cheney, Powell, and Baker (who was vacationing in Wyoming but was represented by Eagleburger) opposed. The president at first leaned toward Scowcroft, but Baker and Eagleburger persuaded him to work with the Soviets and the UN Security Council to gain specific authorization to use force against Iraqi shipping. Baker and Pickering succeeded in gaining Soviet support for, and thus passage of, the UN resolution, and although by then the *Khaneqan* had reached the port of Aden in Yemen, Saddam did not again challenge the blockade.

One outcome of this episode was the closer welding together of the United States, the Soviet Union, and the growing international coalition against Iraq—though not without considerable squawking from Thatcher, who felt Bush should have shot up the tanker without asking the UN's permission. Bush eventually got her to accept his decision, at which point she told him on the phone, "All right, George, all right. But this is no time to go wobbly." Scowcroft loved that expression, and it became an inside joke each time Bush faced a major decision during the Gulf crisis: "You're not going wobbly on us again, are you, Mr. President?"

Another effect of the tanker episode, less noticed but perhaps more significant, was that Bush became resigned to the probability that force would be necessary to resolve the crisis. Asked shortly after he announced the interdiction policy whether he held out any hope of a diplomatic solution to the Gulf crisis, he replied, "I don't see it right now," but added that he believed economic sanctions eventually would change Iraq's attitude. Standing in his kitchen in Kennebunk-port about a week later, however, a somber Bush told Fitzwater that he had come to terms with the likelihood of war with Iraq. "You better get ready, Marlin. Think about what we're going to say, because at any time now we might have a ship sunk or an airplane shot down, or it may be something else that will trigger it, but when that happens, we're probably going to war."

"Some GI Pissing on a Mosque"

The morning after the meeting on the tanker crisis, Bush trolled the Atlantic in search of bluefish. The skies were the color of cold oatmeal and the fishing wasn't great, either: three blues in four hours, not counting the proverbial big one that broke the president's line. But for Bush and his fishing partner, Scowcroft, the hours afloat on August 23 were among the most valuable of the Gulf crisis. As the engines droned, and with few distractions from phone calls or fish, the president and his national security adviser talked their way through their strategy toward Iraq. How long would the blockade of Iraq take to bite, considering the major leak of food and other supplies allowed through Jordan by Iraq's ally, King Hussein? If the blockade did choke Iraq, what were Saddam's options for trying to break out? How should the United States be prepared to respond? If sanctions alone failed to force Iraq to move fairly quickly, how long would the United States be able to maintain support in the coalition and at home? How soon should, and could, the United States move to an offensive option?

The two men assumed without condition that the United States would do whatever was necessary to drive Iraq out of Kuwait, but was that enough? What further objectives should they pursue? The overthrow of Saddam? Destruction of Iraq's chemical, biological, and nuclear weapons programs and its ballistic missiles? As a lesson in the dangers of expanding one's war aims, Scowcroft recalled the U.S. experience four decades earlier in defending South Korea from invasion by the communist North. Soon after General Douglas Mac-Arthur's bold landing at Inchon in September 1950, the United States and its UN allies succeeded in pushing the invaders back to the pre-war boundary at the 38th Parallel. Flushed with the momentum of its victories, however, the United States tried to unify Korea by marching all the way to the border with China. In response China intervened and drove back the American forces. The conflict lasted nearly three more years, cost tens of thousands of additional military and civilian casualties, and poisoned U.S.-Chinese relations for twenty years. All to end up back at the *status quo ante bellum.*

In the Gulf crisis, Scowcroft warned, a war fought not only to liberate Kuwait but also to occupy Iraq and overthrow Saddam could splinter the coalition that Bush had assembled. It could trigger violent resentment by the Arab masses against the United States and the Arab regimes' allies with it. And it could create a power vacuum in Iraq that Iran and Syria might rush to fill.

If it came to war, Scowcroft argued, the United States would have ample opportunity to bomb deep inside Iraq, to destroy its unconventional and ballistic weapons, and to cripple its conventional army as an offensive threat. But those objectives must remain unstated. Nor must the overthrow of Saddam be a public objective. When he retreats from Kuwait, or is driven out, Bush and Scowcroft were assuming, his generals and Baath party leaders would tear Saddam apart like carrion and elevate a new leader who would be eager to restore ties with the rest of the world. Scowcroft didn't like the president's emotional speeches equating Saddam with Hitler; they created expectations that the United States would not come home until Saddam had been killed or captured. But he lost that argument to Bush, who felt the comparison was necessary to sell his policy to the public. Bush cited Winston Churchill's view that World War II need not have been fought if Hitler had been thwarted in his 1936 push into the Rhineland, when he was weak enough to have been deterred at relatively low cost.

Rolling along as they fished, Bush and Scowcroft also discussed the remarkable partnership they had achieved with the Soviet Union under Gorbachev and Shevardnadze and the unexpectedly constructive role it was creating for the United Nations in the current crisis, and perhaps as a model for future ones. Ever since the founding of the UN after World War II, Scowcroft observed, the Cold War competition between the United States and the Soviet Union had prevented the body from functioning. Almost every Third World crisis, Bush agreed, had turned into a "test of will" between the superpowers. Now, with Washington and Moscow cooperating in the Gulf and elsewhere, there seemed an opportunity for what the two men would call a "new world order."

As that phrase became a standard fixture in Bush's speeches, it came in for some gentle ridicule from Scowcroft's colleagues. Gates adopted a sardonic greeting for his boss, paraphrasing Shelley's classic poem on the folly of empire builders: "What new worlds have you for us to conquer today, Ozymandias?" Still, few were more thunderstruck by the new world order than Brad Gates, who had spent much of his ten years listening to his dad, a copper-bottomed Cold Warrior, warning of the menace of the evil empire in Moscow. As Bob Gates took a rare break from crisis management during mid-August and walked along the Kennebunk River with his son, Brad asked, "Let me get this straight, Dad. The Russians are on *our* side on this one?"

The elder Gates chuckled softly and replied, "That's right."

Brad let this sink in a minute and concluded, simply, "Wow."

The world had never seen a coalition like the one Bush cobbled together in opposition to Iraq. To be sure, Saddam Hussein's blunders helped turn the world against him. Yet it remains difficult to overstate the diplomatic virtuosity that Bush displayed in accommodating the interests of coalition members large and small and keeping them united behind an effective policy. From the beginning Bush had to provide political cover to dozens of parties: to the Saudis through the Arab League, to the Soviets through the September summit in Helsinki and the carefully contrived appearance of a "partnership" with the United States, to everyone through the United Nations. Bush had to hold in check hard-line allies like Thatcher and, on odd-numbered days, King Fahd. He had to soothe more dovish allies like the Soviet Union, France, and the Arabs of North Africa. He had to persuade and bribe Iran not to accept Saddam's pleadings for an entente.

At home Bush dared not risk his complex and delicate strategy to the rough-and-tumble of public debate, so he strove to avoid asking any sacrifice that might prompt closer scrutiny. He sent Secretaries Baker and Brady, tin cups in hand, to beg billions of dollars in contributions to the Gulf effort, in oil and in cash, from the oil producers and other wealthy allies such as Germany and Japan. Bush directed part of those contributions to the U.S. Treasury to cover the costs of the deployment, and he shared the rest with poorer members of the coalition such as Turkey and Egypt, whose economies were hard hit by the cutoff of commerce with Iraq. He concealed from the U.S. public and the allies, especially in the beginning, the enormity and duration of the military deployment that he had in mind, the offensive goal he had set privately for the liberation of Kuwait, and the private conviction he had formed that his goal likely could not be achieved without war. That he managed this global juggling act for as long as he did was nothing short of remarkable. "The politics of keeping this coalition together is like a marriage: you have to constantly work at it," Richard Haass observed. "It's also like having friends; everybody wants to have a lot of them, but the price of that is that you have to pay attention to them even at times when you'd rather not."

These demands were uniquely well served by Bush's kinetic, personal brand of diplomacy, through which he had built up warm relationships with other leaders over the years. Also, since becoming president, Bush had stored up some strategic favors owed: for example, from China for his restraint over the Tiananmen massacre, from Japan for favorable resolution of several trade disputes, and from Germany, whose leaders remembered that Bush as vice president had urged Reagan not to embarrass them by canceling his planned and controversial visit to the Nazi war cemetery at Bitburg. Bush once explained to Sununu that before the Gulf crisis he had a general hunch that considerations granted to other leaders would come in handy later. "The UN vote [authorizing the use of force against Iraq] wouldn't have been possible if we hadn't broken our necks to sustain the president's veto of sanctions against China" in early 1990, Sununu said. "The president couldn't tell you exactly what that chip would be used for, but he knew it would be valuable."

Bush's phone log during the Gulf crisis looked like a roll call of world leaders, from Prime Minister Giulio Andreotti of Italy to Emir Zaid ibn Sultan an-Nahayan of the United Arab Emirates. It listed sixty-two calls to heads of state and government during the first thirty days after the invasion of Kuwait (not including any that Bush might have chosen not to record).

In his dealings with fellow world leaders, Bush could keep his requests and assurances private. But as summer turned to fall he was increasingly called upon to explain and justify his policy in public, and there he did not fare as well. He kept shifting his emphasis among

153

various justifications for the U.S. military deployment in the Gulf, as if he were market-testing ads for a new deodorant. One week American jobs were at stake because of Saddam's choke hold on the Gulf's oil. The next week Saddam was on the brink of deploying nuclear weapons. White House aides noticed that polls showed that the main concern of most Americans in the Gulf crisis was Saddam's taking of American hostages, along with other foreigners in Iraq. So Bush emphasized that for a while. Then he shifted to the importance of showing that countries couldn't get away with invading their neighbors.

None of these arguments was without merit or inconsistent with the others, but they were not fitted into a coherent whole. Bush denounced Saddam angrily and continued to compare him with Hitler, while promising that the United States demanded only that he withdraw from Kuwait. He grew emotional when he cited reports of the brutality of Iraq's occupation: the torture, rape, and murder of Kuwaitis. Yet the outrage rang a bit hollow because Saddam had practiced the same brutality on his own people, even dropping poison gas on Kurdish Iraqi civilians, when Bush pressed for closer relations with Iraq. And he knew that Syria, China, and other U.S. allies were scarcely more humane than Iraq.

The United States would not reward Saddam's aggression, Bush insisted, yet in a major address to the UN in October he signaled that if Iraq withdrew from Kuwait, it would receive favorable settlement of its claims against the sheikhdom and could take credit for a new U.S. push for progress on the Palestinian question. "In the aftermath of Iraq's unconditional departure from Kuwait," he said, "I truly believe that there may be opportunities for Iraq and Kuwait to settle their differences permanently . . . and for all the states and the peoples of the region to settle the conflict that divides the Arabs from Israel." When reporters and diplomats seized upon Bush's linkage of these issues, he denied that he had meant what he said. "There's no change in my position," Bush insisted blandly. "There's no flexibility here, and I was surprised when I heard that some were interpreting it as such."

Advisers who had helped craft the speech, however, conceded that Bush had become tangled in his efforts to send different messages to different audiences, both in private and in public. "We were trying to signal Saddam that if he withdrew, completely and unconditionally, good things could happen," said a senior White House official. "But the message was understood differently by the domestic audience and by Israel."

Each time Bush let loose another flurry of mixed messages in a speech or press conference, one reporter told a senior foreign policy official, "my mother calls and asks whether we're going to war."

"My mother calls and asks the same thing," the official replied glumly.

During that October Bush was being pummeled for breaking his "no new taxes" pledge in budget talks with the Congress and for his halfhearted attempts to deny that he had done so. The newspaper headlines read WAFFLE, RETREAT, BLINK, and FLIP-FLOP. The president's approval rating plummeted twenty points in a matter of weeks, and the public doubts began to seep over to his handling of the Gulf crisis. None of this could send the desired message to Saddam Hussein, who, Bush fretted, was probably concluding that he could stare down the irresolute American president. Indeed, although the embargo was blocking 95 percent of Iraq's pre-August imports and almost all its exports, CIA estimates on the effects of sanctions, which arrived on Bush's desk each Friday, reported that rationing and increased domestic farm production would allow Iraq sufficient food to hold out for several months and perhaps another year.

Even as the coalition's noose around Iraq was tightening, the rope was fraying. High oil prices were hammering the economy in the United States and elsewhere. GI's in Saudi Arabia and their friends and congressmen back home were beginning to grumble that the U.S. military was bogged down in the desert with no end in sight. On October 8, a stone-throwing melee between Palestinians and Jews near the Temple Mount in Jerusalem's Old City escalated to gunfire. Israeli police killed seventeen Arabs, some of them shot in the back. Bush and his men held their collective breath, fearing Saddam would use the incident to stir anti-American riots throughout the Arab world. It didn't happen, but it reminded the White House of the unpleasant surprises that could split the coalition. U.S. Ambassador to Saudi Arabia Charles Freeman had been worrying all along about the dangers of cultural clashes between American troops and their hosts. "This will never work," he glumly told a colleague. "All it's going to take is one photo of some GI pissing on the wall of a mosque and the Saudi government will be overthrown." Scowcroft added that "Saddam is playing games, some of them with skill, to try to divide the coalition and create trouble. He's acting as if time is on his side. And he may be right.''

A political adviser to the president said, ''Take a look at your calendar. The sanctions might not really hurt Iraq until eighteen months from now. And if they still haven't moved Saddam to pull out of Kuwait, then we're looking at going to war sometime after that period. Then we're well into 1992 and the primary campaign, with the economy in the toilet and body bags coming home. If you're George Bush, you don't like that scenario. You think if war is going to be necessary, better sooner than later.''

Bush had contemplated an offensive option against Iraq since late August, but only with a few close advisers, not with Colin Powell or his commanders. Their standing orders were to defend Saudi Arabia, but they, like most of the president's top aides, had learned that they could sometimes tell more about Bush's leanings by studying his public comments than they could through channels. They saw that he was moving ever closer to embracing the military liberation of Kuwait. If so, the president was fast getting ahead of their ability to deliver. If he wanted to liberate Kuwait by force, he had some decisions to make and some men and machines to move in a hurry.

Now Bush began telling his inner circle that ''I don't think we have time'' to wait for the sanctions to work—meaning that political support for containment of Saddam could not be maintained for that long, at home or abroad. He asked for a briefing on what an offensive option against Iraq would look like, what additional forces would be required, and how soon they could be ready to attack. Schwarzkopf, at Powell's urging, asked the president for a doubling of total manpower to nearly five hundred thousand, including another three aircraft carriers, the army's elite Seventh Armored Corps, based in Germany, and the First Armored Division, nicknamed the Big Red One, based in Fort Riley, Kansas. It was as if Bush had taken his top two commanders out to dinner and they had ordered all the entrées on the menu.

Powell and Schwarzkopf felt they were only being prudent: they wanted to be sure that if they were to fight, they would have more than enough force at their disposal to prevail quickly and overwhelmingly. But some of the president's civilian advisers saw an additional motive. ''If you look at the history of our military conflicts, the military almost always resists using force, which is probably a good thing,'' said one member of Bush's inner circle. ''What they usually do is say they can accomplish the mission, but only with some enormous force that they know would be almost impossible logistically and politically for the president to order in place." But whenever the military took that tack with Bush—during planning for the Panama invasion, the initial deployment in the Gulf crisis, and the offensive option—he would adopt the manner and expression of a poker player calling a bet. "He would just say 'okay' and give them everything they wanted," this official said. As Powell recalled, "The president listened carefully. Questions were asked. But he never hesitated."

Bush approved doubling the force in late October, though he delayed announcing it until after the November 6 midterm elections. Even then he declined to specify how many more troops he was sending. He had consulted with the major allies, and he cited their support in his announcement of the new deployment, but he informed congressional leaders only hours beforehand to prevent them from mounting effective opposition. In fact, lawmakers felt that Bush misled them about his plans in closed-door meetings between his secret approval of the doubling of the force and his public announcement. And although most Democrats in Congress opposed the dramatic escalation, it was within the president's power to order it unilaterally. The lawmaker's only recourse would be to withhold funds for U.S. troops already in harm's way: a move that would carry great political risks and won no significant support.

"What Balls!"

Bush also outflanked the Congress when he won explicit UN approval to oust Iraq from Kuwait by force if it did not withdraw by a date certain. He sent Baker to Moscow to enlist Gorbachev and Shevardnadze for a Security Council resolution that would endorse the use of "all necessary means" to enforce the UN resolutions against Iraq if it did not comply by January 15. It was an easier sell than expected.

"The first thing we must do is stick together," Gorbachev told Baker. "If we let a thug like this get away with what he's done, then there will be no hope for the kind of new international reality that we would like to see."

The resolution passed on November 29, and the heat passed on to Congress. "It was quite clear that [the UN resolution] would give us

157

such a boost, in terms of international public opinion but also domestic public opinion and public opinion with the Congress," Baker recalled. "It would put us, frankly, in the position of being able to say to a congressman who would not vote for us, 'You mean you are not willing to support the president, but the prime minister of Ethiopia will support the president?' " Of course, as several congressmen pointed out, the prime minister of Ethiopia was not risking half a million of his young men and women. Bush himself had observed to aides early in the crisis, "It's awfully easy for others to say what the United States ought to do."

With the UN resolution, Bush was exuberant. He had his confidence back, and he was ready to pull the trigger again. The next morning, November 30, he issued a dramatic public invitation for Tariq Aziz, the Iraqi foreign minister, to visit him in Washington and for Baker to visit Saddam Hussein in Baghdad. The purpose was not to negotiate or seek compromise over the UN resolutions that required Iraq to withdraw from Kuwait without conditions. Rather, Bush was suggesting, he was offering "to go the extra mile for peace," making certain that Saddam understood he must quit Kuwait or be attacked. Scowcroft later recalled that by late November Bush realized that "Saddam didn't seem to believe us." But Bush was determined to demonstrate, not least to the Congress, that "we have left no stone unturned" in the search for a peaceful solution. He told Scowcroft, "I don't want people to be able to say, 'Well, if you had only done this. . . .' "

Bush had hatched this "peace initiative" a few days earlier, during a visit to Monterrey, Mexico, as he chatted with Sununu and Scowcroft in the courtyard of the ancestral home of Mexican president Carlos Salinas de Gortari. To protect the surprise and drama that he relished, Bush shared his idea with Scowcroft and other top aides only shortly before his announcement, so there was scant opportunity to think through the implications.

The effect, as any of his Arab allies could have told Bush, was to vitiate the strong warning that the UN resolution had sent to Saddam. Now, recalled Saud Nasir al-Sabah, the Kuwaiti ambassador to Washington, Saddam would be "convinced that the United States did not have the guts to go to war or fight for Kuwait." Saudi Prince Bandar, seething with anger, phoned Scowcroft to complain both about the weakness that Bush was signaling to Saddam and about his failure to consult with King Fahd in advance. Several U.S. allies in the Middle

East now feared that Baker, who had always wanted a compromise to get the United States out of the Gulf before any shooting started, was going to cut a separate deal with Iraq at their expense. They wondered uneasily whether they shouldn't make their own peace with Saddam before it was too late. "Anything you did to generate support domestically was inclined to make your international coalition nervous, such as talking to the Iraqis before you go to war," Baker recalled. "Anything you did to beef up the international coalition, such as going to war without talking, made your domestic constituency nervous. And we had to maintain the support of both."

As it turned out, Bush's initiative helped him where it now mattered most—with Congress. Iraq jerked him around on the dates for an exchange of foreign ministers, so Bush withdrew his offer. Instead Baker and Aziz met in Geneva on January 9, with Bush and his top advisers holding their breath, fearing that Aziz would spring some surprise (for example, a partial pull-back that might sway the Congress and split the alliance). But there were no surprises. Aziz refused to accept the sternly worded letter that Baker offered from Bush to Saddam. During a break in the seven-hour talks, Baker phoned Bush to report that Aziz showed no flexibility. During the same break, Barzan al-Takriti, a member of the Iraqi delegation who was Saddam's half brother, observed contemptuously of his American counterparts: "They are weak. They are bluffing."

When the Geneva meeting broke up without progress, Bush strode into the White House press room and declared himself "discouraged." But his sad words were crocodile tears. He looked relieved, even ebullient. Saddam had blown one of his last opportunities. A year later Bush said in an interview with Hugh Sidey of *Time* that he would have gone to war against Iraq even if he had not won authority from the Congress, and his top advisers believe him. But now he would not have to defy the legislature. "The way the Iraqis stiffed us," Gates recalled later, "certainly seemed to help with the vote in Congress." Three days later the House and Senate voted 250–183 and 52–47 to support the UN use-of-force resolution. That left three days until the deadline, January 15.

George Bush is the most gregarious of politicians, with little use for solitude. So it was odd to see him, during his first summer as president, at a picnic on the lawn of his vacation home in Maine, standing

159

apart from the party and gazing somberly out to sea. "Penny for your thoughts," one guest interrupted. "Oh, I was just remembering," Bush replied softly, "that forty-five years ago today, my plane was shot down over the Pacific."

On January 15, as the world wondered whether Bush would make war against Iraq, his friends took note that shortly before dawn the president did something highly unusual. He took a stroll around the south grounds of the White House. Alone. And though his two spaniels romped nearby, Bush, his hair still slick from the shower, seemed lost in thought and paid them little attention. A few hours later, warming himself beside the fire in the Oval Office, surrounded by a handful of advisers who soon would become known as the "war cabinet," Bush scratched his looping signature onto a directive that committed the United States to its most lethal conflict since Vietnam. "There was little sense of drama," Gates reported. "There was more a sense of inevitability."

The normally cautious Bush now had gambled his presidency on the liberation of Kuwait. And from the early hours it looked like a winning bet. America's smart bombs, cruise missiles, and highly trained pilots struck with awesome effectiveness and incurred minimal allied casualties. With well-bred modesty Bush assessed the air war's early results as "So far, so good." He observed, "War is never cheap or easy," and warned against "euphoria." Yet aides said Bush was hard-pressed to contain his own optimism when U.S. casualties for the first two days remained in single digits. On his next predawn stroll he carried a hand-held television to follow live reports from the Gulf. And later, when TV aired the first footage of successful U.S. air raids, he jabbed his index finger at each target in a silent "Gotcha."

On the second night of the air war, U.S. intelligence got a beat on CNN. Seconds after the first Iraqi Scud missiles were launched against Israel, U.S. satellites detected them. Technicians at the Pentagon relayed a warning to Israel Defense Forces headquarters in Tel Aviv, using a new, direct link, code-named Hammer Rick, which Bush had ordered installed shortly before the war commenced. Air raid sirens began wailing across Israel, and minutes later the Scuds smashed into Tel Aviv and Haifa. This news flashed back to the Pentagon, across the Potomac to the Situation Room in the White House basement, then up one floor to the northwest corner suite where

Scowcroft worked. He phoned Bush, who had retired to the White House residence. The coalition the president had painstakingly assembled and nurtured over five months, and now had taken to war, was facing its greatest threat. If Israel retaliated, as it always had done against an aggressor, Scowcroft said, it "could transform the conflict from one of Iraq versus the world into one of the U.S. and Israel versus the Arabs."

Bush had anticipated from the first weeks of the crisis that Saddam would try to lure Israel into the fray, and he had taken extraordinary measures to prevent that. Four months before he invaded Kuwait, Saddam had boasted recklessly of his chemical weapons and threatened that "we will make the fire eat up half of Israel if it tries to do anything against Iraq." Almost immediately, worried that his rhetoric might prompt a preemptive strike by Israel, Saddam sought and received assurances of restraint from Israel, through Bandar and Bush. After the invasion, and after Saddam threatened again to attack Israel if the United States or its allies attacked him, the United States once again begged Israel for restraint. Meeting with Shamir in early December, Bush predicted that if war came, Saddam would do everything he could to draw Israel into the fight and drive the Arabs out of the U.S.-led coalition. For Israel to attack Saddam's missiles preemptively, or even to retaliate against an attack, would "play right into Saddam's hands."

Bush had never gotten along with Shamir. He found the Israeli leader cold and arrogant and felt he had misled him on Israel's construction of settlements in the occupied West Bank. Lacking the personal connection he always sought in diplomacy, Bush stuck to arguments of mutual self-interest. Please, Bush asked Shamir, leave the fighting to us this time. We are there in force. We have the whole world behind us. We are going to remove Iraq as a threat to all its neighbors, including Israel. If Iraq attacks Israel with missiles, the United States will retaliate in every way that Israel would. Bush took from his jacket pocket the results of recent polls in Israel, showing that a majority of Shamir's countrymen agreed that Israel should stay out of the Gulf conflict.

Shamir responded with an unprecedented assurance to Bush that despite Iraq's public threats to attack Israel, Israel would not launch a preemptive strike against his missiles. It would expect the United States to take out as many of those missiles as possible during the early hours and days of the war. If Iraq did hit Israel with missiles,

Shamir said, he could not promise that Israel would not retaliate. Much depended on casualties and on whether Saddam used chemical weapons. Shamir promised, however, to consult with Bush before the Israeli cabinet decided on any military action. In case Israel did decide to retaliate, Shamir suggested, it would be in the interests of Israel and the U.S.-led coalition to share IFF codes—electronic passwords that enable combat aircraft to "identify friend or foe" and avoid shooting down an ally. Bush refused, reasoning that the prospect of shooting down a U.S. aircraft, or being shot down, might deter Israel. Bush instead offered Israel the latest Patriot antimissile missiles and additional cash aid.

Bush and his men also worked to massage this contingency with the Arab allies, who agreed grudgingly that they might not bolt the coalition if Israel retaliated against Iraq, as long as it was undertaken in eye-for-an-eye fashion and did not involve Israeli ground forces. Fear of Israeli involvement even influenced Bush's temperate response to blatant embargo violations by his "old, close friend" King Hussein, who allowed truckloads of supplies to reach Iraq from Jordan's port of 'Aqaba. Bush felt betrayed, yet he resisted the easy step of ordering U.S. warships to shut down the port. He understood that if King Hussein strictly observed the embargo, or had his own port closed, the pro-Iraqi majority in Jordan probably would rise up against him, tempting Israel to intervene.

By 7:15 P.M. Washington time on January 17, when the first missile attacks on Israel appeared on television, Scowcroft had a briefer in his office with maps and satellite information on their points of origin. The big questions likely to determine the Israeli response remained: Were the missiles tipped with chemical warheads? And how many casualties had they inflicted? By 7:45 P.M. Scowcroft was joined by Baker, Eagleburger (who had visited Israel the previous weekend to press for continued restraint), Gates, Haass, and Sununu. Considering that they were now living through one of their worst nightmares of the war, the atmosphere was remarkably calm and macho cool. Baker stretched out on a chair, twirled a key chain on his finger, and composed raunchy limericks during breaks in the conversation. Somebody ordered up sandwiches from the White House mess. Everybody scanned the news wires, intelligence cables, and CNN as they discussed their options, hitting the "mute" button whenever a phone call came through. Bush pointedly remained in his residence, discussing pollution-abatement costs over dinner with EPA director William

Reilly. A phone was within easy reach for frequent updates from Scowcroft.

Cheney arranged for a scrambling of U.S. warplanes to Iraq's western desert, from which the mobile Scuds had been launched against Israel. Baker then moved to a small office nearby and phoned the Israeli ambassador. He expressed sympathy and appreciation for Israel's restraint, asked that it continue, and informed the ambassador that the United States was already retaliating. The same messages were relayed to Israeli defense minister Moshe Arens by Cheney. Baker, at Bush's direction, also placed calls to leaders of the main Arab allies—Egypt, Syria, and Saudi Arabia—urging them to hold tight. About 9 P.M. good news arrived from Israel: none of the Scuds had been armed with chemical warheads, they had caused no deaths, and only a handful of Israelis had been wounded. Baker phoned Shamir shortly before midnight, and Bush followed up within hours, reassuring him of U.S. action against the Scud launchers, offering additional Patriot missile batteries manned by U.S. crews, and urging continued restraint. Shamir did not commit. But although Scud missiles continued to rain down on Israel, it did not respond.

The president, as is his habit at times of tension, escaped the White House on Thursday evening, February 21, for a bit of what he calls "prudent recreating": an outing to Ford's Theater to see *Black Eagles,* the play about black airmen in World War II. Fitzwater observed that the evening out "helped clear his mind" for what Bush knew was to be a long night deciding when to launch the next phase of the war, the ground campaign.

Shortly before Bush left for the theater, Gorbachev had called. He had been meeting with Aziz, the Iraqi foreign minister. Iraq had withstood five weeks of withering and relentless aerial bombardment. Gorbachev told Bush that he had agreed with Aziz on terms for Iraq to withdraw from Kuwait: terms that Bush knew, as he heard them enumerated, were not consistent with the UN resolutions and would allow Saddam to preserve much of his military machine and political prestige. Bush quickly had convened nine of his top advisers, an expanded version of his war cabinet, and instructed them to plot a counter to the Soviet–Iraqi move while he was at the theater. "It was a delicate business," Gates recalled. "We wanted to maintain as good a relationship as possible with the Soviets, but at the same time, we were determined not to back down, not to compromise on the UN resolutions—to make Saddam either surrender to us or face military defeat.''

At 10:20 P.M., when Bush returned to the White House, his war cabinet was waiting in the private study beside his bedroom. It was a warm evening for February; the fireplace was dark. Powell was clad in a green turtleneck and sport jacket. Quayle and Cheney had come in their tuxedos from a dinner given by the visiting Queen Margrethe of Denmark. Cheney had removed his eyeglasses and was absent-mindedly chewing one end of the frames. Like everyone else, he was studying a pair of freshly copied documents in his lap. One was a list of ''criteria'' by which the United States and its allies would judge whether any Iraqi withdrawal was ''unconditional'' and worthy of a break in the air war. The second paper was a single-page argument that deemed the Gorbachev–Aziz peace plan ''unacceptable.'' Bush quickly scanned the drafts, nodded, and said, ''I like both of these. Let's put them together. It's not enough to just say we don't accept the Soviet plan. I went through this with Gorbachev on the phone earlier tonight, and he knows it's unacceptable and he knows the specific reasons why, and we ought to lay them out to the whole world.''

Powell suggested, ''Well, let's set a date and set a time''—an ultimatum for the Iraqi army in Kuwait to ''move it or lose it'' in an imminent ground attack.

Bush replied immediately, ''I think that's a good idea.'' From the weeks before the air war, Bush and his inner circle had agreed that the ground war might have to be started earlier than they would like, before bombardment had inflicted maximum damage on the Iraqi military, if ''political considerations'' such as a move by coalition members for a cease-fire or other compromise threatened to allow Saddam to escape with much of his military intact. This was just such a case.

Powell observed, ''The Iraqis were just trying to stiff us and stiff the whole world, once again.'' Once Bush endorsed the idea of an ultimatum, they turned to what the deadline should be. Bush wanted it as soon as possible. So did Powell. Baker cautioned that the U.S. ultimatum must have allied support and must be seen to allow a reasonable time for Iraqi acceptance and compliance.

''The diplomatic question was the toughest,'' Haass recalled. ''We had twenty-eight partners, and the biggest concern was making sure we could get everybody on board.''

Someone suggested that noon Saturday be the ultimatum hour. Bush said, "I think that's a good idea. What's it do for you, Colin?"

Powell replied, "It's good for me." Noon in Washington would be sundown in Kuwait. Allied forces held the advantage in night-fighting ability.

Bush then asked, "What's it do for you, Jim?"

Baker, always adept at hopping on board when the train is leaving the station, replied, "It's good for me, too, but it's a new item that the allies don't know about, and we need to get back to them about it."

At that point, about 11:15 P.M., Bush said, "Okay, we're agreed, then. It's noon Saturday."

Baker returned to the State Department for a long night of calling the allied foreign ministers with the news. The next morning Bush summoned reporters to the Rose Garden to hear his statement on the Aziz–Gorbachev plan. Fred McClure, the White House legislative affairs director, watched from the wings, unaware of what was coming. When Bush reached the part about the noon Saturday ultimatum, McClure muttered to a colleague, "What balls!"

The morning after the ground war commenced, a Sunday, George and Barbara Bush attended services at St. John's, the Episcopal church across Lafayette Square from the White House. Cheney, with his wife and daughter, sat in the pew behind the president. At one point he passed Bush a note saying that the operation was off to a good start. In one of the most dangerous and worrying operations, U.S. Marines had breached Iraqi defenses along the southern border, picking their way through mine fields and barbed wire and antitank ditches, with only four men killed.

"I Miss the Clarity"

The ground war lasted one hundred hours. Schwarzkopf's armored divisions swung hundreds of miles to the west and encircled the Iraqi army with the now famous "left hook" maneuver. The allied troops and officers, their training and motivation, their strategy and weapons, were too much for the Iraqis. Thousands surrendered; tens of thousands died fighting. U.S. casualties were below even the most optimistic estimates of the war planners: 137 killed, 7 missing, and 467 wounded.

By the fourth day Bush heard rising criticism both at home and from the allies that the war had turned to a rout: Iraqi units were being killed as they tried to flee. Bush called a cease-fire at midnight on February 27, a time approved by Powell but one that left the field commander, Schwarzkopf, feeling he had been pulled up short. As a result, major elements of Saddam's elite Republican Guard units escaped with their tanks and helicopter gunships, but that was not of great concern to the White House. They couldn't say so in public, but Bush and his top advisers all along had planned to leave Iraq with enough of an army to defend itself and to "maintain internal order," as it was put in the Oval Office.

The Bush administration feared, with considerable justification, that if the United States broke the back of the military and secret police, the major institutions of Sunni Moslem control of Iraq, the war could well be followed by prolonged and destabilizing civil conflict, as the Shia Moslems in the south, backed by Iran, and the Kurds in the north fought for control of their turf. Neither the Shia nor the Kurds were capable of exerting dominion over a unified Iraq, the administration reckoned, so the likely consequence of civil war would be de facto partition of the country among its warring factions, with most of the neighbors drawn into the fight, directly or covertly. Iraq could turn into a giant Lebanon, smack in the middle of the industrial world's oil supply. And that, Bush knew, was not in America's interest. Thus, when he called upon "the Iraqi people" to overthrow Saddam, he really meant only to address Saddam's ruling elite. Bush wanted the power structure to remain intact in Iraq, only with a different headman. But he never made that clear to the Shia and the Kurds, who saw Saddam's rout from Kuwait as their big chance and got slaughtered and starved out by the remnants of Saddam's army—often within sight of U.S. troops under orders not to intervene.

It had been raining for several days when, on April 12, a Friday, the sun burst out over Washington's cherry blossoms and tulips. President Bush, scheduled to meet with his national security advisers—Scowcroft, Cheney, Powell, Gates, Sununu, and Quayle—invited them out onto the benches in the Rose Garden. The tone of the session was as sunny as the weather. The main topic was the gratifyingly rapid withdrawal of U.S. forces from southern Iraq. The only discussion of northern Iraq was in terms of satisfaction that Saddam was no longer challenging U.S. warnings that he not fly any helicopters or warplanes north of the 36th Parallel. Kurdish refugees above that line, driven into the mountains by Saddam's vengeful army, were receiving token air drops of food and water from U.S. helicopters, but they were still dying like mayflies—one thousand a day, most of them children and old people, weakened by hunger and exposure and stricken by dysentery. Bush's aides knew that the president was tired of hearing of the Kurds' misfortunes, and no one cared to dampen the mood on this fine spring day.

The following morning, a Saturday, Bush was off on his second fishing trip in as many weeks, this time to Alabama in search of large-mouth bass. On his way he addressed military families at Maxwell Air Force Base near Montgomery, reaffirming his cautious, America-first policy toward the hapless Kurds. He spoke with uncharacteristic heat born of his annoyance with critics who insisted he should do more to help.

"Yes, we want the suffering of those refugees to stop, and in keeping with our nation's compassion and concern, we are massively helping. But, yes, I want our troops out of Iraq and back home as soon as possible," Bush said, his voice rising, to enthusiastic applause. "I do not want one single soldier or airman shoved into a civil war in Iraq that's been going on for ages. And I'm not going to have that." Then Bush took to the water, where Scowcroft, as usual, caught more fish: 16 bass to the president's six.

But there was no escape from the Kurdish problem. Baker had just returned from a visit to the Kurdish refugees and phoned Bush in Alabama to describe the horrors he had seen. What was more, the camera crews with him had seen them, too; night after night, the networks were leading the news with pitiful Kurdish children dead and dying. Congressmen of both parties were growing restive. The Turks were screaming that they lacked the money or logistics to provide aid in the remote mountains and that the unrest there threatened to excite passions among Turkey's own Kurdish separatists. The British and French had warned Baker that unless the United States took the lead, they would move forward with their own plans to offer military protection and expand food and medical aid to the Kurds on the ground inside Iraq. Bush told Baker he would think about it. Then he flew from Alabama to Camp David. There he received a phone call from Prime Minister Turgut Ozal of Turkey, who was every bit as agitated as Baker had advertised. The plight of the Kurds, Ozal insisted, was "an embarrassment to you and a political threat to us, and it will get worse, believe me." Then the prime minister said firmly, Here is what you must do. First, you must get the Kurds down out of the mountains to the flatlands where they can be helped. Second, to get them out of the mountains, you must protect them from the Iraqi military.

This went against Bush's oft-stated instinct to avoid entanglement in Iraq's ferocious tribal conflicts—and even more so against Scowcroft's, Cheney's, and Powell's. Yet as Bush canvassed the European allies, he learned, as Baker had warned, that they were prepared to move without the United States, leaving him to look cold and heartless and, more important, like a man surrendering the leadership of the new world order. By Tuesday evening, three days after his defiant Alabama speech, Bush had turned his policy 180 degrees. He would send ground troops into northern Iraq to protect the Kurds. "So much for our nice, clean victory," carped one White House opponent of the new policy, "and for not getting bogged down in Middle East politics."

The Kurds would be only the first bit of unfinished business in Iraq to gradually corrode what should have been an untarnished triumph for Bush's leadership in diplomacy and war. Iraq's genocide against the Kurds and the Shia raised doubts not only about the wisdom of allowing the Republican Guards to escape, but also about Bush's decision to leave Saddam Hussein in power. Months later, as the recession began to bite in the United States, a bumper sticker inquired "Saddam Hussein Still Has His Job. How About You?" Then there was the emir of Kuwait, who refused for weeks to return to his country and whose shameful performance both during and after his exile was thrown up at Bush by his detractors: This is the man we went to war for?

These criticisms were, of course, unfair. As Bush pointed out on several occasions, restoring the Kuwaiti royals was among the least of the goals for which the United States had gone to war. Bush also stated consistently that "the United States and the coalition did not go there to settle all the internal affairs of Iraq." Those who chided Bush for not "finishing the job" by ousting Saddam seldom thought through the costs and difficulties of such a mission. "Saddam was not going to sit and wait on his veranda for us," Gates said. "We saw how difficult it was to find Manuel Noriega in a much smaller country with a smaller army." Saddam's ouster would have required a full-blown takeover of Iraq, incurring additional U.S. casualties. It would have committed the United States to putting a new government in place and would certainly have splintered the wartime coalition, leaving the United States to do it alone. "Can you imagine how we would be pounded," Gates said, "if we were 'bogged down' in an 'inconclusive civil war' in Iraq?"

Besides avoiding that mistake, Bush posted several positive accomplishments with his victory in the Gulf. He renewed U.S. credibility worldwide and confidence in the U.S. military—not to mention his own self-confidence. He showed how old Cold War adversaries could work for a common purpose. He invigorated the UN as a forum for resolution of international disputes. And he and Secretary Baker employed the new U.S. influence among Israel and the Arabs to bring the parties face to face for the first time for comprehensive peace talks. But even those achievements, ironically, began to work against Bush as the victory in war failed to revive public confidence in the economy and the recession deepened. Pollsters reported that although Americans were mightily impressed with Bush's performance during the Gulf crisis, they resented the fact that he did not apply the same skills to reversing America's economic decline. "If he ever exerted the same kind of leadership on domestic issues that he did in the Persian Gulf," said Representative Leon Panetta, the California Democrat who chairs the House Budget Committee, "there's no question President Bush could have a significant impact."

None of this was the welcome "home" that war hero Bush had expected. He could be excused if he shared the sentiments of a movie character he cited in one of his speeches midway through the Gulf crisis: a character played by John Houseman, a World War II veteran, now desk-bound in Washington. A young colleague asks him snidely, "Do you miss the action of those days, sir?" To which Houseman replies, "No, I miss the *clarity*."

7

"THE ENEMY IS INSTABILITY"

It was a rainy summer Sunday in Kennebunkport, and the Hillcrest Driving Range was abandoned but for two men who, to the amusement of the proprietor, fired golf balls into the gloom while they discussed foreign policy. The older man bore a certain resemblance to Yoda, the wizened and kindly philosopher-warrior of the hit sci-fi movie *The Empire Strikes Back*. He wore blue Bermuda shorts and top-of-the-calf black dress socks, as if he had just come from the office and changed in the car. A dark sedan with a radiophone was parked just behind him.

That was Brent Scowcroft, national security adviser to President Bush, who was vacationing at his family's seaside mansion in Maine. Scowcroft was determined to get in a little practice before his scheduled golf match the next morning with Bush and the president's latest celebrity guest, Red Sox pitching ace Roger Clemens. Scowcroft claimed to be fighting "a nasty roundhouse hook," but you couldn't tell from the high, soft draw he consistently hit with his medium irons.

Asked by his companion what was brewing in the world as of 6 P.M. on August 18, 1991, Scowcroft leaned on his golf club and furrowed his brow. "It's so quiet, it's eerie. And it's been this way for two or three weeks." The only thing moving on the NSC's radar screen was the United Nations effort to negotiate release of hostages held in Lebanon and Israel, and nothing looked likely to break there anytime

170

soon. The Arabs and Israelis, the warring factions in Yugoslavia, and even the Soviet Union—where President Gorbachev was resting at his dacha on the Black Sea—seemed to be joining Bush in taking August easy.

Scowcroft had even had time to write an opinion column in that morning's *New York Times,* defending Bush from critics who accused him of clinging too tightly to Gorbachev, at the expense of the independence-minded Soviet republics, during his recent visit to Moscow and Kiev. In particular the Russian Federation and its first freely elected president, Boris Yeltsin, showed more interest in the American principles of democracy, self-determination, and market reform, the critics charged, yet Bush cared less about advancing those principles than about propping up a Gorbachev government that would let Bush have his way in the Middle East and Latin America. To the contrary, Scowcroft had written, Bush was offering a partnership with Moscow only as long as it pursued political and economic reform and not if it began "moving backward in an effort to restore the Stalinist imperium."

Only hours after Scowcroft stowed his golf clubs, hard-liners in Moscow did just what he and Bush had warned against.

At about 11:30 P.M., Scowcroft was watching the news on CNN in his hotel room overlooking the lobster boats on the Kennebunk River, when the first bulletin moved out of Moscow, reporting that Gorbachev was ill and unable to perform his duties. Within minutes an aide in the White House Situation Room phoned to make sure Scowcroft saw the news. U.S. intelligence so far had little to add. Minutes later his deputy, Bob Gates, phoned Scowcroft, and the two talked briefly until a second, more detailed bulletin moved on CNN, at about 11:45 P.M. Soviet vice president Gennady Yanayev, backed by seven other top Soviet officials, had declared that he was taking over as president. This almost certainly was a coup. Scowcroft picked up his large, white secure phone to Walker's Point, the Bush family's oceanfront summer home, and woke the president to tell him the news. Bush paused a moment, then muttered softly, "Oh, my God."

The coup, like the death of an elderly parent, was stunning but not unexpected—at least not to the Bush inner circle. U.S. intelligence had been picking up rumblings of an attempt to oust Gorbachev for nearly a year, and the reports had recently grown more frequent, more detailed and authoritative. When Soviet foreign minister Eduard Shevardnadze had suddenly resigned the previous December, he had warned publicly that reactionary conspiracies were brewing. In April the CIA had produced an analysis entitled "The Soviet Cauldron" on the seething unrest among opponents of Gorbachev's reforms. In June, Bush had been so concerned that he had phoned Gorbachev to warn him. Secretary Baker, during a June 20 visit to Berlin, met secretly with his Soviet counterpart, Aleksandr Bessmertnykh, to deliver details of the coup warnings that he dared not speak over phone lines that were tapped by the KGB. Only three days before Baker's warning, the hard-line Soviet prime minister, Valentin Pavlov, had asked the Supreme Soviet for enhanced powers but had been rebuffed by the legislators. As it turned out, Pavlov had then joined the coup plotters.

On the Friday before the coup, Aleksandr Yakovlev, a reformist ally of Gorbachev, had angrily quit the Communist party with a public warning that "an influential Stalinist group has formed within the leadership core of the party" and is "making preparations" for "a party and state coup." On the following morning, after he had read Yakovlev's jeremiad in the newspapers, Bush had sat outside on his deck at Walker's Point and had heard in his daily intelligence briefing a vague warning that "reactionaries" in Moscow might move against Gorbachev before Tuesday's scheduled signing of the union treaty, granting new powers to the Soviet republics at the expense of the central government and the Communist party.

Much earlier, in the first months of his presidency, Bush had insistently questioned his CIA briefers about the possibility that Gorbachev could be tossed aside by the Soviet army, the KGB, and/or Communist party hard-liners. His advisers didn't think it likely at the time, and they were right. But Bush had not let go. Although he slowly had developed a good working relationship and even a certain affection for the Soviet leader, he couldn't believe that someone could be so *imprudent* as Gorbachev and get away with it. Now, on August 18, when Bush heard the news from Scowcroft, he felt his instincts had been vindicated.

For the next hour, Bush conferred by phone with Scowcroft, who was following events not only on CNN, but through a sophisticated portable communications link with the White House Situation Room. Before dawn broke on Walker's Point, intelligence analysts were reporting signs that the coup was not exactly going by the book: there were few troops moving, and news reports were being allowed to flow in and out of the USSR. On the other hand, the eight-member "emergency committee" running the coup included heads of the key institutions of repression and control: KGB chief Vladimir Kryuchkov, Interior Minister Boris Pugo, and Defense Minister Dmitri Yazov. And they were well enough organized to hold Gorbachev incommunicado at his Black Sea retreat.

When Scowcroft and Bush talked again at 5 A.M., the national security adviser observed to the president that when coups are led by such major figures, "they usually succeed." Like it or not, he said, the United States might well have to "do business" with the coup leaders. That, he said, meant that Bush's first public statements on the coup must be carefully nuanced. "We don't want to embrace them," Scowcroft said of the putschists, "but we don't want to burn our bridges with them, either." The coup should be described as a "disturbing development," but not "illegal" or "illegitimate." Maybe "unconstitutional"? No, still too strong. Scowcroft finally suggested an awkward but serviceable construction: "extraconstitutional." Bush concurred.

Over the next 72 hours Bush's response to the Soviet coup illustrated the assumptions and instincts that underlay his conduct of great power statecraft. He engaged in frenetic and, on the whole, effective personal diplomacy, placing dozens of phone calls to fellow statesmen, to seek their reactions and mold a consensual response to the coup. As during the outbreak of democratic and market reforms across Eastern Europe and the Soviet Union over the previous two years, Bush and the United States did not play a decisive role. Gorbachev had been the lead actor in pulling back the institutions of Soviet repression. But the historical and economic forces at work were larger than either man. If U.S. policy had not forced the pace of reform, however, it at least had not retarded it—which had been a real possibility. As the USSR had retreated from Eastern Europe, Bush had played the role he plays best: avoiding mistakes of commission. He had taken care not to appear to "meddle" in Soviet and East European affairs and thus to discredit the reformers as stooges of the West.

Now as the outcome of the coup remained uncertain, Bush took care to avoid offending anyone who was in power or might end up there, regardless of whether he approved of their behavior at home. Americans, Bush once observed, are "sympathetic to fostering American values abroad, but they want to be realistic about the price."

The price of mishandling the Soviet coup could be high. As the Soviet army had begun to pull back from Eastern Europe, and the Soviet economy had collapsed, Moscow and Washington had cooperated in many areas: Afghanistan, Angola, Cambodia, Namibia, Nicaragua, and, especially, the Persian Gulf. The Soviet Union had abandoned its old ally Iraq to defeat by the U.S.-led coalition, and Bush had declared the United States the undisputed leader of the new world order. That was his best achievement, and it could be at risk if he were gratuitously to slam the door in the faces of the coup leaders and they prevailed. Already the coup leaders had signaled to Bush that they would remain interested in close collaboration. That confirmed Bush's conviction that with the Cold War waning, allies and adversaries could be found in unlikely places. America's enemy no longer was any one country or ideology. The Gulf War demonstrated that, as did this Soviet coup. These days, as Bush had emphasized early and often, "the enemy is uncertainty; the enemy is instability."

"Tell Those Sumbitches . . ."

While the president had slept for a few hours before dawn on Monday, Scowcroft had summoned his press spokesman, Roman Popadiuk, 41, a basset-faced, dry-witted veteran foreign service officer born of Ukrainian refugee parents and reared on the streets of Brooklyn. Popadiuk found his boss clad in baby blue pajamas, his back against the headboard of his bed, hugging his knees to his chest, gazing at CNN with an almost meditative calm. It was a look Popadiuk had seen before: just before the U.S. invasion of Panama, just before Operation Desert Storm. Scowcroft, like Bush, looked more at ease, even more fulfilled, during crises than in times of quiet.

Popadiuk had already called the wire services with a bare-bones statement that the White House was "aware" of the reports of the coup and was "continuing to seek details." That would do for the next few hours, but as soon as Bush emerged for his scheduled golf match, he was bound to be questioned by the rotating press pool that

174

follows all his movements. Fitzwater, tracked down on vacation in Jackson Hole, Wyoming, had phoned Scowcroft to advise that he ask the president to read a statement and take questions before leaving the Point. Popadiuk agreed: "The president is going to have to talk about this in the morning, and I think it would be better if he did it without a golf club in his hand." It could look very bad: BUSH MISSES PUTT AS STALINISTS RECLAIM EASTERN EUROPE. "This is serious," Popadiuk persisted. "He needs to do something more formal."

Scowcroft shrugged. "I don't know; he's handled serious things on the golf course before." Bush and Scowcroft had formulated much of the allied strategy during the Gulf crisis the previous August while trolling for bluefish and had deflected questions from the press between tee shots. Most of his advisers were reluctant to suggest to Bush that these venues made him look like a sports-mad preppy, and when reporters or Democrats suggested that, it just got Bush's back up. "I've heard some of the commentators telling me how I ought to conduct this business," Bush said during the first hours of the Soviet coup, "but my mind goes back to how it was a year ago, and another very troubling international situation." Message: Let the commentators yap; I've proven I can lead the world without giving up my vacation.

This potential image problem on the morning after the coup was, to the relief of everyone except the president, resolved by the elements. Driving rain, at the front edge of Hurricane Bob, made golf resistible even to the weather-resistant Bush and forced the 7:45 A.M. press conference inside a Secret Service office near the president's home. Bush already had been working the phones for nearly three hours: to the new British prime minister John Major, French president Mitterrand, Baker, and the senior U.S. diplomat on duty in Moscow, James Collins. Major, under pressure from his predecessor, the still outspoken Thatcher, was publicly taking a hard line against the coup plotters. Mitterrand, on the other hand, accepted the coup as a fait accompli. Collins did not have much to add about the situation on the ground; he mentioned that he had a letter from Yeltsin asking for Bush's support but did not give details.

In his opening statement to the press pool—and, via CNN, to the world—Bush called the coup "momentous and stunning," also "disturbing" and "extra-constitutional." At that last one, reporters raised their eyebrows. But there was more. Bush talked of Gorbachev in the present tense, yet in a tone of eulogy, as "a historic figure" whose

175

"contributions have laid a foundation for progress that I am convinced the people in the Soviet Union want to see continue." Bush then volunteered that "I don't know whether to take heart" from a statement by the coup's figurehead leader, Yanayev, "that this does not mean turning back the reforms." When asked for his gut impression of Yanayev, whom reporters had seen Bush chatting with during his visit to Moscow three weeks earlier, the president replied, "Well, my gut instinct was that he has a certain commitment to reform."

In fact, Bush knew better. His CIA and State Department briefings and dossiers on Yanayev painted him as an inertia-bound party hack with little commitment to anything beyond his own perks and survival. Though it was scarcely noticed (and Bush and his aides failed to mention it), Yanayev had accompanied Bush on *Air Force One* when he had flown from Moscow to Kiev. A harsher judge of character than is generally appreciated, Bush had appraised the Soviet VP as unimpressive, a nervous chain smoker with sunken eyes, a cave dweller's complexion, and grooming that was careless even by Russian standards. But Bush was determined not to burn any bridges to the coup leaders. He did mention, hedging his bets, that "coups can fail," adding that "it's too early to say" and concluding, "Let's hope that Yanayev, when he made his statement, was speaking from conviction—his statement being that this will not mean setting back, as I understand it, setting back reform and commitment to go forward."

Then, perhaps aware that he sounded like a man waiting to see which way the wind would blow, Bush declared that although "all this stuff is unfolding," he would take "a firm stand on principle." He would, for example, put all economic aid "on hold" until the Soviet government's commitment to reform was reaffirmed. But when asked whether he would support the call for a general strike by the senior *freely elected* official in the Soviet Union, Russian Republic President Boris Yeltsin, Bush ducked. "Well, we'll just see what happens on that." Listening to follow-up questions, Bush perceived that reporters were implicitly criticizing his cautious reluctance to back Yeltsin, just as critics had assailed his worried, wait-and-see attitude in 1989 toward the Democracy Movement in China and the opening of the Berlin Wall. As he had in those earlier episodes, Bush snapped, "It's not a time for flamboyance or show business or posturing."

It *was* a time, however, to get out of Kennebunkport. Bush was stubbornly reluctant to appear to be caving in to those critics who urged that he stop golfing and fishing and return to Washington. But with Hurricane Bob threatening to flood Walker's Point and possibly disrupt communications links to the White House, his advisers and Secret Service agents got him to fly back to the capital, at least through Tuesday morning.

Robert Strauss, the newly confirmed U.S. ambassador to the Soviet Union, was called to Washington from his vacation near San Diego to be immediately sworn in and dispatched to Moscow. The executive jet that carried Strauss also stopped to pick up Secretary of State James Baker, Press Secretary Fitzwater, and Deputy Chief of Staff Andy Card—all vacationing in Wyoming. On the long flight home Strauss at first was depressed at the prospect of dealing not with the glamorous and collaborative Gorbachev, but instead with what he now expected would be the hard-line leaders of a new Soviet government. But he gradually got himself worked up to deliver some undiplomatically earthy demarches, saying to his colleagues on the executive jet, "I guess I *could* tell those motherfuckin' sumbitches . . ."

"A Prudent Skepticism"

A few years earlier Bush might have told the "sumbitches" himself. He had trained all his life to be the consummate Cold Warrior; to lead the forces of good in what he assumed would be an unending battle. He had been taught that the Soviets would not keep agreements, could not reform, should not be trusted. And he had seen repeatedly the domestic political costs of straying from that catechism. Bush had been a young combat veteran of the war against Japan, studying economics at Yale when Franklin Roosevelt was posthumously reviled by the Republican Right for abandoning Eastern Europe to the tender mercies of Joseph Stalin. Bush had worked as a young oilman in West Texas during the 1950s, when one of his political heroes, later one of his mentors, was the champion Red baiter Richard Nixon. As his interest in politics sharpened, Bush had watched Nixon beaten in the 1960 election by John Kennedy, who relied in part on demagogic charges that the incumbent Eisenhower-Nixon administration had allowed a nuclear "missile gap" to develop between the United States and the Soviet Union.

As a congressman in the late 1960s, Bush had hewed to the Republican party line on containing the Reds. He had denounced the 1963 treaty in which the United States, USSR, and Britain had agreed to test nuclear weapons only underground. And as many initial enthusiasts for America's war against Soviet-backed communists in Vietnam had reconsidered their support as the struggle dragged on inconclusively, Bush had not wavered. He has told friends that he believes to this day that America's only mistakes lay in its failure to muzzle the press and to prosecute the war more ferociously: to win quickly and overwhelmingly. As CIA director in the Ford administration, Bush—along with Scowcroft, Cheney, and Baker—saw at close quarters the potency of American conservatives who opposed the Ford–Kissinger pursuit of "detente" with the Soviet Union. It was during this period that Bush covered his own right flank by caving in to conservatives who felt the CIA's estimates of Soviet military capabilities were understated. He had invited in a "Team B" of outside experts, heavily weighted toward hard-liners, shared classified data with them, and passed along to Ford their report, which differed sharply with the findings of the CIA's own "Team A."

As Bush had prepared for his 1990 campaign, he had watched President Carter, at the June 1979 Vienna summit, embrace Leonid Brezhnev and kiss him on both cheeks, in the Russian manner. Six months later the Soviet army had invaded Afghanistan. The photo of that kiss was widely circulated by the 1980 Reagan–Bush campaign. As vice president and heir presumptive to Ronald Reagan, Bush had worried to confidants that the Old Man was going soft on the Soviets during his last years in office. Reagan had let himself be charmed by Gorbachev, Bush thought, even while convincing himself that he could "handle" the wily Soviet leader. Nancy Reagan, meanwhile, had pressed her husband to think of his place in history books; to take some chances with Gorbachev in the hope of a breakthrough toward peace between the two nuclear superpowers; perhaps to win the Nobel Peace Prize.

Bush's approach to history was to study events for mistakes that should be avoided. And to Bush the lessons of the Cold War were clear: nobody ever got hurt, especially in Republican politics, by taking a hard line against the Soviets, but plenty of politicians in both parties got clobbered for looking gullible. In his 1988 campaign, therefore, Bush had deliberately presented himself as more wary of the Soviets than either Dukakis or Reagan. In June of that election year

Gorbachev was wowing the world with his proposals to the Communist party Congress for the most radical reform since the Bolshevik revolution: a move toward political pluralism and market pricing, away from censorship and bureaucratic control. Dukakis saw this as an encouraging trend for the United States and the West. So did Reagan. Bush saw it as an opportunity to demonstrate his tough-minded skepticism.

In a speech to the World Affairs Council of Northern California in June 1988, Bush warned that "the Cold War is not over" and that the United States must be prepared for "protracted conflict." In subsequent speeches and interviews he suggested that economic reform might only make Moscow a more potent adversary. "The ferment" in the Soviet Union, he said, "could produce a more powerful force with unchanged objectives. Arms reduction could become an excuse for a weak defense and create dangerous instability." His acceptance speech at the Republican convention struck the same cautious tone toward the Soviet Union: "Perhaps what is happening will change our world forever. Perhaps not. A prudent skepticism is in order." Bush vowed to emphasize long-intractable negotiations concerning conventional forces in Europe, over the START talks to which Reagan had given priority. "Despite the drama of nuclear weapons, the imbalance in conventional weapons is a basic source of instability in Europe," Bush told a Chicago audience in August 1988. "Soviet military spending has not slackened," he told employees of a defense contractor in Denver in October. "The Soviet tank armies are still poised to take the offensive in Europe."

Bush's campaign manager, Lee Atwater, often advised in domestic politics that "when your opponent is coming your way, don't go out and meet him in the middle; let him keep coming." As candidate and president, Bush took the same attitude toward Gorbachev. He vowed in October 1988 to keep the pressure on the Soviets by building new U.S. missile systems, saying, "This is no time to reduce our leverage."

Early in 1989 Bush observed to his aides that Presidents Kennedy and Carter, in particular, let themselves be stampeded into "early-term mistakes" with the Soviets. Kennedy had agreed to a June 1961 summit where he let himself be bullied by Nikita Khrushchev. That may have helped persuade the Soviet leader that the young American pres-

179

ident would not resist the deployment of Soviet nuclear missiles in Cuba in 1962. Carter had rushed, after only two months in office, to present a "comprehensive," and widely derided, arms control proposal to Brezhnev.

Bush would avoid such mistakes in part by ordering up from the federal bureaucracy a series of protracted "policy reviews" on U.S. relations with various major countries, regions, and transnational problems like ocean pollution. (This was a trick Bush and Scowcroft had learned from Nixon, who used a similar "strategic review" to put on hold the negotiations the Johnson administration had begun with the Soviets.) Bush's reviews were never expected to inform or influence his policies, but as Baker observed slyly, they served to keep the bureaucracy busy.

The reviews also bought Bush some time to find his feet and build his confidence, an adjustment period he had needed in earlier posts. When he was ambassador to the United Nations, Bush was expected to participate in "four power" talks on the Middle East, among the UN envoys from the Soviet Union, Britain, and France. New to diplomacy, he felt overmatched by the tough and experienced Soviet representative, Yakov Malik. So Bush, according to his deputy, "held himself back" for the first several meetings until he had sized up his counterparts and felt comfortable taking an active role. Once he did so, he won respect for his judgment and mastery of his brief.

As U.S. envoy to China, Bush never felt confident enough to seek a private audience with Mao Zedong. When Secretary of State Kissinger visited Beijing in 1975, Bush accompanied him to a meeting with Mao, at which the Chinese leader commented to Kissinger, "This ambassador is in a plight." Turning to Bush, Mao asked, "Why don't you come visit?" Bush replied, "I'm afraid you're very busy." Mao said, "Oh, I'm not busy. . . . You should really come visit." When President Ford flew to Beijing five weeks later, Bush accompanied him to see Mao. But Bush never took the Chinese leader up on his invitation to return without his bosses.

Bush conceded early on that he felt a similar "intimidation" and "trepidation" at the prospect of dealing with Gorbachev, and he wanted to put off his first summit with the Soviet leader until as late as possible in 1989. Bush had been in Gorbachev's powerful presence several times during the second Reagan term and felt he had not been treated with respect by him or, for that matter, by his pushy and contentious wife, Raisa. In early 1989 when Gorbachev was successfully wooing European public opinion with one bold public arms control initiative after another, Bush looked staid and defensive. Frustrated, he encouraged Fitzwater to dismiss the Soviet leader as "all show biz" or, in the press secretary's more memorable phrase, "a drugstore cowboy."

Meanwhile the policy reviews and the delay associated with them provided the political cover that Bush needed in order to break with his hard-line campaign rhetoric and frame a more constructive approach. He began executing this shift with a series of speeches in April and May, when he "welcomed the changes" Gorbachev was bringing and professed repeatedly "our desire to see reform succeed in the Soviet Union." Groping for some vision of a new U.S. policy toward Moscow, Bush settled for a call to move "beyond containment" of communism and toward "the integration of the Soviet Union into the community of nations." For that to take place, Bush said, Moscow must reduce its conventional and nuclear forces, allow self-determination for central and Eastern Europe, and extend civil and political rights to its own people. Playing on Gorbachev's call for a "common European home"—a phrase that U.S. policymakers read as a call for Western Europe's disengagement from the United States —Bush said, "There cannot be a common European home until all within it are free to move from room to room." Bush offered as his competing vision a "Europe whole and free" and made clear that the United States intended to maintain a strong military presence there.

In these speeches Bush reiterated the challenge hurled by presidents from Kennedy to Reagan for Moscow to tear down the Iron Curtain and the Berlin Wall. Bush also expressed encouragement for the spread of democracy in China. He didn't seriously expect his rhetoric on either subject to have any more effect than did that of his predecessors. And what happened next probably was not influenced by Bush's rhetoric. Still, within days he was reminded of the old advice to be careful what you wished for, because you just might get it.

"I Know the Chinese"

Shortly after midnight on June 3, 1989, only hours after he had returned to Kennebunkport from the NATO summit in Brussels, Bush was awakened with news that the Chinese authorities had ordered soldiers to attack a peaceful crowd of some 100,000 student demonstrators in Beijing's central Tiananmen Square, killing hundreds, wounding thousands, and arresting thousands more. His response was muted. He issued a written statement that began "I deeply deplore the decision to use force." The rest of the statement, however, emphasized how much Bush valued "a constructive relationship beneficial to both countries." He balanced hope that China would "return" to "the path of political and economic reform" with hope for "conditions of stability."

For the next two days Bush stubbornly resisted doing or saying anything more. "I know the Chinese," he told his aides. "I know how to deal with them, and it's not through pressure or sanctions." Scowcroft agreed. Secretary of State Baker, a more astute reader of public and congressional opinion, persistently urged Bush to issue a stronger denunciation of the massacre, accompanied by at least limited sanctions. He warned that if he did not do so, Congress would take the lead and pass tougher sanctions than Bush would like. Bush typically chose a middle path. He wished to be "positioned," he said, on the side of public opinion, while giving as little offense as possible to the Chinese leadership. Two days after the massacre, Bush called a press conference, where he again emphasized that "this is not the time for an emotional response, but for a reasoned, careful action that takes into account both our long-term interests and recognition of a complex internal situation in China." He announced a suspension of meetings between U.S. and Chinese military leaders and of U.S. weapons sales to China, but he made no move against the exports that allowed China to maintain a $12 billion trade surplus with the United States.

In denouncing the massacre, Bush used most of the right words, but anyone watching and hearing him could see that his heart wasn't in it. His first and overwhelming reaction was that of the foreign policy professional and Burkean conservative: he saw the Chinese students provoking rapid change and instability, and it made him uneasy. During the chaotic days after the massacre, unable to reach the Chinese rulers by phone, unable for a time even to verify their whereabouts,

Bush and his top advisers feared they might see China riven by a bloody struggle among its leaders and its army. They warned, in background briefings for select congressmen and journalists, that China's Democracy Movement, however admirable its rhetoric, was little more than a debating society. It did not constitute an alternative leadership; it could not hope to win the support of the major institutions of control: the People's Army, the Communist party, the secret police. It could not, in short, govern the world's most populous country. Bush and company worried that China might lurch backward as it had during the Cultural Revolution of the late 1960s. When it did not— when Deng Xiaoping and Li Peng and the other hard, old men reaffirmed their grip on power—Bush was privately relieved. As Secretary Baker observed, "I don't think it would be in the best interests of the United States for us to see significant instability in the People's Republic of China."

Under pressure from Congress and public opinion to do more to express U.S. displeasure with China's rulers, Bush on June 20 announced a suspension of "all high-level exchanges of government officials" between U.S. and Chinese officials—a commitment he violated shamelessly less than two weeks later. He dispatched Scowcroft and Eagleburger in July on a secret mission to kowtow to the rulers of China: to explain to them that Bush would like to maintain good relations but was forced to placate U.S. public opinion. On December 9, Bush again sent Scowcroft to tell China's leaders, in an obsequious banquet toast, that "negative forces" in both their countries "seek to frustrate our cooperation." Scowcroft referred to the massacre, in the classic police-state euphemism, as "the events" of Tiananmen. After the December visit became public, Secretary Baker told a TV interviewer that it was "the first time we've had high-level United States officials go to the People's Republic of China" since the massacre. Baker was exposed as a liar a week later when CNN reported the secret July trip.

Bush's response to the Tiananmen massacre was telling in two ways. It demonstrated where he comes down in the always difficult balance between maintaining cordial relations with important states and promoting democratic values. It also revealed his penchant for selling different policies to the public than he pursued in private and for bridging the two with deception and misdirection.

On the first point, as Scowcroft's toast made clear, Bush placed his administration clearly on the side of China's rulers and against both their victims and those in the United States who expressed outrage at the massacre. Bush reckoned he knew China, from his fourteen months in 1974–1975 as U.S. envoy to Beijing. He couldn't speak two sentences of Chinese before or after his assignment there, aides said, nor was he conversant with the major academic writings on the country. But he had learned just enough to become convinced that China's history and culture left it immune to foreign influence. And he and Barbara had pedaled their bicycles all over Beijing, just like the locals, and felt they had developed a "feel" for the place.

By the time he became president, Bush felt certain that there was no sense "posturing," as he put it, about democracy and human rights when dealing with Chinese rulers who didn't know the meaning of the words. They would only withdraw angrily from China's quickening intercourse with the rest of the world: from trade, human exchanges, the freer flow of information, and economic reforms. Most important, they would make mischief elsewhere in the world. China was, after all, a major arms exporter, a nuclear power, and a veto-holding member of the UN Security Council. That last venue, Bush argued, was where the wisdom of his accommodating policy toward China paid off. Because in the crunch, when bigger U.S. interests were at stake during the Gulf crisis and China's autocrats could have obstructed every U.S. move in the UN, they instead let their old friend— "Busher Who Rides Bicycle," they called him—have his way.

Bush's tolerance for human rights abuses and autocracy were hardly confined to China. He visited the Philippines as vice president in 1981 and gushed praise for that country's dictator, Ferdinand Marcos, saying, "We love your adherence to democratic principles and to the democratic processes." When he visited Poland as vice president, Bush showed greater warmth toward the martial-law ruler, General Wojciech Jaruzelski, than toward the pro democracy trade unionists of Solidarity.

The deception that Bush employed to maintain his two China policies became a hallmark of his administration. He and his closest advisers regularly misled not only the public, but other senior officials outside the inner circle, to the point that Bush and Baker, Scowcroft, and Sununu were sometimes referred to by their colleagues as "The B.S. Boys." The purpose of the president's lies and misdirections usually was to lay the ground for a policy surprise, a tactic he long had delighted in using to hype the political impact of what otherwise would be seen as modest initiatives.

Even before the Scowcroft missions to Beijing were revealed, for example, Bush misled the press and public in order to build more drama for his first summit with Gorbachev. Asked in mid-September when he might meet with the Soviet leader, Bush said, "I feel under no rush" to do so that year. Five days later, he announced that he and Gorbachev would not meet until the following spring or summer, in the United States. Asked why not sooner, Bush replied that "this was the agreed timetable, and it's agreeable to us." In fact, he had hatched the idea for an earlier summit, to be held in December, during a chat with Scowcroft and other top aides on the balcony of the U.S. ambassador's residence in Paris on the splendid afternoon of July 16 and had almost immediately received Gorbachev's assent.

During the run-up to the December summit in Malta, Bush worked frantically to spin down expectations, lest he be judged a flop in his first *mano-a-mano* with Gorbachev, who was quicker on his feet and prone to steal the show with dramatic public initiatives. Bush and his sherpas emphasized privately to the Soviet side that they wanted a "get to know you" session, without a substantive agenda and without surprises. The Soviets agreed. In public Bush went so far as to describe the affair as not a "summit" at all, but as something more like a heavily chaperoned first date. He insisted that "we have no set agenda." There would be no "specific proposals," Bush promised. "There won't be a surprise." And Bush had promised Gorbachev "in my own handwriting" that there would be "no arms control proposals."

In fact, before they left Washington for Malta, Bush and his closest advisers prepared a laundry list of 21 proposals, including several on arms control, that he tabled during his opening statement at the summit. Bush took great satisfaction in catching everyone unawares— Gorbachev, the press, and the public. "The Soviets were unprepared for this," said one member of the U.S. delegation, "because we had been able to keep it a secret, shockingly enough." Had the president only refused to comment about his plans in advance of the summit, the surprise would not have worked. Reporters would have given more emphasis to private hints from some officials before the summit that Bush was preparing several initiatives. To shut down those stories and maintain the element of surprise, Bush felt he had to lie.

The tactic worked so smashingly at Malta, in terms of press play and polls, that Bush immediately started setting the trap for his next surprise, to be sprung in his first State of the Union address two months hence. At NATO headquarters in Brussels, where he flew from Malta, Bush was questioned about deeper cuts in conventional forces in Europe (CFE) and told reporters that he first wanted to accomplish the cuts he had proposed the previous May. "I'd like to get CFE I in the bank first," Bush said. "We ought to manage that before we start the architecture of something else." In fact, his aides already were preparing a second CFE initiative that Bush would unveil with great fanfare in an otherwise ho-hum State of the Union speech on January 31, 1990.

The day before that address, Bush invited a handful of reporters to an off-the-record lunch. Though the tone was friendly, one guest, ABC's Brit Hume, made the point to Bush that journalists recognize a president's right to secrecy—but not to deception. Hume gently reminded Bush that it's possible to say "no comment" instead of misleading the press and public. The point did not take, however. During lunch Bush was asked what had become a stock question since the relevation the previous month of the two secret Scowcroft-Eagleburger trips to China: Had Bush sent any other top aides on secret missions lately? Rather than refuse to comment, Bush replied, "No." In fact, as Bush spoke, Eagleburger and Gates were on their way home from a secret tour of European capitals, where they had explained to NATO allies the arms control initiative that Bush would announce in his State of the Union address—the speech that Bush had said would include no such initiative. To compound the deception, the arms initiative was omitted from copies of the speech that were circulated to senior officials for their suggestions, leading some to confirm to reporters Bush's assurance that there would be no such initiative in the speech.

Bush went to this well a third time only 12 days later, when he was asked whether he thought it was time for the four powers who had occupied Germany after World War II—the United States, USSR, Britain, and France—to hold a conference on the future, including the possible unification, of that divided country. "No," Bush replied, "not at this juncture." In fact, Bush's negotiators were at that moment working on plans for just such a conference, which was announced the next day in Ottawa.

A spate of stories on Bush's pattern of deception followed, including a devastating segment by Hume on ABC, juxtaposing videotape of Bush promising one thing with tape of him doing another. Bush responded by storming back to the press cabin on *Air Force One* during a predawn flight to Cartagena, Colombia.

"I think we've had too many press conferences," he stated. "I'm not going to be burned for holding out or doing something deceptive." His jaws were clenched and his lips were smushed together in that odd expression he wears when he is nervous or angry or both. He clutched a yellow-highlighted document that appeared to be a summary of the latest news dispatches about his battered credibility. He snapped "No comment" to half a dozen routine questions, refusing even to say whether he had a good night's sleep. "I can't go into the details of that," Bush said petulantly, "because some will think it's too much sleep and some will think it's too little."

Cold War Nostalgia

For all his denials, Bush was always keenly sensitive to what "some would think," particularly when the subject was his cautious and emotionally flat response to the outbreak of freedom in Eastern Europe during his first year as president. As the Soviet army began to pull back from Eastern Europe and Stalinist governments fell, as freedom rang out across the continent and ordinary Americans chatted excitedly about the news in grocery checkout lines and barbershops, Bush wore his grimmest game face. His first and strongest impulse was to fear a breakdown in the stability that had kept the peace during four decades of the Cold War. Bush's soberness was particularly striking in contrast with what everyone, not least his aides, knew would have been the response of his predecessor. Ronald Reagan would have tapped into the national and global mood of uplift; would have ordered up stirring triumph-of-freedom speeches from the pen of Peggy Noonan and delivered them with gusto. But George Bush, the foreign policy pro, concentrated prudently on what could go wrong.

One of Bush's biggest worries was Germany, on both sides of the Iron Curtain. The liberation of Eastern Europe in 1989, made possible in large part by Gorbachev, was accompanied by an understanding on the part of the president and other allied leaders that the Soviet Union would continue to have vital security interests in East Germany. The division of Germany lay at the heart of the Cold War and of the cold stability it had produced. German dynamism had been blamed for several generations of European conflict even before World War II, and the prospect of reuniting West Germany, already an economic superpower, with the untapped potential of the East, scared the Germans' neighbors and allies on all sides, including the United States.

However upsetting it might be to the stability treasured by the great powers, the people of benighted East Germany could not resist the contagion of freedom. In September 1989, East Germans began escaping to the West by the thousands, via circuitous routes through Czechoslovakia and Hungary. Bush warily refused to comment on the situation because, Fitzwater explained, that "might be inflammatory or interpreted as internal meddling." On the previous day, September 12, the administration had ushered Boris Yeltsin, then a member of the Soviet parliament and leading challenger to Gorbachev, in through the back door and up from the basement of the White House, for a meeting with Scowcroft and Gates, during which Bush "dropped by" for about fifteen minutes. The usual protocol for opposition leaders—an Oval Office session with the president, with remarks and photos for reporters—was not followed, Fitzwater explained, because "we didn't want to indicate that we were trying to provide a platform for dissent" against Gorbachev.

The evening after Yeltsin's visit to the White House, Deputy Secretary of State Eagleburger described, in a frank and eloquent talk to foreign policy specialists at Georgetown University, the post–Cold War worries chewed over every day by the president and his top advisers. "For all its risks and uncertainties, the Cold War was characterized by a remarkably stable and predictable set of relationships among the great powers," Eagleburger observed almost wistfully. Then he warned, "Let us not fool ourselves. If it is true that we have emerged victorious from the Cold War, then we, like the Soviets behind us, have crossed the finish line very much out of breath. Both we and the Soviets are faced with a frankly diminished capacity to influence events. . . . Nor is the multipolar world into which we are moving necessarily going to be a safer place than the Cold War era from which we are emerging." Instead, "the chances for instability increase." Eagleburger predicted, for example, that reform in the Soviet bloc and the relaxation of Soviet control over Eastern Europe would result in "putting the German question back on the international agenda."

Bush and other statesmen hoped and assumed the German question need not be answered immediately; that the two states of the German nation would reunite, but only through a quiet and gradual process guided by the four powers who had conquered Hitler's Reich. "It takes time," Bush said in an interview with *The New York Times* on October 23, 1989. "It takes a prudent evolution."

Two weeks later the East Germans took history into their own hands. Faced with accelerating emigration of their people through Hungary and Czechoslovakia, and with growing crowds at the Berlin Wall, the East German government panicked and sent conflicting signals to its security forces. Amid this confusion, on November 9, border guards in East Berlin simply allowed their countrymen to walk to the West through gates that had been closed to passage of all but a privileged few since 1961. Tens of thousands of East Germans poured through in the first hours. And within days the wall itself—for three decades the symbol of communist enslavement of half of Europe, the barbed-wire-topped, German shepherd–patrolled barrier beside which hundreds of men and women had been machine-gunned to death for trying to flee—was being battered into rubble by sledgehammers.

Germans on both sides were ecstatic, as were people all over Europe and the United States. This was a day that freedom-loving people had dreamed of since 1945; fulfillment of a hope for which the Western allies had spent trillions of dollars to keep soldiers under arms and nuclear weapons on alert during four decades of cold and bitter peace. And now it had come so suddenly! People instinctively felt elated, but they also wanted to feel satisfied and proud. They wanted someone to tell them what it all meant. They knew what Ronald Reagan would say. But they would not get inspiration from George Bush. When he appeared before the TV cameras in the Oval Office, he looked as if he had just seen his dog run over by a truck.

And he sounded worse. In a flat, constricted voice, Bush read a brief statement whose prose was leaden with caution and littered with the jargon of a UN bureaucrat. He referred euphemistically to the momentous opening of the wall as "the latest news coming out of Germany" and emphasized the actions of East German autocrats over those of their subjects. "Of course," Bush said, "I welcome the decision by the East German leadership to open the borders." He declared himself, unconvincingly, to be "very pleased." He made a big point of noting that "this, if it's implemented fully, certainly conforms to the Helsinki Accords, the Helsinki Final Act." Answering questions from reporters, Bush managed to cite the Helsinki Final Act twice more within the space of a minute, as if it were some secret code. When reporters offered Bush openings to say something a bit more sweeping, Secretary of State Baker, sitting facing the president, made little hold-it-down motions with one hand.

Reporter: Is this the end of the Iron Curtain, sir?

Bush: "Well, I don't think any single event is the end . . . but clearly this is a long way from the harsh days of the—the harshest Iron Curtain days. Long way from that."

Asked directly why he seemed so downbeat, Bush replied, "I'm just not an emotional kind of guy." He bristled that "we'll have some that will suggest more flamboyant courses of action for this country." Then he tried lamely to blame the hour: "The fact that I'm not bubbling over, maybe it's—maybe it's getting along toward evening." This at 3:30 P.M. The closest Bush came to a frank accounting of his reaction was this: "We are handling it in a way where we are not trying to give anybody a hard time."

His foreign policy advisers later explained that they and Bush were primarily concerned not to "gloat," not to "rub the Communists' noses in it," not to invite a crackdown by hard-liners in East Germany, elsewhere in Eastern Europe, or in the Soviet Union. Bush and the fellow Cold Warriors who advised him were haunted by visions of the Soviet tanks that had crushed previous popular uprisings: in East Germany in 1953, Hungary in 1956, and Czechoslovakia in 1968. They also were haunted by the fresh memory of the Tiananmen massacre. "What happened in China set back the relationship there," Bush explained. Therefore, on the German question, "we keep acting prudently so as not to exacerbate tensions. . . . We can hopefully not contribute to an unforeseen disorder." In this context Bush's ritual incantation of the "Helsinki Final Act" was meant as a signal to communist leaders that the American president chose to view the opening of the wall not as a retreat or defeat for them, but as a routine fulfillment of their international obligations. No big deal.

Such nuanced messages, however, were incomprehensible to the president's American audience. "We just won the Cold War!" said Representative Robert Torricelli, a New Jersey Democrat. "And rather than declaring victory, or even hinting this might be a success, we're lamenting what's going on." House Majority Leader Richard Gephardt, a Missouri Democrat, agreed: "Even as the walls of the modern Jericho come tumbling down, we have a president who is inadequate to the moment."

Bush shrugged off such criticism in public, but in private he let his fury show. "What do they want me to do?" he asked a group of aides, raising his hands like the actors in a Toyota ad. "Jump up and yell, 'Oh, what a feeling'?" In subsequent public comments, however, Bush took pains to brighten his tone. He began salting his speeches with the head-shaking observation that "we are living in fascinating times"—an ironic and unacknowledged play on the old Chinese curse, "May you live in interesting times."

Bush had another reason for nervousness over the speed of communism's collapse in Europe: it created pressure to cash in the so-called peace dividend; to cut U.S. military spending deeper and faster than he deemed prudent. Therefore, on February 6, 1990, a week after submitting a defense budget little changed from the previous year, Bush embarked on a photogenic, three-day pilgrimage to military bases in California and Nebraska, which resembled nothing so much as a Cold War Nostalgia Tour. At an army base in the Mojave desert, Bush clambered atop a tank and watched U.S. troops repel a mock Soviet armored assault. At a top-secret weapons lab he heard briefings on Star Wars. At the headquarters of the Strategic Air Command in Omaha, he wriggled into the cockpit of a B-1 bomber and peered into the bomb bay in which nuclear weapons were cached.

Meanwhile, on the evening of February 7, Moscow time, Mikhail Gorbachev prevailed over Communist party hard-liners at the Central Committee plenum and dramatically ended the Party's 70-year monopoly of power over political and economic life. It was midmorning when the news reached the traveling White House in California. As Bush helicoptered to Berkeley, Fitzwater and other aides told him that Gorbachev's latest reform was sure to lead the evening news and urged him to work a positive response into his luncheon speech to the Commonwealth Club of San Francisco. Bush refused, saying, "I'd be intruding in internal Soviet affairs, and I don't want to do that. Let's leave it for the Q and A."

In his speech Bush provided the caption for those hawkish photos of himself with tanks and bombers: "Some would have me predicate the defense of our people on promising—but as yet unfulfilled—hopes for the future. I will not do that. . . . When it comes to the security of this country, I would rather be called cautious than I would be called reckless." Afterward, during the question-and-answer session with

191

club members, Bush was asked how he could help Gorbachev achieve his reforms. He replied, "I think we can avoid doing dumb things."

What Bush feared most in the Soviet Union and the newly liberated countries of Eastern Europe was a coup led by hard-liners. "The best way to lend support to those types is to give them any reason to say 'The West is out to get us.' " Scowcroft said.

Indeed, when Bush met with reformist politicians and intellectuals during visits to Eastern Europe and the Soviet Union in 1989 and 1991, he found that his concern not to spark a backlash by communist hard-liners was better appreciated there than in the United States. "Intellectuals in Eastern Europe appreciate the fact that the president is very cautious," Bart Kaminsky, an adviser to Poland's Solidarity and a University of Maryland professor, told the *Christian Science Monitor*.

Scowcroft added that the same concern explained the administration's reluctance to recognize the Baltics and other secessionist Soviet republics before Moscow did so. "It tells everyone over there that we're not rushing to take advantage of this situation." Even by December 1991, however, when the Soviet central government ceased to exist, Bush extended diplomatic recognition only to Russia, Ukraine, Belarus, Kazakhstan, Armenia, and Kirgizstan, while withholding it from the other six former republics: Turkmenistan, Azerbaijan, Tadzhikistan, Uzbekistan, Georgia, and Moldova. Bush said the six had not lived up to his "standards of democracy, stability, and human rights" (unlike, say, China, Syria, or South Africa). The more likely explanation, according to Paul Goble, who quit at the end of 1991 as State Department special adviser on Soviet minorities, is Bush's basic discomfort with the rapid change in the former USSR. "Everything has been done late, grudgingly, and with little advance planning."

After being accused first of stiff-arming Gorbachev, by mid-1991 Bush was being widely criticized for clinging to the Soviet leader. The motive usually attributed by his critics was Bush's love of personal diplomacy, particularly over the telephone. And to be sure, Bush had forged a strong relationship with Gorbachev, inspired by the Soviet leader's collaboration in the freeing of Eastern Europe and proven in the Gulf War and in resolution of a half dozen long-festering flashpoints from Afghanistan to Cambodia.

But the larger factor was the desire of Bush and his advisers to see Gorbachev continue, at least as head of some sort of Soviet confederation: one that could maintain central control of the Soviet military and its nuclear arsenal; that could act as guarantor of international agreements on arms control and economic aid. Scowcroft told the president that he feared the breakup of the Soviet empire would result in the sort of "endemic instability" that has persisted in southern and Eastern Europe since the breakup of the Ottoman and Astro-Hungarian empires in the early years of the century. "We are still seeing the results of the dissolution of the Ottoman and Austro-Hungarian empires," Scowcroft said. He, and Bush, feared that the splintering of the Soviet Union would not end with the independence of the 15 republics: "Remember, Russia alone can go into 16 autonomous regions," several of which nurse ancient ethnic enmities.

That fear—of the worst instability imaginable, the nuclear-armed variety—was more powerful than any respect or affection Bush might harbor for Gorbachev. And when in August of 1991 it appeared that Gorbachev might be gone, it dictated strongly that Bush keep the door wide open to anyone of any political persuasion who might be able to hold the Soviet Union together, whether it was Yanayev and his fellow coup leaders or Yeltsin and his reformers.

"Stay in Touch with Yeltsin"

As Bush flew to Washington from Kennebunkport on the afternoon of August 19, the situation was shifting rapidly in Moscow. Yeltsin was loudly denouncing and defying the coup leaders from the steps of the modern, ivory-colored Russian parliament building. Fully expecting the building would be attacked by tanks at any moment, Yeltsin called upon Muscovites to take to the barricades to defend the government they had elected. And while the lumpen majority of the capital's 10 million people displayed the political passivity for which Russians are famous, an enthusiastic crowd estimated at 5,000, many armed with Kalashnikov rifles, hand grenades, and shovels, answered Yeltsin's call and began arranging vehicles and metal scrap into antitank barricades. U.S. intelligence picked up signs that several senior military officers were refusing orders from the coup leaders. A few key units were defecting to Yeltsin's side. What looked like an irresistible power grab only hours earlier now was turning into a real contest.

Word of Bush's morning press conference reached Yeltsin quickly

193

and alarmed him greatly. Noting Bush's ridiculous description of Ya-nayev as a potential reformer, and his refusal to endorse Yeltsin's call for a general strike, the Russian Federation's foreign minister, Andrei Kozyrev, then visiting Paris, responded that "this is no time for ap-peasement, while reactionaries attempt their illegitimate coup." He called the initial reactions of Bush and other Western leaders "ambig-uous and even discouraging" and said that the coup leaders "believed . . . that their efforts had deceived the West." Even before Bush's first press conference on the coup, Yeltsin had phoned James Collins, the deputy chief of mission at the U.S. embassy in Moscow, and pleaded: "We need your help." He had sent through Collins an urgent letter for Bush, imploring the president to "demand the restoration of the legally elected organs of power" and the "reaffirmation of the post" of President Gorbachev. This last formulation cleverly appealed to the shared interest of Bush and Yeltsin to emphasize the "post" over the person of Gorbachev.

Bush, however, was slow to get the message. During their phone conversation early on the morning after the coup, Collins had pro-vided Bush little detail on the Yeltsin letter. That would not come until Collins cabled the letter to Washington, where at about 11 A.M. EDT, it spooled off a printer in the White House Situation Room. An aide rushed a copy upstairs to Gates, who realized its significance. He phoned Scowcroft on *Air Force One* en route back to Washington and read the letter to him. Scowcroft then briefed the president. The Yelt-sin letter included what for Bush were magic words, asking for "op-erational contacts." Translation: Phone me. By now Bush had seen Yeltsin on CNN standing up to the coup leaders with thousands of Russian citizens and soldiers rallying to his side. Perhaps Yeltsin would come out on top. Bush moved to position himself for that possibility.

Immediately, the flying White House shifted its support somewhat toward Yeltsin and away from Yanayev and company. Bush and Scowcroft agreed that the president should not be seen, in political parlance, "walking back the cat" with a message that corrected the one he had sent only a few hours earlier at his press conference. That task fell to Scowcroft, who strolled with studied casualness back to the rear press cabin of the jet, ostensibly to inform the dozen reporters there that Robert Strauss would be sworn in as ambassador on Tues-day morning. He then invited questions and hardened the White

House line, calling the coup "quite negative" for U.S. interests. While "Yanayev has tried in his statement to appear moderate," Scowcroft said, the coup clearly was sprung "for the purpose of setting back the reforms." Scowcroft noted that Yeltsin had mounted "a dramatic challenge" to the coup leaders.

Preparing for Bush's unexpected return to Washington, workmen rushed to move the furniture back into the Oval Office, which was being painted during his vacation. Gates was analyzing the latest intelligence on the coup and leading deliberations by the administration's crisis-management team, known as "the Deputies" and comprising the number two officials at NSC, Defense, State, CIA, the Joint Chiefs of Staff, and, in this case, Treasury. While the Deputies usually conferred via secure teleconferencing facilities, the high policy stakes this time brought them face to face at the White House.

Bush, along with Scowcroft, Powell, and Sununu, sat in for part of the second Deputies session at 5 P.M. in the Roosevelt Room. (Bush dislikes the Situation Room. It is too dramatic, too much like *Dr. Strangelove.*) Bush was told that U.S. intelligence was picking up signs of "hesitancy" on the part of the coup leaders. As soon as the coup was announced on Sunday night, he was told, U.S. intelligence specialists had rushed to their offices and had run a postmortem check of satellite photos and communications intercepts over the past 72 hours for any large movements of Soviet troops and internal police units, as well as any urgent phone or radio messages among top officials and security forces. The intelligence analysts had come up virtually empty. Either the plotters had acted with uncommon skill and stealth or the whole enterprise was "half-assed." The Deputies were leaning more and more toward the latter explanation.

"All we had to do was to contrast it with the imposition of martial law in Poland" in 1981, said Gates. Troops and tanks had been slow to move. No opposition politicians had been rounded up. Foreign journalists had been allowed to continue transmitting reports. News broadcasts to Moscow from the outside—the BBC, Voice of America, Radio Liberty, CNN—had not been jammed. Deputy CIA director Richard Kerr told Bush: "This does not look like a traditional coup. It's just not professional. They seem to be trying to take control of the major power centers in phases, and you can't do a phased coup."

Bush related that Mitterrand that morning had commented on the erratic behavior of the putschists and had predicted that "this may be the first time that a coup fails" in the Soviet bloc.

Bush also mentioned that he had talked to Eastern European leaders, including Czech president Václav Havel, Polish president Lech Wałesa, and Hungarian prime minister József Antall. All three worried that the Soviet coup might offer opportunities for hard-liners to return to power in the former Soviet satellites—an understandable concern given the history of Soviet-sponsored crackdowns after periods of liberalization in their countries. He had done his best to reassure the East European leaders and had encouraged them to "retain calm" in their country and not to do anything that might appear provocative. For his part, he would emphasize that the coup should not be seen as an "East-West" conflict. He also would state publicly that he considered the gains of democracy in Eastern Europe to be "irreversible." Yet Bush and his national security advisers grimly agreed that in the unlikely event that the Soviet army marched back into its old quarters in Eastern Europe, there would be little the West would or could do militarily.

The Deputies had asked the State Department to prepare a complete list of possible U.S. sanctions against the coup leaders, and the agency had grunted out an 11-page, single-spaced response, involving virtually every economic aid and exchange program between the United States and the Soviet Union. Reviewing the list, Bush was particularly concerned that the United States do nothing that could be interpreted as breaking his campaign promise never to let U.S. foreign policy require any sacrifice of U.S. farmers by imposing a grain embargo such as Carter had ordered after the 1979 Soviet invasion of Afghanistan. (Never mind that Bush was entering the second year of an embargo against Iraq, another big market for U.S. farm exports.)

Shortly after 6 P.M. Monday, Bush issued a written statement, his toughest yet, saying that "we are deeply disturbed" and "condemn" the "unconstitutional" and "misguided" and "illegitimate" use of force by the coup leaders. Bush expressed support for the Russian president and quoted approvingly from his letter. "It was diplomacy through the media," said Popadiuk. "This was a clear signal from us to Yeltsin." The Russian president and his supporters quickly got the message and were ecstatic. The crowds surrounding the Russian Federation building would swell to more than 50,000 by Tuesday, and throngs more than twice that size were gathering in Leningrad.

Bush rose early on Tuesday. Before sunup he had stretched, showered, dressed, breakfasted, and taken his thyroid medicine. He had scanned the papers and the morning news on TV, checked in a couple of times with the Situation Room. Scowcroft now felt fairly certain that the momentum was shifting rapidly away from the putschists and toward Yeltsin, who was shown on TV rallying his people from the top of an abandoned Soviet army tank. It was now late afternoon in Moscow, Scowcroft observed, and the coup leaders were wringing their hands instead of cracking heads and taking charge. If they hadn't done it in the first two days, he reckoned, they weren't going to do it at all.

By 7:15 A.M. Tuesday Bush was seated at the personal computer in his small hideaway study just off the Oval Office, pecking out the last words of a "To Do" list:

1. Make an assessment [of the Soviet coup]. Meet with advisers on U.S. influence, arms control, economic aid.
2. Get Marlin back to Kennebunkport.
3. Contact South American leaders: [Venezuelan president Carlos Andrés] Pérez. Also [Spanish prime minister Felipe] Gonzalez.
4. Make sure our message is consistent and steady.
5. Stay in touch with Yeltsin.
6. No politics. Don't answer [House Majority Leader] Gephardt or other critics.
7. Get our information out to our people: [Republican senator Richard] Lugar, others on TV talk shows.
8. Change work schedule. Meetings at Kennebunkport. Soviet experts. Domestic advisers: Darman, Porter.

This was vintage Bush: reaching out in every direction at once, even in the midst of what was shaping up as the collapse either of Soviet reform—or of Soviet communism. He was thinking ahead to his return to Kennebunkport later that day: he would need Fitzwater there to brief the press, rather than the Deputies who had sufficed before the coup. Bush was thinking that on Monday he had phoned a dozen European leaders, plus the prime minister of Japan, but he had not talked with any Latin American leaders. His concerns were both for manners—he didn't want anyone to feel left out—and for coalition building. He now wanted solid international condemnation of the Soviet coup (and he would get it, with the sole exception of the pariah states of Cuba, Iraq, and Libya).

Bush was also aware that he had looked wishy-washy on Monday and that he must stick with his new, tougher line against the coup leaders. He was intensely annoyed that even after his brilliant performance over the past year in the Gulf crisis and war and aftermath, Democrats such as House Majority Leader Gephardt and the "self-anointed experts" on television had continued to criticize everything he did and offer "unsolicited advice." Bush groused to several aides that these "talking heads" had pestered him during the Gulf crisis, and "they're doing it again." Well, he wouldn't give them the pleasure of a reaction. He would leave that to reliable Republican foreign policy surrogates such as Senator Lugar of Indiana.

Finally, Bush was concerned that his absorption with the Soviet coup might give fresh ammunition to Democrats who complained often that he paid too little attention to domestic and economic policy. This line of attack, he knew from the polls, was scoring among some swing voters, so he had better head it off. In addition to meeting with Soviet experts at Kennebunkport, therefore, he would be sure to let the press see him meeting with Budget director Darman and domestic policy chief Porter.

After typing his "To Do" list, the president turned to an item he had omitted: he had the White House operators try to reach Gorbachev at his dacha in the Crimea, as they had tried the previous day, but "the blinds [are] still down," Bush told his aides. He then reached Yeltsin by phone and expressed his support and that of the dozens of leaders he had consulted. "We respect you," Bush told Yeltsin. "You've been duly elected there. We pray for you, and we hope that you're successful." Yeltsin thanked Bush and told him the crowds around his building had grown to 100,000. He had sent emissaries to see Gorbachev, but they had been turned away.

Bush then met with a dozen of his national security advisers. CIA director William Webster delivered a 10-minute update on military units defecting to Yeltsin, estimates of his popular support, and actions taken by the coup leaders. Bush emphasized that regardless of the outcome of the coup, the United States should continue to pursue arms control negotiations with the Soviet Union and should eschew any grain embargo that "hurts us more than it hurts them." Otherwise, he said, the United States should "keep as much pressure as possible on the coup people."

198

Almost everyone present felt the talk with Yeltsin had hardened Bush's resolve more than anything he had heard from his aides. "Before that," Fitzwater explained, "we didn't know whether there was anybody for us to support" against the coup leaders. Scowcroft added, "There was only one leader with his head above the parapet in time of peril, and that was Yeltsin. He was doing a magnificent job. . . . He was saying to the coup plotters, in essence, 'No, this will not happen' "—the same message President Bush had hurled at Saddam Hussein after he invaded Kuwait. Scowcroft remarked, "There was great admiration here for that performance."

Over the next 24 hours, faced with widespread international opposition and—most important—mounting resistance from their own troops and citizens, the coup leaders lost their nerve. Several tried to flee Moscow, but all were caught. Gorbachev was returned to Moscow and restored to the presidency—though not for long, as it turned out. The coup, intended in part to consolidate power in the Soviet central government, instead hastened the independence of the republics and the demise of the Soviet Union, which by late December would cease to exist.

The coup had failed, Bush explained, because "the coup plotters underestimated" the Soviet people's devotion to "democracy and freedom." True enough. But as one White House official noted, "So did we, for the first 12 hours or so." When the lone Chinese man in the white shirt had been shown on CNN standing down a column of tanks after the Tiananmen massacre, Bush had been as emotionally moved as any of his countrymen. But he also knew a futile cause when he saw one. Bush had made a similar assessment of Yeltsin and his followers on the first day of the Soviet coup. But the odds had shifted when the Russian president had rallied army units and officers to his side, and Bush had shifted with them, doing what he could to help. The man in front of the tank had looked like a loser, the man on *top* of the tank a winner.

That, of course, was not the way Bush would portray his decision making. In the retelling, he had stood always and bravely by the side of Yeltsin and his freedom fighters. Bush also felt, with greater justification, that the coup had vindicated his policy since 1989 of cautious and disciplined avoidance of any gloating over the collapse of communism, of any word or action that might trigger a crackdown by Communist party hard-liners—a policy that had been heaped with ridicule and scorn by domestic critics who demanded a more flamboyant response. Under interrogation, several of the coup leaders said they had long been suspicious that Gorbachev was securing his own position at the expense of the Communist party and the apparat, by selling out to the United States and the West. Had Bush provided more ammunition to Gorbachev's opponents, in the form of provocative statements, they might have moved earlier, before Yeltsin's election and the consolidation of the forces of reform. And earlier, the coup leaders might have succeeded.

Claims for the great benefits that had resulted from Bush's discipline and prudence summoned echoes of John Kennedy, when he spoke of Eisenhower as a man "praised primarily for what he did not do: the disasters he prevented. . . ." Bush and his aides pointed with pride to the democratic and market reforms still under way in Eastern Europe and the Soviet Union and its successor states, and claimed that this proved the effectiveness of Bush's policy. And sometimes they could cite credibly the specific pitfalls that Bush had avoided and the likely adverse consequences had he not avoided them. But other times their argument sounded like the silly ad campaign for popcorn, which claimed that the snack repelled unsightly alligators. "And if you don't believe it, think: When was the last time you saw an alligator in a movie theater?"

Whether Bush had helped win one for democracy, or had astutely *picked* a winner, or both, the bottom line for domestic political purposes was that he shared richly in Yeltsin's victory. First the Gulf War and now this: the long, twilight struggle of the Cold War was going to be won on his watch. A second term for Bush seemed a certainty. So, at least, thought Senator Al Gore, the Tennessee Democrat who had been considering another run for the presidency but decided against it as soon as the coup collapsed. So, too, thought Stephen Hess, a liberal political analyst at the Brookings Institution, who observed of the Democratic party's challengers to Bush: "When you think of the need for leadership in a dangerous world, the names of Bill Clinton and Paul Tsongas and Tom Harkin don't come to mind."

Despite Bush's deliberately leaked exhortation that his aides should avoid inserting partisan politics into foreign policy, the president's intensely partisan eldest son, George W. Bush, universally known as "Junior," couldn't help but exult on *Air Force One* during the flight back to Maine: "Do you think the American people are going to turn to a *Democrat* now?" Not even the sputtering economy, it seemed,

200

could beat Bush. As he prepared for a press conference in Kennebunkport a week after the coup, Budget Director Darman told him, "Mr. President, you could go out there and tell them that a depression is upon us and no one would even notice."

8

CLASS PRESIDENT

Those who know George Bush well, admirers and detractors alike, describe him almost invariably as a "classy" guy, and the characterization is apt. Bush is exceptionally well mannered, modest, restrained, generous, and considerate of others. He has always been, even in the White House, attentive to his friends and devoted to his family. He is publicly grateful for the privilege to which he was born and is quick to sympathize, at least in words, with the disadvantaged. A sense of noblesse oblige, of the noble obligation that comes with inherited advantage, was drilled into Bush by his parents. It accounts for his interest in public service and his lifelong work on behalf of such charities as the United Negro College Fund, beginning in the 1940s, when such an association was not only unfashionable, but potentially hazardous in politics. He is, at bottom, a difficult man not to like, whatever one thinks of his politics.

There is in Bush, however, a gritty ruthlessness and will to power often missing in men born to comfort and connections. Sporting companions say they see flashes of this trait on the golf course or tennis court, where, though he is always polite, it is clear that he hates to lose. He plays best when his opponent is about to close out the match, and he has made a career of coming from behind. In politics Bush has always done whatever he thought was necessary to win, even if that meant blatant pandering on taxes, thinly veiled race baiting, misrepresenting his opponent's record, and hinting that his rival was unpatriotic.

One source of this ruthlessness, friends say, is Bush's memory of watching his father defeated for the U.S. Senate by opponents who distorted his support for family planning and used it against him. Another was his own struggle to win election as a leader of the nascent Republican party in Texas during the 1960s. His Eastern Establishment roots posed a liability, and catering to white resentment of the civil rights movement offered a way to offset that. As Bush was hit hard from left and right, he determined to give as good as he got. He learned to use class and race, both to inoculate himself against charges of elitism and to take the initiative against more liberal opponents. His artful posturing and his often divisive campaigns masked a class agenda that has not changed much in 30 years.

In his first political race, a 1964 bid for the U.S. Senate, Bush was attacked by the right-wing John Birch Society. Its pamphlets alleged, among other reckless charges, that *Redbook*—the women's service magazine owned by the McCall Corporation, of which his father-in-law, Marvin Pierce, was then president—was an official journal of the Communist party. At the same time, Democratic incumbent Ralph Yarborough was alleging that Bush was "the darling" of the Birchers: an "extremist" who would bombard North Vietnam with nuclear weapons that "create leukemia and cancer in babies"—and a Yankee "carpetbagger" to boot. Bush fired back by calling Yarborough a "liberal" who "sets class against class, race against race." Bush sought to link race and class by encouraging white fears that new civil rights laws would bring lower-class blacks into their schools and neighborhoods and into competition for their jobs.

Bush told blue-collar workers that "the new Civil Rights Act was passed to protect 14 percent of the people. I'm also worried about the other 86 percent." He promised to "develop attractive job opportunities both for our growing population and for those displaced from . . . jobs by the new Civil Rights Act." In the 1964 Democratic primaries, when George Wallace mounted an openly segregationist challenge to Lyndon Johnson and won from 30 to 45 percent of the vote in three northern states, Bush concluded that "there must be a general concern from many responsible people over the civil rights bill all over the nation." He interpreted Wallace's showing as indicative of broad public support for his opposition to the bill, which he called "unconstitutional."

Bush required considerable coaching to overcome his upper-class image during his 1964 campaign. Jim Leonard, a native Texan who managed Bush's 1964 race, asked him to stop wearing button-down shirts (as John Kennedy had done during his 1960 campaign for president) and to stop using ten-dollar words like "profligate." He had Bush tour the state by bus with a country-western band called the Black Mountain Boys, who were useful not only in attracting crowds, but also in lending the Greenwich-born candidate more of a down-home flavor.

Though Bush lost the 1964 race, he received more votes than any Republican in Texas history; 200,000 more than the GOP nominee for president, Barry Goldwater. And he learned some important lessons, including the need to blur his use of racial appeals as well as his attacks on the liberal welfare state. He had, for example, denounced Medicare as "socialized medicine"—which, of course, it was and is —but after 1964 Bush began to realize that socialism could be politically potent when its beneficiaries were middle class. In a speech at the University of Texas in June 1965, Bush declared, "I generally favor the goals of the Great Society." He disputed the notion, however, "that a Great Society can or should be built solely by the federal government, or any government."

Bush won election to Congress in 1966 but was defeated in his second try for the Senate in 1970 and in his bid for the Republican presidential nomination in 1980. In both losses Bush was hurt by his privileged, East Coast Establishment background. "One of the ways that Reagan beat Bush was that he was able, usually in subtle ways, to contrast himself with Bush's elitist image," said Lee Atwater, who had worked for Reagan in 1980. Bush had won strong support from the traditional Wall Street and country club Republicans, but in most states Reagan had beat him among primary voters with lower education and income. "One of the most potent and most consistent factors in American politics is the distrust and resentment of elites," Atwater observed. Many swing voters are convinced that "various elites and special interests are stacking the deck against them."

When Bush put together his 1988 campaign, he moved to address his image problem by hiring Atwater, who was steeped in the status anxieties and resentments of working-class whites in his native South Carolina. Atwater war-gamed how he would run against Bush if he were working for the Democrats and decided that he would connect the voters' reservations about Bush's privileged and insular upbringing with their fears about the Republican party's economic agenda. He would revive the latent image of the GOP as "a bunch of rich, old snobs" and link it to a devastating caricature of George Herbert Walker Bush: chauffeured to the Greenwich Country Day School during the Great Depression, spanked by his father with a squash racket, prepped at Phillips Andover Academy, inducted into the nation's most elite secret society at Yale as well as the suspicious Trilateral Commission, bankrolled in the oil business with family money, launched into politics with the help of Washington politicians who played golf with his senator father, and concerned publicly that his partisans in Iowa—of all places—might be prevented from attending the party caucuses by their daughters' debutante balls.

If he were running against Bush, Atwater would build TV ads around pictures of the Republican nominee as a foppish-looking ambassador to the UN during the early 1970s, with his half-rim eyeglasses, long hair and sideburns, and flashy neckties. Pictures of Bush playing golf, and in tennis whites, dancing a silly pirouette to celebrate winning a close match. Pictures of the sprawling oceanfront Bush family mansion in Kennebunkport, with a voice-over saying, "No wonder he wants to cut capital gains taxes on the wealthy. . . ."

Don't get him wrong, Atwater cautioned. He loved and admired Bush and believed such attacks would be outrageously unfair; they would discount his decency and service to his country, his hard work and his sympathy for those who had not had his advantages. Still . . . Atwater drawled with a mischievous grin, "If I was managing the Democrats' campaign, I think I might be able to beat George Bush."

Instead, with Atwater's help Bush struck first by painting Dukakis as the elitist in the race. He employed indirect racial appeals. And he used effectively both economic appeals and symbols of class kinship to weld a diverse coalition. Bush played to his base of Wall Street and country club Republicans, but also to a wider audience with his "no new taxes" pledge and another refrain: "I won't let them take it away from you." The latter pitch was applied to several accomplishments, from peace to prosperity, that he attributed to the Republican reign in the 1980s. But it also resonated at a deeper level with many swing voters who felt they had something—a secure job, a nest egg, a piece of land, a safe neighborhood, good schools—that the envious lower orders of society, led by Democrats, might try to confiscate.

205

Matching this message was a television ad campaign that writer Alessandra Stanley wickedly dubbed "Presidency by Ralph Lauren." These ads featured gauzy, slow-motion shots of Bush, looking tanned and chiseled, surrounded by his happy, well-behaved children and grandchildren, all tastefully attired in natural fabrics. The settings were a picnic on a spacious lawn and a lobster boil in a country kitchen—both from the Bush family compound in Kennebunkport, whose size and expensive oceanfront placement are carefully obscured. Instead the viewer gets a montage of what Stanley calls "upper-class totems": white wicker chairs on the porch, a pedigreed springer spaniel, little girls in Liberty print dresses, leather-bound books, patchwork quilts. All casual, yet understatedly elegant: the "whole atmosphere of the good life" that designer Lauren strives to conjure in his ads. "Without Ralph Lauren and his expert molding of American taste, George Bush (Andover '42, Yale '48, a.k.a. 'Poppy') might never have been elected," Stanley wrote. "For more than a decade, Lauren has been hooking middle-class and lower-middle-class Americans on WASP aesthetics and pseudo-English gentility." Hugh Barnard, publisher of the *Retail Marketing Report,* agreed. While Bush's aides were still fretting about how to overcome their candidate's preppy image, Barnard was advising his subscribers that "the American public has become more conservative and tradition-conscious. . . . They want stability and classiness."

Although this trend played to certain of Bush's strengths, he and his aides hedged their bets with stylistic appeals to voters who might look warily both upon Ralph Lauren and trickle-down economics. Bush emphasized his affinity for country music, touring by bus with C&W bands just as he had two decades earlier in Texas—except this time he was able to recruit headline talent: the Gatlin Brothers, Crystal Gayle, and Lee ("I'm Proud to Be an American") Greenwood. Bush injected more of a Texas twang into his voice. "Fair" became a two-syllable word. He no longer intended an action; he was "fixin' to" do it. Bush did not excise all fancy words from his vocabulary, but, mindful of the advice of his first campaign manager, he spelled them out syllable by syllable, as if reading them for the first time. Even "ed-jew-cay-shun" got this aw, shucks treatment. He had his picture taken throwing horseshoes rather than playing golf or tennis. Campaign officials discouraged photos of the Bush spread in Kennebunkport. The owner of an expensive speedboat and an avid angler for the exotic bonefish of the Florida Keys, Bush now emphasized his love of fishing for the humble largemouth bass and attended the Bass-masters exhibition in Alabama. He also let it be known that he liked to unwind with a beer (domestic, of course) and a big bag of pork rinds.

Dukakis, meanwhile, gave the Bush campaign a couple of scares on the populist front. In Detroit on Labor Day, Dukakis railed that Bush "wants to give those who make $200,000 a year or more a tax break of $30,000. That's more than the average teacher makes. That's enough to send your son or daughter to Michigan State for four years. The down payment young couples could use to buy their first home. And who do you think is going to pay for that tax break? Look at your kids." A few weeks later Dukakis roused farmers in the hamlet of Idalou, Texas, with a speech by President Kennedy's wordsmith, Ted ("Ask not what your country can do for you") Sorensen, which powerfully linked the Republican party with big business and the neglect of rural America. "By the 1920s, most Americans had electric power," Dukakis said. "Not rural Americans. The big utilities refused to supply them. Not profitable enough, they said. The Republicans agreed. And the utilities refused to let the farmers pay for the lines. They called it socialism. The Republicans agreed. Franklin Roosevelt knew better. . . . He had faith in America's farmers. . . . They beat the Republicans and the utilities and their lobbyists. Hundreds of thousands of farmers formed cooperatives. Your parents and grandparents signed up their neighbors. With their own hands, rural Americans dug the holes, set the poles, and strung the wires. All over America, the lights came on."

Watching on television, Atwater fretted, "If he keeps this up, we're in trouble." He needn't have worried. Though Dukakis occasionally talked the populist talk, he just couldn't walk the walk. He was a cold, dour technocrat, as were many of his top advisers. His campaigning style had been hard-wired decades earlier in the hyper-rational, "good government" political culture of affluent, well-educated, liberal Brookline, Massachusetts, where any appeal to emotion was considered bad form.

Dukakis had little effective response when Bush began calling him "the man from Harvard" and declared with theatrical suspicion that "there's an elite inside the elite there, and everyone knows who I'm talking about. . . . I'm talking about a handful of people who have

207

served in these Democratic administrations that come out of the same liberal philosophy.'' Even Dan Quayle got in on the act, calling Dukakis ''conceited'' and alleging that he ''looks down on America.''

From the first weeks of the general election campaign, the Bush team beat Dukakis to the populist punch, defining the Democrat, rather than Bush, as someone alien to the ''values'' and attitudes of the white working class, on ''issues'' ranging from school prayer to the Pledge of Allegiance. ''We preempted the Democrats, labeling *them* as the elitists,'' Atwater crowed after the election. ''We were able to catch the populist vote, which is a lot of the swing vote, by presenting ourselves as the campaign that understood the resentment against elites, the Establishment, the big institutions, and we were able to define those as liberals, Harvard, and people who coddle criminals.'' The Democrats' failure to mount any sustained attack on Bush as an elitist, Atwater said, shaking his head in wonderment and pity, ''was the biggest surprise of the campaign.''

As soon as the election was past, Bush dropped most of his working-class affectations. It turned out that his favorite snack was not pork rinds but popcorn, and beer gave way to vodka martinis (on the rocks with lots of olives) and white wine. Many of his cabinet members and top advisers were chosen from Dukakis's ''Harvard boutique'': among them Attorney General Thornburgh, Treasury secretary Brady, Budget director Darman, and domestic policy chief Porter. All but one of Bush's cabinet were male, as were all but one member of his senior staff. The cabinet and senior staff each included one black. Not only minorities and women, but also white ethnics were under-represented among Bush's top advisers. Episcopalians, millionaire inheritors, and prep school graduates were vastly overrepresented.

Bush once again strapped his watch to a striped-cloth band that had been banished during the campaign as too preppy. He similarly resumed wearing shirts with white collar and cuffs over striped or pastel-colored bodies: ''what Roger calls my 'elitist shirts,' '' Bush joked in a reference to his savvy campaign adman and image adviser, Roger Ailes. During the 1988–89 transition, Bush vacationed at three pleasure domes—a Florida beachfront estate, a Texas quail-hunting preserve, and a Kentucky bluegrass Thoroughbred farm—owned by William Stamps Farish III, an oilman, polo player, horse breeder, and manager of the president-elect's million-dollar blind trust. At a lavishly catered fund-raising event, held on the lawn of Farish's five-thousand-acre Kentucky spread and attended by 3,500 wealthy contributors, Bush announced that he had named one of Millie's puppies after Farish. Bush once again joked that the "III" was "not going to help with my elitist image." But Bush wouldn't have to worry about that until the next campaign.

Do It Yourself

Bush's election had at least two immediate and salutary effects. The first was that the denizens of official Washington, and increasing numbers of real Americans as well, began copying Bush's well-bred and well-publicized thoughtfulness in writing graceful, personal notes to friends and acquaintances. Puzzled hosts and hostesses in the capital found their mailboxes stuffed with overnight thank-you notes even for informal drinks parties and backyard barbecues. The second effect, perhaps coincidental, was that voluntary community service began to rise. A Gallup poll in 1990 found that 54 percent of the Americans surveyed said they had done some volunteer work that year, up from 45 percent in 1988. This trend was confirmed in 1990 and 1991 by scattered reports from volunteer referral agencies across the country: New York City's major referral center reported inquiries up 28 percent in 1991 over 1990; Houston's was up 20 percent; Kansas City's was up 16 percent.

Bush had, of course, emphasized voluntarism throughout his fall campaign, beginning with the "thousand points of light" metaphor penned by Peggy Noonan for his acceptance speech at the New Orleans convention. That phrase attracted much snickering, but Bush was dead serious about the idea. It stood at the center of his approach to poverty, homelessness, illiteracy, juvenile crime, and most other social problems. As a political tool during the 1988 campaign, Bush's pitch for voluntarism served multiple purposes. It allowed him to appeal to more moderate suburban independent voters who liked the Republican promise of lower taxes and smaller government but had been turned off by the gluttony and callousness of the Reagan years. And it allowed Bush to do so without alarming conservatives suspicious of new government programs.

Still, Bush's approach was not entirely political, and it was not without risk. One of the unspoken sources of Reagan's appeal, for people who had inherited money or an expensive education or other advantages, or had otherwise been lucky and found themselves a comfortable niche in the system, was his message: Relax. Stop feeling guilty about the "less advantaged." If they worked as hard as you do, and embraced your values, they wouldn't be in such a fix. Bush wanted to change that attitude, so he added a line to his speeches: "Any definition of a successful life must include service to others." It was a theme many of his countrymen were ready to hear. The turn away from the excesses of the 1980s was only part of the reason. Americans of all political persuasions also were growing exasperated at the failure of government at any level to accomplish anything tangible in their lives and neighborhoods. And as baby boomers had their own babies and settled down, they developed more of a yearning for the sense of community they remembered from their childhood, or at least from television. They wanted that for their kids.

Bush fleshed out his "points of light" philosophy in a Rose Garden speech to a group of distinguished volunteers and other community leaders in mid-June 1991, when he was coming under fire from the Democrats for lacking a domestic policy to match the vigorous foreign policy he had demonstrated in the Gulf War. This criticism moved Bush to personally pen the clunky, key phrase of his speech—"an America whole and good"—to match the vision he had earlier voiced for "a Europe whole and free" after the collapse of communism. "America's problem-solving does not begin or end with the Congress nor with the White House," he declared. "It is through you that we can solve our most pressing problems. . . . Only the combined light from every school, every business, place of worship, club, group, and organization in every community can dissolve the darkness."

Bush's "points of light" program, soon ensconced in a suite of White House offices and bolstered by a private foundation, could claim success in encouraging voluntarism, removing liability insurance hurdles to it, and publicizing nonprofit programs that worked. More Americans were visiting elderly shut-ins and coaching Little League baseball. But the "points of light" did not, and could not, cast much light on the inner city and the underclass. Middle-class volunteers might be willing to dish out stew to the homeless at a well-staffed downtown soup kitchen, but they would not venture into inner-city neighborhoods terrorized by gun-toting drug gangs. They could not provide ghetto children with equal opportunity to health care, to decent schools, to money for college, to job training. And on these issues Bush had no coherent approach.

It was not that he had none to choose from. Darman, the hyper-pragmatic budget director, along with his archenemies among activist conservatives—Housing secretary Kemp, drug czar Bennett, Quayle chief of staff Kristol, and White House aide Pinkerton—all suggested novel, antibureaucratic programs to attack the problems of the under-class by expanding the opportunities available to them. But they could win no sustained support or interest from Bush. He would often ask impatiently, "Why does government have to do that?" Some of his aides gradually realized that Bush saw the "points of light" not so much as a complement to a domestic policy strategy, but as a substi-tute for one.

Bush's attitude flowed from his class background and worldview; from the conflict between noblesse oblige and institutional reform. Noblesse oblige has always been about the dispensing of favors from haves to have-nots, not about the restructuring of government and society. Indeed, the first purpose of noblesse oblige, from the time of Edmund Burke, was to defend the established hierarchy, with its in-herited privileges and inequality of opportunity; to round off the sys-tem's rougher edges, give it a kinder face, and make it seem less objectionable; to contain the pressures for institutional reforms. In this way Bush's promotion of voluntarism and philanthropy, and his shunning even of those reforms pressed by conservative activists, nicely served the interests of the most privileged Americans, with their tax exemptions for inherited assets and other government subsi-dies and preferences, who served as Bush's natural political base.

A second effect of noblesse oblige traditionally has been not so much to better the lot of its recipient permanently, but to make the donor feel better about himself, particularly in his relationship with his conscience and his God. Gregg Petersmeyer, who runs the White House Office of National Service, observes that " 'Points of Light' isn't supposed to be about other people. It's supposed to be about you . . . about making service fulfilling to the giver." Ray Walker, a psychoanalyst and cousin to George Bush (though something of a black sheep in the closely knit Bush–Walker clan), told Barry Bearak of the *Los Angeles Times* that "the family misses the point that all this altruistic public service is also serving *you*. It gives you power and a sense of goodness. . . . That's the complexity of the thing. God help us from people who think they are going around exercising their goodness!'' Walker added that his family and the Bushes never made the leap from their sense of noble obligation to genuine empathy. ''Does anyone from the family understand what it is to be poor? No. And the bigger question is: Do they understand their own ignorance?''

The late Alexander Ellis, who had married George Bush's sister, Nancy, had observed of his brother-in-law in 1987: ''Certainly he cares about the poor in the religious sense. He knows it's right to have that concern. But I'm not sure what kind of *feeling* he has for the poor. It wouldn't be a priority for him. It wouldn't be where the resources would go.'' Ray Walker added, ''There is a Christian innocence to George. His life has been without moral ambiguity. He feels that he has been granted goodness and that his success proves the goodness was warranted. But this has all come to him without introspection, without any grappling about right or wrong. George plays it safe. . . . He plays for the status quo.''

Even as he applauded and encouraged voluntarism in his June 1991 speech, Bush made clear that he felt the status quo in America needed only some minor improvements. ''Every American should take pride in this country's fundamental goodness and decency,'' he said. He lauded the volunteer leaders and philanthropists in his audience as ''those who make America the land of opportunity''—a telling phrase, because Bush generally believes that equal opportunity is not so much a slippery goal to be relentlessly pursued as a state of grace that America already has achieved. During discussions of equal opportunity, Bush often brings up examples of disadvantaged Americans such as his appointee to the U.S. Supreme Court, Clarence Thomas, a black man born to desperate poverty in Pin Point, Georgia, who worked his way up through college and law school and the federal bench. If Thomas could do it, Bush reckons, that proves sufficient opportunity already exists for those with sufficient drive and persistence.

To be sure, Bush would support certain social programs to attract certain groups of voters, as he did during his 1988 campaign—and as he did, in a different direction, in suddenly developing an interest in welfare reform as the 1992 campaign heated up. But what Bush believes deep down, according to his friends, was what he had espoused in 1964: a Great Society should be created by voluntary efforts and moral persuasion rather than by government.

The government's main domestic task, as Bush sees it, is to promote the interests of established businesses and investors. And not just by freeing the markets. "The marketplace," Bush declared, "cannot solve all of our problems." In fact, Bush did not trust the workings of the marketplace even to protect the interests of established businesses and investors; that was why he constantly sought to micromanage the tax code by adding "incentives" for particular industries (and campaign contributors). He is pro-business, not pro-market.

When a shipyard worker gets laid off from his job, Bush expresses sympathy for the individual, but he sees the layoff as the invisible hand of the free market at work. And if that worker doesn't find another job within a few weeks, Bush is not inclined to stretch out his unemployment benefits. But when a real estate developer or business owner falls on hard times, or has trouble finding bank loans or investors for his latest enterprise—well, in that case, the workings of the market are unacceptable to Bush. He wants to move heaven and earth, even write new loopholes into the tax code, to help those businessmen. In February 1992, promoting to an enthusiastic audience of business lobbyists his anti-recession proposals, including generous tax breaks for real estate and capital gains, Bush cited by name a North Carolina businessman who wanted to build a convenience store and gas station. "He just can't do it," Bush lamented, "under our present system."

Bush believes that if only government took care of the owners and managers of capital, they would, in turn, take care of domestic policy. They would, first, provide jobs. Then they and their employees would, under his exhortation, provide charity, in the form of cash donations and voluntary services. Wealthy philanthropists and civic-minded businesses would lead the way, along with churches, private hospitals, clubs, associations, and individual volunteers, to feed the hungry, house the homeless, shape up the flunking schools, and train ghetto youths for jobs. A great deal of such community service was already under way, of course, before Bush began talking about it, and it increased after he took up the cause. But even devoted volunteers decried the idea that their work should be a substitute for presidential leadership to improve equality of access—particularly for children born into poverty—to basic health care, education, and job training. What Bush offered was a trickle-down social policy to match his trickle-down economic policy. His message to the country on domestic policy, essentially, was: Do it yourself.

. . .

Bush recommends to others a self-reliance that he has not had to practice in his own life. His family provided crucial help at every stage of his career. This went beyond the obvious head start for which Bush publicly calls himself "lucky": being born to well-educated and attentive parents who imbued him with sound values, who reared him in a safe neighborhood, and who gave him the best health care and education that money could buy. Bush's family also introduced him to many of the other families who run America's government and commerce.

In his autobiography, *Looking Forward,* and elsewhere, Bush portrays himself after graduation from college as boldly breaking with the comfort and connections of his East Coast roots: striking out on his own to find his fortune in Texas; working his way up from "painting oil rigs" to running his own multimillion-dollar company. But he blurs a few telling details. Fresh out of Yale, Bush was offered a job in Odessa, Texas, with Dresser Industries, on whose board his father sat and whose chairman, Neil Mallon, was one of his father's closest friends and a fellow member of Skull and Bones, the elite secret society at Yale. Mallon didn't have any children of his own and promised George Bush, "You'll have a chance to run it someday," according to Bush's brother Prescott. The new red Studebaker station wagon that Bush often describes as the chariot of his independence was bought for him by his family. He drove the car out; Barbara and their first son, George W., followed by air.

Bush was immediately well liked in Odessa and nearby Midland, as he had been at all his schools and in the navy. He was friendly, smart, hardworking—like most of the hard-charging young war veteran Ivy Leaguers out to make their fortunes trading mineral rights in the West Texas oil country in those years. One thing that distinguished Bush from the others was the capital provided by his family—mainly his uncle, Herbert Walker, but also his father and other relatives, as well as Uncle Herbie's business associates. They staked young George to $300,000 in the first tranche, back in 1950 when that was real money, and tripled their investment within a few years. "George would've been just another carpetbagger," said Midland old-timer J. C. Williamson, "if he hadn't rode in on a silk carpet."

When Bush got interested in Republican politics in the late 1950s, his father introduced him to Vice President Richard Nixon, an occasional golf partner, and to Gerald Ford, then the Republican leader in the House. When Bush was elected to Congress, he became the first freshman since 1904 to be given a seat on the powerful tax-writing Ways and Means Committee. The chairman, Wilbur Mills, explained, "I got a phone call from his father telling me how much it mattered to him." Ford, too, interceded with Mills. In 1970 Nixon, then president, encouraged Bush to try again for the U.S. Senate, with an assurance that if he lost, he would be "taken care of." He did and he was: Nixon named him ambassador to the United Nations.

Bush, however, seemed to take all these introductions and connections and assists for granted. After all, most of his peers had similar networks and had received even more money from their families. Bush had not met anyone outside his social class until he got to know the handful of scholarship students at Phillips Andover. And despite his parents' best efforts to remind Bush and his siblings that other children did not live as well as they, it was a difficult case to make when the Bushes had one of the more modest incomes and homes in their part of Greenwich. In that community, *really* wealthy people lived off their investments; Bush's father Prescott Bush worked for a living, as a banker and then as a U.S. senator. "We never felt that Dad had any kind of wealth at all," recalled Jonathan, Bush's younger brother. "We had a cook and a maid and a chauffeur, but other kids had a lot more."

There was considerable truth in the line coined during the 1988 campaign by Jim Hightower, the Texas agriculture commissioner and a populist Democrat: "George Bush was born on third base and thinks he hit a triple."

"The Fairness Issue"

Bush's class biases and blind spots are most evident in his attitude toward taxes. He is against them, of course—but only for certain people. He believes that taxes must be kept low on the owners of capital, so they will be encouraged to take risks rather than just collecting interest on their tax-free bonds and playing golf all day. He believes implicitly that taxes need not be so low on workers as on investors, because workers will not be "disincented" so much; they, after all, have no choice but to work. Republican senator Phil Gramm of Texas once stated Bush's philosophy more bluntly than Bush would. Explaining why he wanted to cut taxes on the wealthy, Gramm said, "I want to induce my friends to invest in jobs, and all of them are rich."

When he first campaigned for office in 1964, Bush was a traditional, responsible, fiscal conservative. He espoused small government, low taxes, and balanced budgets. He believed that domestic spending must be pared before taxes could be lowered across the board, lest the deficit swell, driving up interest rates and the cost of capital to businesses. But his upbringing among well-heeled investors and bankers, and his experiences as an oilfield entrepreneur and a member of the tax-writing Ways and Means Committee in Congress, left Bush with a taste for "targeted" tax cuts, aimed at the owners and managers of capital whom he considers to be the engines of the economy. That the beneficiaries of these special tax breaks also financed Bush's oil companies and election campaigns was, to his mind, only a happy coincidence.

One of the few domestic themes on which Bush, as candidate and president, has demonstrated rhetorical passion and persistence is his crusade to cut the capital gains tax—that is, the tax on profits from the sale of assets like stocks and bonds, real estate and timber, Oriental rugs and paintings. Cutting this tax obviously would benefit the owners of such assets: fully 60 percent of the savings would flow to the best-paid 1 percent of taxpayers, who earn more than $200,000 a year. But Bush and his supporters claim these benefits will trickle down to average Americans, as investors and entrepreneurs rush to expand existing businesses and start new ones, thus creating new jobs. Bush has often portrayed his capital gains proposal as a silver bullet that would instantly enrich the economy and heal the society. If only Congress would "reward investment and stop punishing success," Bush told the Philadelphia Chamber of Commerce in early 1992, it would "set America's doers and dreamers free. . . ." Liberal economist John Kenneth Galbraith reformulated Bush's theory as follows: "If the horse is fed amply with oats, some will pass through to the road for the sparrows."

Economists might be closely divided on whether Bush's capital gains tax cut would spark enough investment and economic efficiency to make up for the loss in revenue that the Treasury would collect at the old, higher rate, but several things are clear. The benefits to the wealthy would be certain, immediate, and large; the benefits to the average wage earner iffy and eventual, and the threat of a heavier burden of debt repayment for future generations substantial. That Bush embraces this parceling out of risks and rewards is one measure of his class agenda.

Further evidence of Bush's loyalties can be found in the way he crafted his proposed tax cut of 1989 to deliver the lion's share of its benefits to already wealthy investors who are sitting on stocks and real estate that has appreciated over the years and would reap a windfall by paying lower taxes than they expected—lower taxes than working people pay on their wages. Why, Bush was asked, if his purpose is to spur new investment, does he not target his proposed tax cut to future profits from new investments? He replied with disarming frankness that cutting taxes on existing investments was the only way to make his tax *cut* appear to be a revenue *gainer,* at least in the short term, as investors rush to realize their gains at the new low rate. "There are also revenue aspects of it, so that when you turn over [investments] you're actually going to increase revenues to the federal government," Bush said. This wrinkle would allow Bush to cut taxes without swelling the budget deficit during his term as president. In the longer term, of course, the Treasury would receive less in capital gains taxes, and the shortfall would have to be covered through higher taxes on others or (less likely) through spending cuts.

Bush might be given the benefit of the doubt on capital gains; he might be accepted as sincere in his desire to create jobs for the jobless rather than merely enrich the already rich—if he had not so starkly exposed his class agenda in two other episodes. In early 1990, as he struggled to cut the capital gains tax, Bush helped to turn back efforts in Congress to cut regressive federal payroll taxes on middle-income wage earners. Then, later that year, he agreed to increase regressive excise taxes as part of the initial budget accord that spared the wealthy at the expense of the working class.

The payroll levies for Social Security and Medicare (together called "FICA" on workers' pay stubs and often referred to simply as Social Security taxes) nearly doubled during the Reagan administration and shot up by another 9 percent during Bush's first year as president. As a result, by the end of the 1980s three-fourths of Americans paid more Social Security taxes than they did in federal income taxes. The rise in Social Security taxes also more than wiped out the Reagan-era cuts in federal income taxes, so that most Americans ended the decade paying more to Uncle Sam than they did in 1980. Under the combined weight of FICA and federal income tax, some middle-income wage earners by 1990 were paying Uncle Sam as much as forty-eight cents of every new dollar they earned—a marginal tax rate twenty points higher than that paid by those who earned more than $200,000 per year.

Neither Reagan nor Bush cut taxes overall. They cut them for the wealthy; they raised them for everybody else. Under Bush the U.S. government collected just as much in taxes—about 20 percent of national income—as it had under Jimmy Carter. The difference was that the bottom three-fifths of families, ranked by household income, were paying more taxes than in 1980, so that the top tenth could pay less— and so that the top 1 percent could pay *much* less.

This arrangement nicely served Bush's wealthy core supporters and campaign contributors. But it appeared to be in danger in early 1990, when Senator Pat Moynihan, the scholarly and iconoclastic New York Democrat, pressed for a radical rollback in Social Security taxes and for putting the system on a pay-as-you-go basis. The idea attracted great attention in the press and won initial support from an interesting collection of populist Democrats and supply-side Republicans. But Bush opposed both reforms, blandly in public and fiercely in private lobbying of the Congress. Now it was clear: Bush favored tax cuts for the wealthy, but not for ordinary wage earners. It was also clear that Bush's main interest was not in creating jobs. Economists from such conservative institutions as the Heritage Foundation and the U.S. Chamber of Commerce were in agreement that the Social Security tax, split equally between employees and employers, was the most direct obstacle to job creation in the tax code and that cutting the tax could create a million new jobs. Still, the Democratic leadership in Congress joined Bush in opposition to the Moynihan proposal and killed it.

This was a classic case of the Washington Establishment—Democrats and Republicans, Bush and the Congress—closing ranks to repel a common enemy. Like Toto in *The Wizard of Oz,* the impish, bow-tied Moynihan was threatening to yank back the curtain on one of Washington's most cherished and heavily guarded myths: the Social

Security "trust fund." Though Bush and others had long portrayed it to the taxpaying public as some sort of separate, protected pool of retirement savings, the "trust fund" is nothing of the sort. In truth it does not exist except as a bookkeeping device, created to convince taxpayers that they are saving for their retirement when they are, in fact, financing the ever-expanding general operations of the federal government. The annual "surplus"—$63 billion in 1991—of Social Security taxes collected in excess of retirement benefits paid out was not socked away in little safe-deposit boxes under the names of contributors and future retirees, as Bush and others often implied, but instead was immediately spent exactly as income-tax collections were: for the whole range of government programs, from air force jets to meat inspectors' salaries.

Thus, if Social Security taxes were cut, and more money were left in the hands of average wage earners, federal spending would have to be cut and/or income taxes would have to be raised on better-paid Americans, neither of which were attractive prospects to the leaders of Congress or to Bush. In one of the most revealing explanations for his opposition to the Moynihan tax cut for wage earners, Bush said, "I think it's a disguise for increased taxes around the corner"—increased taxes, that is, on better-paid taxpayers.

For that reason Bush used demagogic rhetoric to scare retirees into viewing the Moynihan plan as a threat to their benefits. "I don't want to see the benefits of Social Security cut," Bush said when asked in a press conference why he opposed the Moynihan plan. Asked the same question in a private interview later that day, Bush said, "I don't want to tamper with the Social Security system. . . . I may not be the swiftest guy in the world, but you're not going to get me out saying to the old people 'Well, we don't know about these benefits. We're not sure they're going to be covered. . . .' That's exactly what the Moynihan proposal does."

Once they caught their breath after dodging Moynihan's bullet, Bush and his aides were struck that the Democrats would not act to help the middle-income workers whom the party rhetorically claimed as its base: not if the price of that help was to cut spending programs and tax subsidies that were fiercely defended by the special interests —real estate developers, retirees, the Israel lobby, dairy farmers, the builders of the B-2 bomber—to whom Democrats, as much as Republicans, were beholden for campaign contributions and bloc votes. Bush and his aides long had feared that the Democrats, having failed to "go populist" during the 1988 campaign, would launch a serious assault on Bush during his presidency by using "the fairness issue." But the Democrats in Congress now looked as if they were no more capable than was the hapless Dukakis.

The opportunities and risks of this situation were not immediately clear to Bush, who took office seeking to bind the wounds of his slashing campaign and promised a break from Reagan's confrontation with Congress. Bush vowed at his inauguration to serve as "president of all the people," specifically including those who voted against him. Like any politician, though, he attended first to the interests of his supporters. He believed in the system, in which "the legislature and the executive do battle as part of our system of checks and balances." And he took a sharply adversarial view of his role. Bush would lead the Republicans in vigorously representing the interests of their core supporters, and he assumed the Democrats in Congress would represent theirs. The two parties would compete and compromise, and the national interest would be served. That was the theory, and Bush made it work with early bipartisan agreements on such previously divisive matters as the Clean Air Act and aid to the contra rebels in Nicaragua.

On the central, lunch bucket issues of who pays and who gets, however, the system worked quite differently: Bush and his Republicans fought like tigers to promote the interests of corporations, wealthy investors, and the upper-middle class. And so did the Democrats.

"More Will Than Wallet"

The bipartisan sellout of the working class found its next expression in the closed-door "budget summit" in the autumn of 1990. This episode was best known as the moment when President Bush broke the central promise of his 1988 campaign: no new taxes. What got less notice was the cleverness with which Bush and his lieutenants, Sununu and Darman, traded their consent to raise taxes for the Democrats' agreement that those taxes should rise mainly on the working class and mainly in the form of regressive new excise taxes, including 12 cents more per gallon on gasoline. So accustomed were they to sticking middle Americans with the bill that Bush and the Democratic elders were blindsided—as was the journalistic establishment in Washington and New York—when their proud handiwork, a bipartisan deal to reduce their budget deficit, was angrily shouted down by ordinary taxpayers across the country.

The second budget agreement, reached weeks later, was less regressive than the first, yet once again Bush and his core supporters got the best of the deal through structural changes in the all-important rules that govern the budget game. The most lauded and laudable change required that if Congress cut a particular tax or increased spending on a particular program—say, highway construction—it had to offset the cost by providing new revenues or by cutting other spending programs. The bad news, however, came in complex provisions little noticed at the time, which effectively froze the federal budget into rigid categories. Under these strictures, cuts in defense spending could not be used to finance tax cuts or new spending programs.

The budget deal thus represented a smashing triumph of the status quo. Amazingly, Bush got the Democratic Congress, for the first time in U.S. history, to *codify* the status quo on the central questions of who gives and who gets. Together, Bush and Congress froze into place the Reagan-era shift in tax burdens that favored the well-to-do at the expense of the working stiff. At the same time they made it almost impossible for Washington to finance new expenditures, whether pork barrel contracts for a congressman's cronies in the road-paving business or urgently needed unemployment benefits. Bush and the Congress erected unprecedented barriers to government's ability to deal with social, economic, and international changes—and they did so at a stupendously inopportune moment. The Warsaw Pact and the Soviet Union were collapsing, rendering pointless much of America's Cold War defense spending. New nations and governments emerged overnight and pleaded for U.S. aid, trade, and advice along the uncharted path from Stalinism to democracy and market economics. Meanwhile the U.S. economy slipped into a recession that Washington, lashed to the mast of its budget deal, did little to address.

As unemployment rose and consumers retrenched, influential lawmakers of both parties in late 1991 sought to jump-start the economy through tax cuts. They only confirmed how embarnacled the status quo had become. The leading Democratic plan for "middle-class" tax relief, presented in October by millionaire Texas senator Lloyd Bentsen, would have showered more than half of its benefits on the 20 percent of American taxpayers who earned more than $50,000. President Bush's alternative was his by now hoary proposal to cut the capital gains tax, aimed at taxpayers who earn more than $200,000. Those were the terms of the 1991 debate in the Washington of Bush and Bentsen: Should government further enrich the wealthiest 1 percent or the wealthiest 20 percent?

Bush did not stop there. During his 1988 campaign, ridiculing Dukakis's plan to boost federal revenues by catching more tax cheats, he had said, "I don't want to put an IRS agent in every kitchen." But in early 1991 it was revealed that what Bush meant was that he did not want a taxman in every corporate boardroom. While drafting its budget for fiscal year 1992, the White House proposed secretly that the IRS shift enforcement resources away from wealthy individuals and companies, whose lawyers often stall cases for years, and toward middle- and lower-income taxpayers, who generally pay up without protest and provide immediate revenue. IRS commissioner Fred Goldberg, however, rejected the White House plan, calling it "no-good tax policy."

Nothing came of the 1991 tax cut proposals, like so much that Bush and the Democrats proposed to one another. Domestic policy by then had developed into inconclusive trench warfare. Congress refused to allow straight up-or-down votes on Bush's initiatives, while Bush vetoed much of the legislation that Congress managed to pass. Bush's blocking strategy was remarkably successful, with 28 of 28 vetoes sustained through May 1992, but it was inherently negative and left the widespread impression that government just wasn't working anymore.

In fact, as Bush well understood, even as government abandoned the working class, it was alive and thriving as never before for *some* of the people. Federal domestic spending, which crept up by only 1 percent a year under Reagan, ballooned by 10 percent in each of Bush's first two years as president, mainly to accommodate interest on the Reagan-era debt (running at $286 billion a year by 1992), the bailout of spendthrift savings institutions whose depositors' money had been siphoned off by get-rich-quick land developers (cost: $300 billion from 1989 to 1991), and the inexorable growth in subsidized retirement and health benefits for the upper and upper-middle classes.

As Darman reported in the "generational accounts" buried in the 1993 federal budget, the average 30-year-old will pay $201,100 more in taxes in current dollars than he will ever get back in benefits. Meanwhile the average 70-year-old already has received as much as he paid into the system and will receive another $65,100 more in benefits before he dies. Young workers are subsidizing retirees who, on average, make more money than they do. But Bush did not wish to "tamper with" this regressive system.

Tax subsidies grew under Bush precisely because their main benefit fell to corporations and the well-to-do. The tax deduction for interest on mortgages of more than $200,000—a plum for the best-paid taxpayers—costs the Treasury $5 billion a year. The write-off for mortgage interest on vacation homes costs another $400 million. The tax exemption for inherited investments constitutes a $5 billion annual giveaway to the wealthiest Americans. While more than 35 million working Americans cannot afford health insurance, their taxes help finance a $43 billion annual subsidy for corporate health plans, most of which provide lavish benefits for top executives.

These, of course, were not the kinds of federal spending that wealthy and upper-middle-income voters had in mind when they decried "waste" and "welfare." And neither Bush nor the Democrats dared to jump in front of a popular gravy train. When Bush declaimed at his inauguration, "We have more will than wallet," he had it exactly backward.

"The American Dream"

A central paradox of Bush's life is that it has been such a compelling adventure, so full of richly varied experiences—in the Pacific war, Texas, China, an array of top Washington jobs, constant foreign travel, national political campaigns—and yet it has left him so out of touch with the basic concerns and dreams of his countrymen. The point is not the one conceded by some of his friends and relatives, that he lacks any understanding of what it is to be poor. The poor are taken care of by Bush's sense of noblesse oblige. What is more significant for Bush as president is that he lacks any fingertip feel for what it is to be a member of the wage-earning middle class in America.

223

At every stage of his career Bush was a member, and usually the leader, of an elite. He was surrounded by other white, well-educated, well-connected men with money behind them and bright futures ahead. Just as he was driven to elementary school by a family servant, Bush has been chauffeured almost everywhere for the past 25 years. He does not know what it is to sit at the kitchen table with the family checkbook at the end of the month and try to make the shrinking paycheck cover the bills. It has been decades since he shopped for groceries (his forays for bagels and pastries don't count), picked up his own laundry, prepared his own tax return, or stood in line at the post office or the Department of Motor Vehicles.

Even as stagnating incomes and unemployment force average Americans to prune their expenses, the Bush household budgets at the White House, and before that at the vice president's mansion, have grown comfortably each year, providing the president with everything from daily fresh flowers to a staff of 40 (mostly black and Filipino) domestic servants. Bush has added to the White House grounds a personal putting green and horseshoe pit. His weekends at Camp David are financed by the taxpayers, as are his vacations fishing in Florida or hunting in Texas. Once, when a senior aide to Bush asked if he could miss an upcoming presidential trip, Bush said yes but asked why. The aide explained, as delicately as possible, that he had been away from home on other presidential trips for quite a stretch and needed to pay his bills, wash his clothes, mow his lawn, and so forth. Bush asked in sincere puzzlement, "Don't you have people to do those things for you?"

The insularity of his life affects Bush's politics and policies in ways both subtle and direct. When he addresses the urgent issue of health care reform, for example, Bush speaks as a man who has had his and his family's health insurance provided free by the government for almost all of the past quarter century, yet he rails against the Democrats' comprehensive plans as "socialized medicine"—just as he railed against Medicare in 1964. In every speech on the subject Bush emphasizes that "the quality of health care in America is second to none" and cites as evidence the number of foreigners who travel to the United States for heart-bypass operations and expensive optional surgery. All of this is true for Bush's friends at home and abroad who can afford to fly off to see the top specialists at Johns Hopkins or the Mayo Clinic or M.D. Anderson Cancer Center. But the issue for most

Americans, as Bush seems not to understand, is not so much quality as affordability.

Similarly, Bush dismisses those who worry about U.S. economic decline by declaring, "You travel anywhere around the world and you will find we are the undisputed, respected leader of the free world." It does not occur to him that most Americans do not travel abroad or that, amid the recession, many can't afford to travel in the United States. Nor does it occur to him that most Americans judge their country's standing not by what foreign kings and prime ministers think of it, but by such homely measures as their own hourly wages, which declined for 60 percent of families during the 1980s and which, after ranking fifth among industrial nations in 1975, dropped to eleventh by 1990.

When he considers federal tax policy, Bush cites the need for lower capital gains taxes and lower marginal rates of income tax on the wealthy, but he seldom talks about the tax bite on middle-class families, many of whom pay a larger share of their incomes in taxes, and higher marginal rates, than do the wealthy. As evidence, Bush need look no further than his own tax return. In 1990, *Money* magazine reported, he paid 23 percent of his $452,732 income in federal taxes, versus the 28 percent paid by the average two-earner family with an income of $52,000. That family faced a top marginal tax rate of 54 percent, versus 31 percent for the president. The main reason for this disparity is that the Social Security tax hits middle-income families harder than it does the Bushes and others in their income bracket. Another reason is that the Bushes and other wealthy families have more ways to cut their tax bills through itemized deductions. (A third factor, not reflected in the federal tax figures above, is that the Bushes pay no state income tax. Although he owns no home in Texas, the president declares it as his domicile because, unlike the District of Columbia or the state of Maine, Texas has no state income tax.)

Bush thinks he stays in touch with the concerns of average Americans, according to his aides, because he reads the polls and a selected handful of the thousands of letters sent to him each week, because he often phones his many friends and acquaintances across the country, and because he travels the country to give speeches and to visit schools and factories. But Bush's friends tend to be prosperous fellow Republicans. And his destinations and audiences are heavily weighted toward upper-middle-class suburbs and Republican business groups.

Most of the people seated on the dais or at his table are corporate and civic leaders and major campaign contributors.

When Bush campaigned in recession-battered New Hampshire in early 1992, he steered clear of the unemployment offices and visited mostly unrepresentative factories that still enjoyed strong business. One New Hampshire businessman who was flush back in 1980 had been ardently wooed by the Bush campaign, which wanted endorsements and cash contributions, but by 1992, when he had fallen upon hard times, he was shunned by the president and his campaign. When reporters in February 1992 asked how he was doing politically in California, Bush answered instinctively in terms of campaign cash: "I understand there's two extraordinarily successful fund-raisers in place out there, so that should say something. Maybe that will get people thinking confidently."

The depth of the recession first began to get through to Bush not through his staff or cabinet advisers, but through corporate executives and other big campaign contributors who sat with him at state dinners and campaign fund-raising events. Many of those businessmen represented real estate interests, which got far more attention than average working people when Bush put together his antirecession plan in early 1992. Former Reagan aide Lyn Nofziger, who knows Bush and many of his advisers, observed that "George Bush is in trouble because these guys over at the White House don't understand the American people. They never had to worry about a job, and they don't understand people who have to really worry about a job. As a result, they came at this matter of the economy rather casually."

On the rare occasions when he does meet with working-class Americans, Bush seems more interested in the photo opportunity and in opening himself to their questions than in asking about *their* lives and concerns. When he took a group of road-paving workers to lunch at a diner near the Dallas–Fort Worth Airport in December 1991, for example, Bush steered the conversation toward Texas football and bass fishing and never asked about their worries or finances. Had he asked, as some reporters did afterward, he could have learned that several of his luncheon guests were worried about layoffs at the nearby General Motors plant and other major employers and were unhappy about their tax bills.

But the conversation need not have been all "gloom and doom," as Bush would put it. The workers also would eagerly have told the president about their dreams: to earn promotion to foreman, find a job with security and good health insurance, buy a new home, send their kids to college, save for retirement, maybe start a small business and keep it in the family. Theirs are dreams expressed in a full-page Nike ad appearing in magazines in early 1992, featuring a photo of Carlton Fisk, the durable, 21-year-veteran major league baseball catcher, over the legend: "I Don't Want Fifteen Minutes of Fame . . . I Want a Career. . . . I Don't Want to Sell a Company. I Want to Build One."

Bush has something different in mind when he talks, as he does often, about the American dream. He stated his version of it in his autobiography, where he talks about the dream he shared with other young Ivy Leaguers who moved to Texas in the 1950s: "There wasn't anything subtle or complicated about it. We all just wanted to make a lot of money quick." He reiterated that vision as president when, even as he accepted tax hikes and opposed tax cuts for middle-income wage earners, he said, "I want to reward everyone who believes in the American dream, trying to make it work. I want Congress to cut the long-term tax on capital gains." It is this dream—to build a company and then sell out, invest the profits, and live off the proceeds—that Bush's economic policy is designed to promote and defend.

9

MANAGING THE DECLINE

Dan Rostenkowski, the chairman of the House Ways and Means Committee, had been friendly with the president since the mid-1960s, when both were junior members of the powerful tax-writing panel. In January 1989, from the inaugural podium on the west front of the Capitol, Bush singled out his old Democratic pal with a conspicuous wave and a loud, "Hi, Danny." Not long afterward Rostenkowski became a frequent visitor to the White House for lunch or cocktails. He told jokes and ribbed the commander in chief: had Bush shown more perseverance during his four years in Congress, Rostenkowski often kidded, he might have become the ranking Republican on Ways and Means. Bush would reply with one of his favorite conversation stoppers: "If you're so goddamned smart, how come you're not the president of the United States?"

But in one bull session in early 1990, the burly Chicago pol dispensed with the kidding. For over a year Bush had balked at a bipartisan package of spending cuts and tax increases designed to reduce the deficit, lower short-term interest rates, and stimulate investment. Bush had long feared a backlash if he broke his "no new taxes" pledge. But now, both men knew, the measure was essential to keep America competitive. Unless the deficit was trimmed, the United States would continue to lose its edge in investment, productivity, rate of growth, and standard of living to Japan and Germany. Rostenkowski decided to give Bush a shove. He drained the mirth from his voice and suggested to Bush that he make an appeal to common sense —explain to Americans that they would surrender financial and political primacy to Japan and Europe if they continued to spend beyond their means.

"Tell the people," said Rostenkowski, "that if we don't balance our budget, we're going to be number two, and they'll say, 'The hell we will!' If you challenge them, Mr. President, they will accept whatever sacrifice you say is necessary. If you lead, they'll follow."

Bush's half-joking reply to Rostenkowski was a harbinger of things to come. "It's easy for you to say."

Intellectually, Bush knew Rostenkowski was right. A Phi Beta Kappa economics major at Yale, Bush had long recognized that Washington had to stop living beyond its means. In 1968, when the budget deficit stood at $25 billion, Bush was one of a dozen Republicans tapped to rebut Lyndon Johnson's State of the Union message. "The nation faces this year just as it did last a tremendous deficit in the federal budget," Bush said then, "but in the president's message there was no sense of sacrifice on the part of the government, no assignment of priorities, no hint of the need to put first things first." He had decried profligate proposals of his rival Ronald Reagan during the 1980 Republican primaries as "voodoo economics" and a "free lunch approach."

But Bush had traded in his grave doubts about Reaganomics in exchange for a long-coveted post on the 1980 Republican ticket. As vice president he watched quietly while Reagan reaped the political benefits of the multi-trillion-dollar borrowing and spending binge that followed over the next eight years. During the 1988 campaign, Bush had further hobbled himself by pledging to cut the deficit without new taxes or cuts in popular entitlements, which had become by the campaign's end not merely a promise, but practically the reason for the campaign itself—and one of the few popular "convictions" the candidate could claim as his own.

As president Bush was stuck. Having jumped on the supply-side bandwagon, Bush could hardly pull a U-turn and admit it had all been a big mistake. He could not disown the policies on which he had staked his candidacy and suddenly lament eight years of deficits, rising merchandise trade gaps, and net foreign investment imbalances. He couldn't admit to the magnitude of the nation's economic problems, as Rostenkowski suggested, because he would be expected to propose a comprehensive strategy for reversing the decline. Any such strategy would be painful, particularly for Bush's core supporters, who had prospered in the 1980s. Besides, a reversal would raise the question of whose policies got America into the mess. Bush might joke about his plight in private—"Let's face it," he told members of Washington's exclusive Gridiron Club in 1989, "if I was funnier than Ronald Reagan, I would have won in 1980. And he'd be here tonight trying to laugh away the Bush deficit"—but he couldn't speak as honestly to the American people.

Bush wasn't interested in reversing the decline; he wanted merely to manage it, to protect his constituents—and his presidency—in an era when most Americans faced diminishing returns.

"Most Americans Are Not Becoming Better Off. . . ."

The long-term economic problem was complicated by the fact that Bush faced a strong probability of a recession sometime during his term. In political terms the two headaches were related: if Bush could make headway on the deficit, he would send a signal to financial markets that America's continuing indebtedness was ending. That, at least in theory, would help bring down interest rates and perhaps avoid a deep recession, or at least soften its blow.

On the other hand, it might not work out that way—particularly if the recession came early or stayed late. Traditional cures for the rising unemployment and stagnant growth that often accompany a recession —more public spending and costly tax cuts—would contribute to the long-term problem of deficits, indebtedness, and high interest rates. If a recession lingered, Bush might have to take steps that, in the name of solving the short-term problem, exacerbated the long-term one.

For most of his term, the long-range problem took preference for one reason: its effects were already being felt. Reagan had left behind a debt the likes of which the country had never seen. During Jimmy Carter's last year in office, the federal deficit had stood at $73.8 billion; eight years later, Reagan's last year in office, the deficit had more than doubled, to $155 billion. Gross public debt tripled to $3.2 trillion by 1990, up from $914 million in 1980. With outlays running ahead of revenues, the Treasury was forced to borrow money to cover the gap to keep the government running. The cost of this borrowing was itself out of control: by 1992, $286 billion of the $1.2 trillion annual budget went *exclusively* to paying interest on the debt—larger than the 1991 deficit itself. Debt-financed consumption and disinvestment in the future spread from the government to private firms and households. Personal consumption—as well as the personal credit to cover such purchases—soared in the 1980s. Corporate and consumer debt, while lagging the rise in public debt, nonetheless jumped in the 1980s. Many of the goods purchased—food, clothes, cars, and VCRs—contributed little in the way of long-term investment in the nation's future.

For the first time in decades, moreover, Americans looked overseas for the credit to finance their consumption. The United States went in less than a decade from the world's biggest creditor to the world's biggest debtor. In the three short years between 1981 and 1984, noted Benjamin Friedman, the Harvard economist, Americans squandered the "entire net foreign asset position that three generations of Americans had accumulated since 1914." Between 1985 and 1987, Friedman added, Americans "accumulated the world's largest foreign debt for the next generation of Americans to service." In aggregate terms every American family began the 1980s holding an average $2,500 credit from a foreign debtor but ended the Reagan years owing $7,000 to a foreign creditor. By the end of the decade Americans were importing cars, Walkman headsets, and computers and exporting land, logs, and deeds. As Friedman noted, "Foreigners have already begun to settle [American] debts by taking possession of office buildings in American cities, houses in American suburbs, farmland in the heartland, and even whole companies. We are selling off America and living on the proceeds."

Economists differed on the costs and benefits of foreign investment, but they almost all agreed that the government's soaring demand for credit was sapping private investment at home. Multiple claims on limited credit caused interest rates to rise, making it more expensive for American businesses to invest in plant, equipment, and research that would enable Americans to compete in the world market. The government's insatiable demand for credit was twice that of the nation's personal savings, diverting private capital away from more productive investments and into paying the interest on the debt. The deficit, expressed as a percentage of personal savings, rose from roughly 50 percent in 1980 to more than 125 percent in 1990. In part as a result, fixed American investment as a percentage of GNP began to drop, from nearly 12 percent in 1980 to around 9 percent a decade later. When the nation should have been investing in the future, it was mortgaging it. As a country, Americans were like those retirees who tooled around the country in shiny Winnebagos sporting bumper stickers that read "We're Spending Our Children's Inheritance!" "We are about to enter an era of annual $400 to $500 million deficits that will truly wreck the country," said Senator Warren Rudman, the New Hampshire Republican. "We will be facing a situation, at the end of this century, that will not be very pretty to look at financially. We will have foreign governments in a position to dictate terms and conditions of money they will loan us. And interest rates will go high. And the economy will be seriously impaired. And the standard of living will decline."

Meanwhile America's competitors overseas invested heavily in plant and equipment. Japanese private investment soared, from 16 percent of its gross domestic product in 1980 to 23.4 percent ten years later. Despite the fact that Japan's economy is roughly half the size of that of the United States, the Japanese actually *outspent* Americans in capital investment by $62 billion in 1990. During the same period, American investment in plant and equipment stalled, at 12.6 percent of GNP. The picture was even darker in the area of federally funded research and development. As a percentage of GNP, federal investment in nondefense research and development trailed that of Japan and West Germany by as much as one-third in 1988. The U.S. government spent less than 2 percent of GNP on basic research, while Japan spent nearly 3 percent and Germany 2.5 percent in 1989. The relative decline in research and development had predictable effects. American companies—and individuals—began to win a smaller percentage of patents issued by the federal government. American companies' grip on domestic and worldwide market share, in a number of key industrial sectors, began to shrink.

As a candidate Bush dismissed these trends as fantasies peddled by pessimists. Early in his acceptance speech at the 1988 GOP convention, Bush distilled the race into "two very different ideas of the future. What it all comes down to is this: My opponent's view of the world sees a long slow decline for our country, an inevitable fall mandated by impersonal historical forces. But America is not in decline. America is a rising nation."

But as president Bush faced a poor alignment of stars. Unchecked, the lag in savings and investment would mean that Japanese and German workers—not Americans—would have access to the most modern equipment. Over time these nations would surpass the United States in productivity and eventually the American standard of living would fall. By the end of the 1980s this pattern was already in motion. Most economists agreed that America, while still a land of enormous human and physical resources, had insisted on consuming more than it produced for so long that it was in decline *relative* to more frugal and provident countries and relative to its own frugal and provident past. Concluded the U.S. Office of Technology Assessment in 1991, "While citizens in the United States still earn more and live better than citizens of Japan, most Americans are not becoming better off, and most Japanese are."

Felix Rohatyn, senior partner at Lazard Frères & Co., and a Democrat, described the problem as daunting but not insurmountable. "We've had a very consistent set of economic policies that consist of borrowing huge sums of money, mostly from abroad, of not investing it but consuming it, of having the physical facilities of this country degrading, of not teaching our children, and of losing our competitive position abroad while our financial system has gone to pieces. . . . We have some very basic problems. It took us ten to twelve years to get into them, and it's going to take us ten years to get out of them."

"You Have to Lead"

Bush began to extricate himself from his "no new taxes" pledge immediately after his election, when he expressed a sudden wonder at the size of the federal deficit. "I've started going into the numbers finally, and they're enormous," he said in one interview with *Time*. The U-turn had to be carefully executed: while polls showed that Americans expected Bush to raise taxes, they also believed any immediate repudiation of the tax pledge by Bush would demolish much of what he stood for as a politician and might even jeopardize his reelection. Bush's advisers engaged in endless calculation: to back away would prove costly at any time; to do so in the first year would be calamitous. As a senior official explained, "If he could make it one year, he wanted to make one year."

But as the same official put it, "The question was, 'What was the definition of one year?'" Bush huddled with his economic advisers during the transition to discuss gently breaking the tax pledge before 1989 was out. What emerged from these discussions was a two-step approach that envisioned reaching a relatively easy, "no new taxes" agreement with Democrats in Congress on the pending FY 1990 budget, then beginning a second round of negotiations for a multiyear deal that might include taxes and could be concluded by the end of the 1989 calendar year. Long-drawn-out negotiations were key to peddling the Bush strategy in public: the more protracted the parley, the more the public would see that both parties were being forced to make painful sacrifices and gutsy compromises. "The concept of the talks," said one official, "was that it could only make sense if it were extracted over a period of time in tough negotiations so people could see that you really didn't want it, you were dragged kicking and screaming, and so on and so on." The talks would give Bush the cover to abandon the "no new tax" pledge. Correctly drawn, the final package would be worth the cost: a long-term "solution" to the deficit that would remove the issue for the remainder of the first term and set the nation at least on the path toward growth.

In April 1989, Bush and Democrats in Congress completed step one, initialing a blueprint that neither cut spending nor raised taxes and was quickly dubbed "the slide-by budget." Rather than reducing the deficit, the deal employed the same old smoke and mirrors that had allowed Washington to ignore the nation's fiscal problems for nearly a decade: nearly $2 billion in "savings" came from removing the U.S. Postal Service from the budget; another $5.7 billion came in asset sales, one-time-only cash infusions; some $850 million was "saved" simply by transferring farm subsidy payments into the previous fiscal year. And with a mere stroke of the pen, negotiators credited more than $400 million to the Treasury by removing a charge for unused food stamps from the books. Bush called the deal "a manageable first step."

But Bush never took the second step. Budget director Darman spent the rest of the year trolling around on Capitol Hill, talking up the prospect of a long-term deal. The ingredients were no mystery: in exchange for "discussing" new taxes, Bush wanted Democrats to agree to spending cuts, particularly in the fast-growing entitlement programs such as Medicare and farm subsidies. House Democrats, particularly Speaker Tom Foley and Budget Committee chairman

Leon Panetta, were interested, but their counterparts in the Senate were not. Meanwhile, at the White House, an unreal euphoria set in. So effectively had the deficit been papered over that Bush concluded that he could postpone the hard bargaining for yet another year.

By 1990, though, Bush could stall no longer. Democrats on Capitol Hill knew that he would have to abandon his tax pledge or oversee more than $50 billion in automatic cuts required by law. When corporate profits began to soften in the spring, Bush saw an opening. In May, with little warning, he agreed to new negotiations with the Democrats, explaining that a suddenly sluggish economy made him do it. "What is at stake here," Bush privately told a group of lawmakers at the time, "is the overall economy." For most of an entire week, coincidentally, Bush made no public appearance. But, suddenly, deficits mattered.

After that almost nothing went right. By agreeing to hold negotiations without winning anything in return, Bush let the Democrats outmaneuver him for weeks. Through the summer of 1990, the Democrats stymied the White House by refusing to pony up cuts in cherished entitlements, shrewdly recognizing that delay worked to their advantage in an election year. Democrats also knew that they did not need to wield the spending knife as long as most of the House Republicans opposed cuts in entitlements just as avidly, if not quite so publicly, as they did. An internal administration survey in August 1990 revealed that House Republicans could agree on only $5 billion in entitlement cuts—a fraction of the amount Bush sought from Democrats. "The major miscalculation was that we gave up 'Read my lips' and got nothing in return," said a senior administration official. "And then the Democrats backed away and let us twist in the wind."

Bush made things worse by staying behind the scenes, giving up the tax pledge in a halting, little-by-little fashion. He turned over control of the talks to Darman, whose taste for clever stratagems sometimes got the better of him, and Sununu, whose powers of persuasion tended to be nuclear. After Bush announced in May that he would seek negotiations, Sununu bent over backward to deny that taxes were on the table—when, as one administration official put it, "any fool could plainly see that they were." A month later the Democrats did it again, this time forcing Bush to sign a statement allowing that "tax revenue increases" would be part of the final package. "You know what this means?" Marlin Fitzwater asked as the chief of staff handed him the statement. "It means no more 'Read my lips.' " Sununu, accustomed to bullying lawmakers and reporters in New Hampshire, said with Queen of Hearts–like stubbornness, "No, it doesn't. Just look at it. It means just what it says."

No one was fooled. The next morning the *Los Angeles Times* announced across its front page, BUSH ABANDONS VOW; BACKS A TAX INCREASE. The *New York Post* was more pointed: READ MY LIPS—I LIED. One of Sununu's White House colleagues said later, "What was intended for that meeting was a softer move, not as hard a move, and the hard move was supposed to come after being dragged kicking and screaming and at a time when the world would also see a whole lot of benefits. It didn't happen that way."

The squabbling over tactics masked the real damage to Bush. Throughout the fall of 1990, Americans realized they had elected a president who was scared to engage in a debate about the nation's most fundamental problem. Rather than state clearly from the beginning what the problems were, what needed to be done to address them, and what he wanted in a budget deal, Bush disengaged from the process. It wasn't that he was incapable of tough negotiation and compromise: throughout the budget talks Bush was up to his elbows in the daily bargaining required to keep his fragile anti–Saddam Hussein coalition intact. But he refused to bring that kind of energy to bear on matters at home. Both by temperament and design, Bush avoided leadership when the country most needed it.

When the negotiators emerged from weeks of seclusion and unveiled their compromise deal in late September, Bush acted as if the long-term economic future of the country were a burdensome distraction. Copies of the proposed package had hardly been distributed when Democratic backbenchers complained that higher excise taxes on cigarettes, beer, gasoline, and home heating oil—and a lack of new taxes on the wealthy—made it too regressive to support. House Republicans, who had largely been ignored by the White House for most of the year, revolted because the final package lacked a capital gains tax cut. On October 6, the House of Representatives rejected by a vote of 179–254 the deal that had been months in the making.

Bush's advisers split deeply over what to do next: some, such as Darman, wanted to cobble together a new bill and rush it through. Others, led by Dan Quayle, wanted to stonewall the Congress, shut down the government, and force Democrats back to the table. Bush, suddenly back in the picture, had a lot of explaining to do. His trademark campaign promise was in pieces, his popularity was plunging, and his party was in chaos. Pressed by reporters to explain whether a budget deal was worth such a high price, Bush rattled off a series of excuses that betrayed his own central failings. "I'm not interested in talking about that. I'm interested in governing. But let me tell you this. I expect others will be talking about that. Fine. Take the heat. Take the hit. There have been changed times. It didn't work out the way I want. I don't have the horses in the Congress to do it exactly my way. So you have to govern. You have to lead. And that's what I'm going to do."

But he never did. Ten days later, as the talks entered yet another "final" round, whatever remained of Bush's backbone collapsed. The Democrats, as adroit as the White House was feckless, upped the ante just as the deal was closing, pressing Bush to accept a higher top marginal tax rate in exchange for a cut in the capital gains tax. Bush indicated at first that the swap was acceptable. But later that day he met with Republicans who spoke against it, arguing that the Democrats would not be satisfied with a small hike and would eventually come back for more. He listened quietly and said nothing but left several aides with the distinct impression that he was leaning toward accepting the swap. After the session, Senator Robert Packwood of Oregon appeared before reporters to announce that the president had given the deal thumbs down. Sununu, meanwhile, told a group of lobbyists the same news: the deal was off.

The next morning headlines charged Bush with changing his mind on taxes yet again. BUSH WAVERS ON TAXING RICH AS SENATORS PROTEST said *The Washington Post*. Livid, Bush called Sununu into the Oval Office. "What happened?" he demanded to know.

"That may have been my fault," Sununu replied, not exactly explaining how he had shut down the deal without Bush's go-ahead. Steamed, Bush quietly turned on his heel, strode out an open door into the Rose Garden, and slammed the door behind him. At the time, the incident was popular among White House aides because it seemed to reveal Sununu's treachery with unusual clarity; what it really revealed was Bush's refusal to seize control of a government in crisis.

Later that day, jogging around a baseball diamond in St. Petersburg, Florida, Bush was asked by reporters if he would accept the deal Sununu had scotched just hours before. Most of the damage had been done, but Bush's sarcastic reply fell well short of a profile in courage: "Read my hips."

It was the closest an American president had come to publicly telling his critics, "Kiss my ass."

"I Just Wanted to Get Some Attention. . . ."

The budget fiasco only deepened the president's resolve never again to squander precious political capital on the nation's long-term economic problems. Instead he seemed all the more determined to turn the tables—to advance economic proposals calculated to brighten his political future.

The most notable of these was the push in 1990 for a Mexican free trade agreement. Reagan had completed free trade negotiations with Canada in 1988, lowering barriers on a broad range of trade between the two nations. Bush had promised to seek a similar pact with Mexico during the 1988 campaign. The idea had intrigued him for years: as vice president he had become convinced that instability in Mexico might someday jeopardize the United States; nothing would better stabilize the nation than strong economic ties to a thriving continent. Bush had one eye fixed on the long term, too: as Europe consolidated into a single market, and the Far East gave signs of similar integration, a free trade zone stretching from the Yucatán to the Yukon made considerable economic sense. The sooner the United States moved to lower barriers in the West, the sooner it would be positioned to take advantage of new markets and defend itself in the event of a trade bloc war. Bush—and many outside experts—believed that a free trade agreement with Mexico would be one of the more durable accomplishments of his presidency.

Bush saw other benefits, too. Ever since his days as a representative from Houston, he had longed to loosen the Democratic party's grip on Hispanic voters and lure more of them into the Republican fold. He had seen emigrant Cubans become Republican regulars in south Florida, where his son Jeb was a leading party official. He knew that Hispanics' devotion to the Catholic church and widespread opposition to abortion provided the GOP some leverage against traditional Democratic party affiliation. "I ask you to consider immersion in my party," Bush told the 59th annual convention of the League of United Latin American Citizens in July 1988. "It is a house with big

238

doors. If you would once walk in, I believe you will like much of what you find inside.''

A trade agreement with Mexico was a useful lever with these voters. The White House believed small- and medium-size businesses stood to gain the most from exporting to Canada and Mexico—mostly because many large companies already were involved in export trade. The fastest-growing segment of small- and medium-size companies was Hispanic-owned: in 1987 more than four hundred thousand Hispanic-owned firms had generated $25 billion in GDP and created more than half a million jobs. Many of the proprietors retained a strong interest in enhancing the welfare of Mexico and Mexicans. As Bush told the U.S. Hispanic Chamber of Commerce in September 1991, ''When we seal the free trade agreement, Hispanic-owned firms in the United States will enjoy strong natural advantages—bonds of family, language, understanding the culture . . . all of these will gain value as business assets.''

But there were still other benefits for Bush. The prospect of a free trade agreement would anger American labor unions—which feared the exportation of jobs to cheaper labor markets south of the border —and force the Democratic party's leadership into an unpleasant choice between two important members of their beleaguered coalition. ''Just think of the politics down the road,'' said David Demarest, the White House communications chief, in early 1990. ''This puts the Democratic party in a very odd position.'' Indeed, under pressure from labor unions, the Democratic National Committee adopted a resolution in 1991 opposing the quick consideration of the free trade talks. Said one Bush aide, ''James Baker and Bob Mosbacher are both from Texas. Both are more interested in politics than policy. Both want to see George Bush campaigning in Mexican American neighborhoods in Chicago and New York saying he is the father of the free trade agreement. They both see an unbelievable opportunity.''

Meanwhile, in a corollary effort spearheaded by Commerce Department secretary Mosbacher, Washington launched a nationwide push for increased exports to help create jobs, boost competitiveness, and improve America's trade position. In the first such program of its kind, Mosbacher lectured owners of small and medium-sized businesses in 27 cities around the nation on the ways and means of exporting. But the National Export Initiative also had a political angle: one of the unstated benefits of the tour was that it also enabled Mosbacher, Bush's finance chairman in 1988 and his general chairman in

1992, to make contact with hundreds of businessmen and would-be campaign contributors in the months prior to the 1992 election. Politics, explained a senior adviser to the 1992 campaign, "wasn't a design, but it was a benefit."

After a year of giving high technology the back of his hand, Bush suddenly warmed to the idea of quietly helping America's leading edge makers of high-technology goods. During his first year in office, Bush allowed top aides to quash any attempt by subordinates to get behind federal support for emerging technologies. During the Reagan years such assistance was derided as "industrial policy" and by definition inconsistent with free market principles. Pentagon technologist Craig Fields, director of the Defense Advanced Research Projects Agency, was fired after he invested $4 million in a California high-speed-integrated circuit company rather than allow a Japanese firm to invest in the concern. When the administration threatened in 1989 to cut off support for SEMATECH, a consortium of microchip manufacturers backed in part by the U.S. Treasury, Intel president Andrew Grove sent Darman a violin so he could have something, Grove wrote in a note, "to play while the American semiconductor industry burns." One widely repeated story held that the attitude inside the administration toward the chip industry was summed up by a senior official who was said to have remarked, "Microchips, potato chips, what's the difference?" Apocryphal or not, the perceived attitude angered business types.

But by 1991 Bush had fully reversed field. In 1990 Sununu heard from electronics and other high-tech lobbyists that it made no sense to leave a natural constituency out in the cold when both Bush and the industry stood to gain so much from cooperation. By the end of that year, well-funded groups of corporations, academics, and labor groups began to agitate publicly for a more forward-looking technology policy—and Democrats, at least, were beginning to pay attention. In response Bush had not only poured millions of dollars into joint research programs with business in high-speed computers, advanced car batteries, and other fuel cells, but his top aides began quietly to seek advice from business lobbyists about where to target scarce federal research dollars in the areas of manufacturing processes, ceramics, and other advanced materials. When the Department of Energy announced that the nation's 726 national laboratories would be opened to joint research projects with business, Secretary James

Watkins called it "a major change in the way we do business." Bush began to make public appearances in 1991, at which he boasted of his visionary support for these technologies. Bush called an agreement on electric car batteries in late 1991 "an idea whose time has come. . . . Electric vehicles represent the next technology milestone in the auto industry, and we intend to beat our competitors to that milestone." Such funding, said one senior official later, "*is* our competitiveness policy."

To disarm business types put off by his environmental and civil rights initiatives, Bush turned a bureaucratic backwater inside Dan Quayle's office into one of the most powerful bodies in the White House. Despite its name, the Council on Competitiveness had very little to do with competitiveness; instead it was empowered by Bush to review major regulations to insure that the costs to business did not outweigh the benefits to society. As vice president, Bush had spearheaded Ronald Reagan's regulatory relief task force, and once elected, he reacted strongly to any news item suggesting that his administration was reregulating American business. But as president, Bush's "kinder, gentler" initiatives on child care, clean air, and disabled Americans had sparked a new wave of regulations that added billions to the cost of doing business. By late 1990, when the new laws began to take effect, businesses howled. Caught between two colliding commitments, Bush tried to appease both sides, collecting kudos for his new laws while working to ameliorate their effect on a core constituency.

The council operated like a kind of private ombudsman for business inside the White House: Quayle and his aides spoke with industrialists who disliked specific regulations or who had received no satisfaction with the regulatory process, encouraging them to contact the council with their complaints. "The only thing I can say to you," said Quayle, "is now's your chance—come and tell us what regulations and what rules are burdening to the private sector." Businesses and lobbying outfits often faxed revised regulations and proposed rule changes to the council on issues ranging from clean air to landfills. Repeatedly the council's conservative young staff attempted to reinsert the preferential language into the regulatory code. The council's primacy was a godsend for Quayle, who had been seeking for two years to establish himself as something more than just an administration toastmaster; as the council's power grew steadily in 1991, so did Quayle's influence.

241

The hot-wired process angered EPA's William Reilly, as well as some Democrats in Congress, who charged that the environmental president was engaging in an old-fashioned bait-and-switch. "They want only enough substance to justify a television commercial," said Senator Al Gore, the Tennessee Democrat, "then behind the scenes, they gut the law."

After ignoring regulatory policy for eighteen months, Bush pivoted, recasting himself as an enemy of the federal rule maker. He defended the council aggressively in public, lamenting the "hammering" his vice president was taking for his work on behalf of deregulation. There was indeed nothing illegal about granting special access to the regulatory process to big business executives or their lawyers and lobbyists. But Bush and Quayle provided no comparable back door to workers concerned about job safety; neighbors concerned about pollution, noise, and traffic; consumers concerned about collusive pricing and distribution arrangements; or taxpayers concerned about special corporate tax breaks.

Overseas, Bush ran errands for big business, too. For the first time he and members of his cabinet became traveling salesmen for American corporations abroad, quietly peddling American products, buttonholing foreign officials, and even, in some cases, closing the deals. America's rivals had been doing this for years: former British prime minister Margaret Thatcher rarely went anywhere without going "to bat" for British companies seeking contracts overseas. Other national leaders invited CEOs along when they traveled abroad on state visits. If Washington had historically refrained from lending business a hand, it was because business hadn't needed a lot of help. For most of the postwar period, American merchandise was so superior to foreign competitors' that intervention was unnecessary. But as French, German, Japanese, and British businesses began to turn to their governments for help, American manufacturers began to press Washington for similar assistance. The free market Reaganauts nearly always refused.

But by 1989 America couldn't afford the old complacency—and neither could Bush. In a virtual sea change in U.S. policy toward exports and exporters, Bush cabinet officers became commercial officers, touting American goods on every foreign trip. Quayle was perhaps the most involved: pleading, for example, with Bolivian and Polish officials to buy new airliners from McDonnell Douglas rather than Airbus. The State Department required new ambassadors and their aides to take two-week commercial training seminars designed to help the diplomats become part-time commercial attachés. The embassies became a kind of early-warning system for business opportunities. In early 1990, for example, the entire administration swung into action on behalf of American Telephone and Telegraph's effort to win a $2 billion Indonesian telecommunications contract after embassy officials in Djakarta heard that Tokyo had mounted a last-ditch campaign to win the contract on behalf of the NEC Corporation. Quayle, Baker, trade representative Carla Hills, Eagleburger, and Mosbacher intervened by telephone, by letter, or in person. Bush wrote a letter to the Indonesian president. In the end Djakarta split the contract in half.

The commercial casework was a "three-fer": it sent a clear signal to foreign governments that good relations were a two-way street, provided the Bush White House with a way to address America's competitive problems without calling public attention to them, and made it harder for businesses fed up with Washington's sluggish response to the decline to lodge high-level complaints. As long as Washington was bringing home the bacon, big business was less likely to complain about Bush's neglect of the deficit, debt, and interest rates. "It's important because it keeps the business community from saying 'You guys aren't helping us,' " said one Commerce Department official who left government in 1990. Once again Bush showed considerable creativity in his work on behalf of established businesses and their interests but gave short shrift to the economy as a whole—or to Americans who didn't merit such casework.

The program reached its apogee and nadir in January 1992, when the president arrived in Tokyo with 18 CEOs in tow to demand access to Japanese markets for American-made autos, auto parts, computers, paper, plastics, and other manufactured goods. Though Bush had initially envisioned the trip as a conventional diplomatic swing with a small trade sideshow, he converted it into a full-blown trade mission when the economy worsened and Democrats in Congress began to tag him as a do-nothing president in the middle of a lingering recession.

The trip was long overdue: an American president had not toured Japan on a state visit since 1982. While other American officials had pressed Tokyo for market access, no president had made market opening the top priority of a state visit. Simply having plaintive CEOs along would have some impact; after all, Tokyo ran a protectionist economy, closing many of its markets to imports while capturing mar-

243

kets abroad through a slow and patient process that often included government-aided research and development, price discipline, occasional dumping, and, typically, matchless quality. Japan's success was a complicated mixture of first-rate work, pure hustle, and periodic dirty pool, and most Americans knew it. Bush's trip, he said repeatedly, was about "jobs, jobs, jobs."

But Bush refused to accuse the Japanese in public of breaking the minimum rules of free trade; instead he begged Japan for trade concessions for American industries that were synonymous with the nation's decline. Instead of demanding fair play for America's best products and services, Bush seemed to be asking for sympathy for its worst. Rather than trumpeting America's ability to compete, Bush was seen as accepting the nation's inability to compete.

It was a stunning reversal of political symbolism. At every point Bush seemed to point to, rather than deny, the decline: The CEOs he had invited along at government expense were in some cases paid six times as much as their Japanese counterparts. Bush's presence at the grand opening of the first Japanese Toys "R" Us store made a telling statement about Washington's definition of competitive exports. Instead of American business titans mau-mauing Tokyo, the reverse occurred. Bush stood by as Japanese automakers pronounced Detroit's products inferior and explained that they agreed to trade concessions only to avoid embarrassing Bush and his hosts. That one CEO in Bush's party, Robert Stempel of General Motors, had announced just days before departure that the industrial giant would permanently lay off 74,000 American workers did little to help matters. Nor did the fact that many of the guests were contributors to the Republican party's campaign coffers.

Just when Bush seemed to have run out of ways to prostrate himself at the feet of the Japanese, he got sick—succumbing to gastroenteritis at a state dinner, vomiting on Prime Minister Kiichi Miyazawa, and appearing worldwide with his head cradled in the lap of his host. He dismissed the incident later, with a self-deprecating joke: "I just wanted to get some attention."

Into The Tank

Bush and his advisers had long feared a recession, but when it arrived in August of 1990 one could almost hear a sigh of relief from the White House. Though defined as two or more consecutive quarters of negative economic growth, the recession actually began in mid-July 1990 and lasted through the first quarter of 1991. For nearly six months the White House aides avoided the "R" word, hoping a recession would not take root. "The economy at best is in a lull," White House economist Michael Boskin explained in November, "but we do expect that lull to be relatively brief and relatively minor."

Like most of their private sector counterparts, administration economists blamed the recession on the sharp spike in oil prices following the invasion of Kuwait in August and the evaporation of consumer confidence it caused. They calculated that the recession would probably last no more than about ten months—typical for slumps since 1945. Classic countercyclical remedies would at best require several months to legislate in Congress and take two or three times that long to have any effect. Brady, Boskin, and Darman argued additionally that new tax cuts or additional spending would unravel the hard-won 1990 budget deal, increase the deficit, and prove counterproductive once the recovery was rolling. These men all believed market forces and the Federal Reserve Board would right the economy's course.

Unlike his foreign policy team, Bush's three-man economic team was not exactly rigged for action. Each man had his own reason for opposing intervention. As the chief economic spokesman for the government, Nicholas Brady had never been particularly well respected in financial circles, where he was regarded as an incurious and none-too-energetic investment banker of the old school with little understanding of the complexities of the modern financial world. Born on a 4,000-acre New Jersey estate, Brady believed that recessions, although uncomfortable for the lower classes, had a way of "cleansing the economy" of underperformers. He believed debt of any kind was bad, even evil, and was given to say that when he was in the private sector, he never had to incur debt to buy a company. White House aides would joke to themselves in reply, "That's right, he bought the company the old-fashioned way—he inherited it."

Michael Boskin, the president's chief economic adviser, was regarded as an astute analyst and a mainstream conservative on policy.

He was also a formidable bureaucrat. Boskin turned the dormant Council of Economic Advisers into a revitalized force in the Bush White House, burying senior officials and Bush himself with memos on scores of subjects each month. Aides marveled at how easily the mild-mannered Stanford professor got along with the president. An avid tennis player, Boskin became one of Bush's regular partners on the court and off and had plastered the walls of his large Old Executive Office Building suite with dozens of nearly identical pictures of himself with Bush on the tennis court, with Bush in the Oval Office, with Bush at state dinners.

Rounding out the economic team was Darman, the 20-year veteran of both Republican and Democratic administrations who thrived on his own complexity. Arrogant, brash, and by his own estimate brilliant, Darman was easily the most powerful—and frustrated—of the three. Simply because of the lack of money available, the budget director exerted an influence over domestic policy and politics that was nearly comprehensive. Thus, while he longed to solve the big problems facing government, Darman's real value to Bush was his unique ability to unravel and solve the arcane, day-to-day problems of politics and government few people understood or knew about. His moderate views and feel for compromise made him an enemy of the Republican right wing; though he could be charming when it served him, his Machiavellian machinations aroused suspicions among Democrats, too. Darman was so proud of the much maligned 1990 budget deal that invasive action on the recession seemed to him unthinkable.

Guided by these three men—along with Sununu, who shared their caution—Bush decided to do what he did best: avoid mistakes, not make things worse—indeed, to do nothing. The slowdown had arrived with almost perfect timing for Bush; if he could emerge triumphant from the looming Persian Gulf War, survive a relatively brief recession, and see a recovery by mid- to late-1991, reelection in 1992 seemed virtually assured. In the meantime he would rely on the Federal Reserve to bring interest rates down and let the economy heal itself. Doing nothing seemed to be the most prudent course, but it was also for Bush an unusually risky gamble: at the depths of a slowdown, he was betting his reelection on an economic recovery he would not even try to influence.

Few questioned Bush's strategy at the time. Few, in fact, were paying much attention. Instead Americans were facing east, fixated on Bush's massive deployment of combat forces to Saudi Arabia. And they liked what they saw. By January 1991, for the first time since 1986, a clear majority of Americans again began to feel good about the country. Overcoming five years of doubt and pessimism about the nation's direction, Americans reported suddenly that they believed the country was "on the right track." White House pollster Robert Teeter explained at the time, "The war had changed the basic attitude of people in this country. Half the people in this country have never seen us win anything. They've never had a team to root for."

Following the war, the tidal wave of good feeling that washed over the nation seemed certain to benefit the economy—and the president. Bush's personal approval rating skyrocketed into the high eighties, briefly surpassing 90 percent in some postwar polls. One survey by *The New York Times* revealed that fully 100 percent of white southern males between the ages of eighteen and twenty-four who were polled approved of Bush's performance as president. If a relative handful of Americans disapproved of his handling of the Gulf conflict, an equal percentage believed Bush's visage deserved to be chiseled into the side of Mt. Rushmore. Bush predicted that the victory would not only lower oil prices, but restore Americans' confidence and get them spending again. "The fear and uncertainty caused by the Gulf crisis were understandable," Bush said in an address to a joint session of Congress in early March. "But now that the war is over, oil prices are down, interest rates are down, and confidence is rightly coming back, Americans can move forward to lend, spend, and invest in this, the strongest economy on earth."

The postwar euphoria only underscored the White House's determination to rely exclusively on monetary policy to jump-start the recovery. Even that seemed to be working: the Federal Reserve lowered the discount rate three times between December 18, 1990, and April 30, 1991, from 7 percent down to 5.5 percent. Economic activity began to pick up in the second quarter of 1991. Hiring boomed in April and May; citing factory orders and auto sales, Federal Reserve Board chairman Alan Greenspan hinted in June that the recession had ended. Vice Chairman David Mullins asserted on June 18 that "it is difficult to escape the conclusion that the economy probably has bottomed out in the last month or so or is in the process of bottoming."

But what Bush—and indeed economists across the map—failed to calculate was how the recession differed from previous contractions. This was no mere slowdown: while inventories, interest rates, and inflation were in better shape than in the last recession in 1981–82, the economy was much more heavily freighted with debt than ten years before. Unlike the recession of 1981–82, which centered primarily in the agricultural and industrial sectors of the nation's midsection, the 1990–91 recovery was slowed by three simultaneously occurring economic factors: the crash of the savings and loan industry, overlending by banks, and overbuilding by developers on both coasts. The nation found itself with years of excess commercial real estate—in some places five to ten years of excess capacity.

Overseas, the collapse of communism in Eastern Europe increased the demand for capital and slowed growth. The federal government's bailout of the savings and loan industry—and subsequent asset sale—put hundreds of millions of dollars' worth of unwanted real estate on the market as the recession got under way. Meanwhile, a zero-inflation policy at the Federal Reserve depressed the money supply and undercut the administration's reliance on lower interest rates to end the recession. Burdened by debt and self-doubt, consumers curtailed consumption, and business slowed production. Americans hunkered down, reduced their debts, and decided they would wait it out.

The White House also mistook the nation's satisfaction with the Gulf War for the general mood. As quickly as the polls had seemed to turn for Bush in the winter, they turned against him in the spring. The "right track/wrong track" numbers reversed in April, as again the majority of Americans began to wonder about the long-term economic stewardship of the nation. The mood, pollsters noticed, was far darker than it had been ten years before. By the end of 1990, with unemployment at 6.8 percent, consumer confidence was lower than it had been during the 10.8 percent unemployment of the 1982 Reagan recession. The third quarter's anemic 2.4 percent growth was enough to technically end the recession but not enough to inspire new hiring. Moreover, growth of 2.5 to 3 percent didn't *feel* like a recovery. Nor did it look like one: a record 88,000 businesses would fail. Housing starts would plummet to a low not seen since 1945. The average age of cars on the road would rise to eight years, the highest since 1950. Jobs disappeared that were never going to "come back." Such blue-chip companies as Allied-Signal, General Motors, Lotus, McDonnell Douglas, Tenneco, Time Warner, and Xerox announced permanent layoffs. IBM reported its first quarterly loss *ever*. Macy's declared bankruptcy.

Though Bush and his advisers appeared to ignore the recession during the summer of 1991, there was considerable handwringing behind the scenes. Federal Reserve Board chairman Greenspan's four-year term was due to expire in August, and the White House withheld announcing the chairman's reappointment until the last minute. Though Bush and his economic advisers had complained publicly and privately about Greenspan's tight money policies, particularly during the first two years of the administration, the president and the Federal Reserve chairman were close. In June of 1989, after Greenspan had spent a night in the hospital with heat exhaustion, Bush had telephoned to joke, "If you raise interest rates, I'm going to put a crimp in your oxygen line." As 1991 unfolded, and the recovery was slow to take hold, the White House again grew impatient with Greenspan's approach. Bush's aides fretted that Greenspan feared inflation more than recession. Though he had lowered interest rates, he was holding growth in the money supply to a stringent 2.5 percent, fearing an inflation-fueling recovery.

In mid-summer 1991 Bush met several times with Brady, Boskin, and Darman to discuss ways to bring the pinch-fisted Greenspan around. Boskin and Darman believed the economy could sustain growth of at least 2.75 percent without serious risk of inflation, and they wanted Greenspan to endorse that goal before the White House announced his reappointment. It was a standard rule of monetary policy that the rate of growth plus the rate of inflation should equal the rate in the growth of money supply. If inflation were running at 2 to 3 percent, with a sustainable growth rate of 2.75 percent, then the supply of money in the economy needed to grow by 5 to 6 percent. Boskin and Darman wanted Greenspan to agree to money supply growth in this range before Bush sent his name to Capitol Hill for renomination. Bush agreed, and it fell to Treasury secretary Brady as chief economic spokesman to deliver the message to Greenspan.

A few weeks later the same group reassembled to discuss money supply, which had not budged from the 2.5 percent range. "Goddamn it," said Darman. "Look at this money supply. It's right down at 2.5 percent. This guy is going to take us into the tank!"

Brady looked up in surprise and asked, "That's what we wanted, isn't it?"

A bit alarmed, Darman and Boskin then explained the old rule that for real growth of 2.75 percent, money supply growth needed to be closer to 5 or 6 percent, depending on inflation. "Now wait a minute," replied Brady. "What's the difference between the real growth rate and the growth of the money supply?"

The backstage maneuvering was overshadowed by Bush's continued good fortune overseas. The failure of the Soviet coup in August made worries about money supply "cones" and growth targets seem of little significance. Said an administration official during Bush's vacation in Kennebunkport, "The latest economic numbers were only a minor setback. We're still coming out of the recession. The focus is still on the Soviet Union and the Middle East peace conference, and we think it will stay there. We have foreign travel planned to Rome, Australia, Asia, Pearl Harbor. We'll cram some domestic travel into September and October."

In September the ground began to move under Bush's feet. Longtime GOP contributors told Bush that the economy was in worse shape than he thought. At a September 19 campaign fund-raising dinner at the Westin Century Plaza Hotel in Los Angeles, the president was "ambushed" by a handful of Orange County developers complaining about the weak economy. When Bush replied that his advisers told him otherwise, the GOP money men became angry and informed the president that it was no coincidence that his economists were not in private business. Leaving the session, Bush turned to former California governor George Duekmejian and cracked, "Well, that was a lot of fun."

Paul Lego, CEO of Westinghouse, gave Bush an earful during a September state dinner for King Hassan of Morocco. At a White House meeting later that month, IBM's vice president and chief lobbyist, Kenneth Dam, gave Bush advance warning of Big Blue's layoff plans and pressed the case for restoration of the 10 percent investment tax credit. In November, complaining about the lack of affordable health care and riding a wave of anti-Washington populism, Democratic senator Harris Wofford came from more than 40 points behind to defeat Bush's former attorney general, Richard Thornburgh, in the Pennsylvania Senate race. The race was a kind of wake-up call to Bush, who began to straddle the political problem by announcing, "People are hurting," while reminding Americans, "This is a good time to buy a home." (That was true, of course, but as Robert Mosbacher later pointed out, "It's a rotten time to sell one." Bush was still resisting action. As he said in Rome in early November, "You notice when tax cuts were proposed two weeks ago, long-term interest rates shot right through the roof. I have a responsibility to see that I don't make proposals which will set back the economy not just in the long run, but in the short run."

250

Bush's poll numbers dipped to new lows. In a *Time*/CNN poll in late November, only 46 percent of all Americans approved of his handling of his job; 18 percent approved of his handling of the economy. Perhaps more disturbing was a new number about a new question, one pollsters were just beginning to ask. In an early December poll taken by Peter Hart and Robert Teeter for NBC News and *The Wall Street Journal,* 63 percent of those surveyed said the United States was in a "state of decline." Politically, an explanation or, better yet, a scapegoat was needed. Bush accused congressional Democrats of failing to adopt his growth package of tax cuts for the last three years. Dan Quayle went further, calling it "the George Mitchell" recession after the Senate majority leader. "I'm going to keep saying it over and over again because it's true," said Quayle.

A group of private economists Bush met with on November 22 told him he couldn't wait for the Federal Reserve to end the recession; he needed to reassure the country that he had a plan.

In December 1991 Bush changed course. With the first primary in the nation less than two months away, and the recession's symptoms still lingering, Boskin, Darman, and Brady told the House Ways and Means Committee that the administration was contemplating middle-class tax cuts. It would be another six weeks before Bush actually decided whose taxes to cut, but he was coming full circle. If his reelection had just a year before been predicated on raising taxes and lowering the deficit, it now depended on cutting taxes and increasing the red ink. "We can't sit back and hope for the best," he said.

The long-term problem would have to wait. Deficits, all of a sudden, did not matter. Reelection did.

10

"I'LL DO WHAT I HAVE TO"

Bush's shell game had come to an end. His clever plan to do only so much, and nothing more, had run aground. He could no longer mask his fear of change with forced optimism. His custodial approach to leadership no longer satisfied those who feared a long decline. Bush was learning the hard way that he could not drift through the second half of his term without an agenda and still be reelected. Recalled one Bush hand, "Lee Atwater used to say, 'You can make a lot of tactical mistakes, but you can't make a lot of strategic mistakes.'

"We were for the highway bill and for the energy bill and that sort of stuff, but nothing was a real priority. And nothing was ever particularly well honed, because of that overriding view that we don't need anything else when it's all said and done. That idea—that we don't need priorities, we don't need George Bush to be promoting specific initiatives—was a *big* strategic mistake."

More than that, the do-nothing approach raised legitimate questions about why Bush was running for a second term at all. If Bush had so little he wanted to accomplish at home after 1990 except the occasional crime bill—and, in the end, Bush had backed away from that, too—what was his agenda for a second term? White House officials knew that the problem was deeper than mere poll numbers. As one official put it, "If you asked sophisticated voters, if you held a gun to

252

their heads and said, 'Tell me four things George Bush is for, or you die,' they couldn't tell you."

Not standing for anything had served Bush well for nearly three years. But as the recession lingered, as the nation's mood became more pessimistic, and Bush came under attack from both right and left, it became a liability. Bush's predicament was obvious: it's okay to be a status quo president when things are going well. But when times turn bad, a status quo president is the last thing you want to be. Coasting through 1992, said one White House official, "might have been fine if we hadn't had this recession and the president's popularity had remained where it was during and just after the war. But now we're going to the well for something new and there's nothing there. It's empty."

With his usual pragmatism and more than a hint of desperation, Bush threw his old strategy out the window. After insisting for months that his top priority was drugs or education, he announced that his "number one priority is jobs and economic growth." After three years of making no attempt to focus on a single message each day and each week, Bush returned to old-fashioned, Reagan-era communications tactics. After working to defend the status quo, Bush recast himself as an agent of change. In a year-end interview with David Frost, Bush said that he believed he was beginning to convince Americans that he wasn't out of touch. "I think people now know that we are trying hard. I don't think they did at first. I think also you got a whole wealth of other performance out there that the American people are grateful for. But I'm certainly going into this as a dog-eat-dog fight, and I will do what I have to do to be reelected."

"Our Program of Change"

Bush was a bit late unveiling his long awaited plan for revitalizing the economy in January 1992. By the time of his State of the Union message, the recession was technically over. According to the statistics, the recession ended ten months earlier in March 1991. But Americans didn't feel that the country was recovering. Besides, even if the economy was righting itself, Bush was now slumping badly.

In his speech, Bush used the recession as an occasion to reincarnate himself as an agent of reform and conviction. Bush unveiled a package of tax cuts designed to stimulate the sagging economy and revive his sagging political fortunes. He unilaterally lowered the withholding tax on millions of American workers and proposed that Congress enact a $5,000 tax credit for first-time home buyers, a $500 increase in the personal exemption, a boost in first-year depreciation allowances, partial restoration of breaks for "passive losses" for real estate developers, a 15 percent investment tax allowance, and a cut in the capital gains tax. Bush suggested that Congress create a new kind of savings account akin to IRAs and permit Americans to dip into existing IRAs for education, health costs, and home purchases. Bush's hour-long speech sounded comprehensive: he spoke of both the short-term and the long-term economic problems, proposing new ways to encourage investment and serving up his reheated ideas in the areas of education, crime, and energy. Using rhetoric that had served him so well in the Persian Gulf War, he explained, "We are going to lift this nation out of hard times inch by inch and day by day, and those who would stop us had better step aside, because I look at hard times and I make this vow: This will not stand."

There was far less to the speech when Peggy Noonan's oratory was stripped away. The false bravado was for the benefit of voters in economically hard-hit New Hampshire, where in three weeks' time Republicans would choose between Bush and conservative commentator Patrick Buchanan. White House officials made little attempt to deny that the plan was largely a diversion: if Congress passed Bush's plan, that would naturally be fine. But in the far more likely event that Congress ignored or rewrote the plan, Bush would have at least taken a stand, earned some chits with the real estate interests and other important constituencies, and positioned himself to blame Democrats later if the recession lingered. Secretary of Housing and Urban Development Jack Kemp publicly dismissed some of the proposals as "gimmicks." But few other officials had the guts to admit that Bush's real economic recovery plan had little to do with the budget or Congress. As one who did said in late February, "The only thing that is moving us out here now is Alan Greenspan. The only thing that is giving Bush a chance at reelection is the Federal Reserve."

If there was a common thread in the new proposals, it was the way Bush was running against himself. After spending much of 1990 fighting and winning a politically costly deficit reduction deal, Bush backed away from both his hard-won measure and the cause itself. He referred to the deficit only once in his State of the Union Speech. If his budget plans did not add to the deficit, they certainly did not reduce it. Darman told Congress the morning after Bush's speech that the deficit would probably not drop below $200 billion for the remainder of the decade and then added that the carefully constructed walls between defense and domestic programs could be dismantled under certain circumstances. Elsewhere Bush abandoned the long-term economic problems for the short-term political fix. In the name of boosting savings, he proposed creating a new kind of tax-free investment instrument that only subsidized more consumption by permitting savers to withdraw the money to pay for college, health care, and homes. Meanwhile Americans who had taken steps to accrue savings through insurance-paid annuities would have their tax breaks reduced. Bush's plan, said *Business Week,* "is 180 degrees off course. It amounts to inviting consumers to go on a long spending spree while mounting a frontal attack on long-term savings."

Bush announced that he was instituting a 90-day moratorium on all new federal regulations to "stop the ones that will hurt growth and speed up those that will help growth. There are certain things that a president can do, and I am going to do them." Coming from Bush, who had championed the enactment of a new clean air act, a child care measure, a civil rights bill, and a sweeping revision of laws protecting disabled Americans, the executive order halting new regulation was akin to the announcement made by the police inspector in the movie *Casablanca* that he was "shocked" to discover gambling in his favorite casino.

Without a trace of irony, Bush declared in his State of the Union, "I understand that politics is for some a game—and that sometimes the game is to stop all progress and then decry the lack of improvement." Yet by ignoring the recession for nearly two years and then challenging Congress to pass his plan—unaltered—in seven weeks Bush was playing the game like a champ. Just 13 months after Sununu had declared that Congress could go home for the rest of the term and never come back, Bush now blamed Congress for not acting swiftly enough. His ads urged New Hampshire voters to cast their ballots for the president in order to send Congress a message. In a flyer mailed to more than 100,000 Republican households, the Bush–Quayle 1992 campaign boasted that "President Bush is fed up with Congress's inaction."

Bush began to tell voters that "government is too big and spends too much" and boasted about the 246 discretionary programs he had slated for elimination. Together these would save nearly $1 billion in outlays, or almost one-tenth of one percent of the entire federal budget. But he proposed to boost spending on 177 other programs and requested an overall increase in domestic spending of nearly $52 billion, or roughly 6 percent. Elsewhere, increased spending—even on programs he once had tried to eliminate—was okay, particularly if it meant votes. Bush proposed to accelerate outlays for federal loans to farmers for ownership and operation expenses, loans for rural housing, and grants for waste treatment plant construction, though his budgetary gnomes had repeatedly tried to eliminate such programs. Two days after his State of the Union speech, Bush unveiled a national health care reform proposal that would expand government spending by $100 billion over five years. The long-awaited proposal might have been better received had he bothered to explain how he intended to pay for it. Instead, just as he had done with prior budgets, Bush offered Congress a range of ways to underwrite the program—provided, of course, that the lawmakers made the hard choices. "Here are the options," a White House official said. "You make it all add up." Months would pass before Bush actually submitted his plan to Congress.

Bush abandoned his own tax plan almost as quickly as he had cobbled it together. Less than a week after the speech, his aides asked the Ways and Means Committee to adopt a narrower package of seven tax incentives: a first-time credit for home buyers, new allowable withdrawals from existing IRAs, restoration of the passive-loss loophole for real estate investors, an investment tax allowance, changes in the alternative minimum tax, and a cut in the capital gains tax. Missing from this list was the proposal to increase by $500 the personal exemption for families, which just days before he had described as "one thing we can do right away . . . and it's what we can afford." Though it would have had no immediate impact on the recession, the increased exemption was the main initiative in Bush's package that had middle-class appeal. It was also expensive, costing the Treasury $25 billion over five years. Because Bush had no way of paying for the giveaway without breaking the budget agreement, he had included it in the second half of what was a two-part budget proposal. Bush asked Congress to move quickly on the first part to jump-start the economy and then turn its attention to the larger, and more expensive, second part. This is an old Washington gimmick: two-part budgets are almost never fully legislated: their chief advantage is that they allow a president to take credit for proposing popular items that will never be enacted. Sam Skinner, the White House chief of staff, explained that there was no need to rush into law items included in the second part because "the things in our intermediate and long-term agenda aren't going to generate economic activity this year."

But in the middle of a tougher-than-expected primary fight, the bait-and-switch only reinforced old questions about whether Bush stood for anything. Buchanan seized on the streamlined package and charged Bush in advertisements with abandoning both his own plan and American families just as he had abandoned the "no new taxes" pledge taken four years before. Bush responded a day later, calling Buchanan's ads "lies." But as *The Washington Post* editorialized: " 'This will not stand,' the President said in his State of the Union address, and now we know what he meant. It wasn't the recession he was talking about, but his program for combating the recession."

There were other missteps that solidified the view that Bush's new convictions might be as ephemeral as his old convictions. During his hurried visits to New Hampshire, Bush could barely hide his expediency, transmitting his strategy with unusual transparency: "But the message is—I care." He refused to engage Buchanan directly or even mention his name, perhaps heightening the voters' sense that Bush was out of touch. On his primary-eve tour through the state, he invited along actor Arnold Schwarzenegger, perhaps thinking that the Hollywood hunk would distract Granite Staters from their woes. And in an interview with *The Boston Globe* on the Sunday before the vote, Bush denied that he had ever taken the "no new taxes" pledge in 1988.

The cynicism was almost more than the market would bear. New Hampshire voters handed Bush a narrow 52.9 percent of the vote. Buchanan won 37 percent, and a long list of write-ins and also-rans won another 10 percent. Though Bush pronounced himself "delighted" with the results, he had failed to win 47 percent of the votes cast—a bad omen for any incumbent and a potentially crippling one for a sitting commander in chief. Privately, White House officials were chagrined. "The president," said a top campaign official, "was paying the price for a very poor economy and a perception of noninterest, noninvolvement, and nonunderstanding of the recession over a lengthy period of time. The voters felt abandoned and ignored, and the president is paying the price for that."

Buchanan posed enormous problems for Bush. On the one hand, the conservative commentator had never held elective office and was hardly a serious threat to Bush's renomination. Republican party rules kept him off the ballot in South Dakota and New York. Most of the primaries after New Hampshire awarded delegates on a winner-take-all basis. In states where proportional rules applied, Buchanan had few delegates slated. Then there was Rule 16-B: adopted in 1980, the little-known Republican party regulation held that only a candidate who had won a majority of delegates in each of five states was eligible to have his or her name placed in nomination at the convention. Teeter wasn't being overconfident when he told reporters on the morning after the New Hampshire vote, "Buchanan is not going to get the nomination."

Nonetheless, Buchanan threw much of Teeter's preconvention strategy into neutral. Anxious to make certain that the party's right-wing base was on board, Teeter had hoped to spend most of the early months of 1992 shoring up Bush's shaky support among conservatives. As in 1988, Bush believed that the party's right-wing base had to be safely nailed down by midsummer when the appeals to more centrist voters got under way. Buchanan's continued presence in the race made that task harder. He was attacking Bush from the right, likening the president to "warmed-over Jimmy Carter" and linking him to higher taxes, pornographic art, and racial quotas to redress employment imbalances. Perhaps worst of all, the former Nixon speech writer was good at it. "If you belong to the Exeter–Yale GOP club," Buchanan said, "that's not going to bother you greatly because, as we know it, it is not their children who get bused out of South Boston into Roxbury. It is the sons and daughters of Middle America who pay the price of reverse discrimination advanced by the Walker's Point GOP to salve their social consciences at other people's expense."

The stand-for-nothing president was suddenly confronted with a challenger who, like him or not, knew what he stood for. The clash of convictions was devastating: the underdog scared the incumbent president into a full retreat from his record. When Buchanan attacked National Endowment for the Arts chief John Frohnmayer for subsidizing obscene art, Bush promptly fired him. Buchanan's aggressive isolationism rendered Bush mute for weeks on most foreign policy matters and foreclosed action for weeks on aid for the emerging ex-

Soviet republics. Around the Bush campaign, a popular joke held that if Buchanan came out against animal rights, Millie and Ranger would be in deep trouble.

On the eve of the March 3 primaries and caucuses in five states, and after almost two weeks of private, sometimes agonized, consultation with old friends and longtime political advisers, Bush announced that his decision to sign the 1990 tax bill had been the "biggest mistake" of his presidency. "If I had to do that over, I wouldn't do it," he said. But Bush based his renunciation of one of his few domestic achievements not on policy, but politics. "Look at all the flak it's taking," he said. As he told an interviewer a few hours later, "Anytime you get hammered on something, I guess you want to redo it." When polling revealed that many country club Republicans in Georgia still held the 1990 tax reversal against Bush, he repeated his recantation three times in a single 24-hour period to various interviewers. Aides rushed to release the transcripts to television networks on the morning of the vote.

The bald expediency of the tax U-turn set off howls of derision from both parties and even members of his own administration. "It's like Pogo," a campaign official said a week later. "We've met the enemy and it are us." Said another, "What we are doing is simply unbelievable."

Buchanan would fade as an electoral threat, but Bush's game face was on to stay. As he often does when cornered, Bush ratcheted up the rhetoric about how strong his "beliefs" and "principles" were, as if he could erase his deeds with words. "So often," he said, "politicians do the easy things, the popular things, but it is the tough things that tell you something about character and honor and leadership." Bush added, "I've learned that life means nothing without fidelity to principles. . . . the presidency is not a popularity contest. I think you elect a president to say what America needs to hear, even when it's not what people want to hear."

Bush then turned to old-fashioned vote buying to shore up his precarious position. New Hampshire won accelerated small-business loans and federal contracts. Five days before the March 10 primary in Florida, the state received federal aid with a project to restore the Kissimmee River. While in California, Bush announced $800 million in road-building and waste disposal aid for projects along the Mexican border. Campaigning in Oklahoma, he announced steps to aid the beleaguered natural gas industry. And on the eve of the Michigan primary, Bush unveiled plans to offer credits of up to $1,000 to consumers who trade in gas guzzlers for more fuel-efficient automobiles. (The oil and gas industry had opposed the gas guzzler idea, but primaries in the states where they were prominent had already taken place.) None of this presidential pork conflicted with what Bush continued to deride as a "government that is too big and spends too much."

As the seven-week deadline for congressional action on his "growth package" expired, Bush unloaded on Congress with both barrels. In an East Room speech delivered just minutes after the Democrats had enacted an alternative package that raised taxes on the wealthy, Bush vetoed the Democratic measure, called for term limits on members of Congress, and set forth a long list of congressional pork projects he wanted removed from the budget. "It is time for Congress to either lead, to follow, or simply get out of the way," said Bush. "On every one of these challenges, there are two very different ways of looking at the world. One is reformist. The other protects the status quo. And that difference is driven by values. The special interests and the foot draggers do not believe in the kind of change that we seek, change which respects markets more than government dictates, which recognizes fundamental American values and the difference between right and wrong, which rewards excellence and punishes wrongdoing. . . . The failure of Congress to move on our program of change means only one thing: it is time for a new Congress."

Bush began to give speeches about what aides referred to as "the five pillars of reform" in education, health care, legal liability, regulation, and welfare. Just as he had transformed himself four years earlier from the man who saw no need for "radical new directions" into someone who boasted, "We are the change," Bush was suddenly posing as the agent of reform locked in mortal combat with a "do-nothing . . . Democratic-led, status quo Congress." In a press conference on April 10, Bush used the word *reform* seven times in his opening statement. "I'm very optimistic about change, now," he said.

Why hadn't Bush attacked these problems earlier in his term? "Well, that was a good question, and I think that politics drives some things. . . . I think a lot of the issues we're talking about . . . get much more clearly in focus every four years and then you go ahead and try to follow through and do something about them."

260

"Pretty Close to Deadly"

If there was a consolation for Bush in the early primaries, it came, naturally, from the Democrats. The field had never been heroic to start with. By late March voters had winnowed the field from five men to two. Unapologetic liberal Tom Harkin of Iowa and Congressional Medal of Honor winner Bob Kerrey of Nebraska had called it quits when their campaigns emerged fireproof. Former senator Paul Tsongas, a neoliberal Greek-American from Massachusetts, had suspended his campaign after winning New Hampshire but flaming out in the South and Midwest. Left standing were Arkansas governor Bill Clinton, who had survived allegations of marital infidelity and draft dodging, and Jerry Brown, former governor of California, whose unlikely antipolitical message was oddly well tuned to a year marked by voter disgust with politics and politicians. Best of all for Bush, none of the A-team Democrats, such as New York governor Mario Cuomo or House Majority Leader Richard Gephardt, had by April entered the race. Though Bush had problems, so did the Democrats.

For months Teeter had been polishing a two-pronged strategy that made the most of Bush's strengths and provided alibis for his weaknesses. Teeter's first line of attack was the Cold War pivot, a "that was then, this is now" explanation for Bush's obsession with foreign affairs and neglect of domestic matters. According to this construct, the president had been unexpectedly and necessarily distracted by a string of world historical events beyond the nation's borders since taking office in 1989. He had neither intended nor particularly liked this distraction. But his prudent management of these epochal changes helped to create stable new nations, set millions free, and solidified America's position as the world's undisputed leader. As Bush said, "We liberated the entire world from old fears, fears of tense endless confrontation, fears of nuclear holocaust. And now our children grow up freed from the looming specter of nuclear war. And having won the Cold War, we did more, we led nations away from ancient hatreds and toward a table of peace, and we did still more than that. We forged a new world order, an order shaped by the sweat and sacrifice of our families, the sweat and sacrifice of generation upon generation of American men and women. And think of it—two years ago the Berlin Wall came tumbling down, and last year the Soviet Union collapsed. Imperial communist became a four-letter word: d-e-a-d. Dead. And today, because we stood firm, because we did the right things, America stands alone, the undisputed leader of the world.''

The genius of the Cold War pivot was that while most people were still mulling his claim of authorship for the changes overseas, Bush swiveled and confessed that such distractions had forced him to neglect domestic affairs. "The biggest thing that has happened in the world in my life, in our lives, is this: By the grace of God, America won the Cold War. . . . Now we can look homeward even more and move to set right what needs to be set right." A few weeks later Bush honed the message to a finer point: "If we can change the world, we can change America."

Bush opened up a second thematic front that Teeter believed would constitute, after the economy, the biggest issue of the fall campaign. In focus groups and in polling over the previous three years—long before the Los Angeles riots of May 1992—Teeter detected that most voters had become deeply concerned about what they perceived to be a general breakdown of civil order in major cities. While Democrats made much of the fact that most Americans believed the country was on the "wrong track," Teeter believed that embedded within this anxiety was what he called a shared sense of "family values." Said Teeter, "It's that whole idea for which the average guy can give twenty-five examples. It's no one issue. Watching television day after day after day, whether it's thirteen-year-olds shooting each other over tennis shoes or whether it's teenage pregnancies or dropout rates, or AIDS or drugs or whatever it is; one after the other, the average voter says the social fabric of this country is coming apart."

Like the Cold War pivot, the family values pitch worked on several levels for Bush. First, it changed the subject, moved the focus away from the state of the economy, and provided Bush with a way to tap into voters' anxiety about the future at a time when many of those same Americans believed Bush was out of touch with the country. The growing list of problems identified by voters in polls, Teeter argued, only bolstered the case for an experienced commander in chief like Bush. "You've got 75 to 80 percent of the people in the country saying we're on the wrong track," he said. "The question is going to be, if you take all those problems that people think exist, they're going to pick somebody they want to lead the country and make the decisions on how to deal with those problems. That's what the election is going to be about."

"Family values" would enable Bush to remind Americans that he shared their simple sense of good and bad, and their sense of right and wrong, their hopes and, more particularly, their fears—even if they didn't care for his performance or disagreed with him on a host of more specific public policy questions. While rank-and-file Democrats might rightly fault Bush for letting urban and family problems fester in his three years as president, Teeter knew that most of those who worried about the problems of the cities spilling out into the suburbs in the form of drugs, robberies, and rapes also believed that the problems were inherently unfixable. The cities, believed many in the suburbs, could not be saved. Thus, real action wasn't as important as right-mindedness.

Indeed, "family values" was Bush code for his belief that government cannot solve the nation's problems. Bush and his wife, Barbara, seemed to believe that merely by setting an example as good parents, grandparents, and citizens, they could do as much as any government program to encourage strong families. Explained Teeter, "He says it publicly and privately—'Barbara and I have spent hours talking about it, and one of the things we think we can do is live a good example.' And that helps, and talking about it helps, and then you take a series of government programs and try to solve these things problem by problem and try not to do things that make the problems worse. All those things go together." Teeter then added, "I don't think there is any massive visionary federal program that is going to address those programs in total or even just one of them. You can't do it. The country is just too pluralistic." Bush put it another way: "I think people understand when Barbara hugs an AIDS baby or reads to a child. I think they understand what we're saying. And that is family is important."

Teeter was particularly struck by evidence that fear of the cities increased in direct proportion with the distance from urban areas. The dissatisfaction with what was perceived to be taking place inside America's urban cores terrified most suburbanites—who, coincidentally, made up a majority of voters in 1992—and simply horrified voters in exurban or rural areas. In this way, "family values" was also a "kind and gentle" appeal to racial resentments. Bush and Teeter knew that after several decades of racially charged political campaigns—many of which they had helped orchestrate—candidates no longer had to play directly to racial fears. Racial code was now so thoroughly embedded in the political landscape that it took only a little scraping to bring grudges to the surface. And what was more, four years after his campaign manager had vowed to make Willie Horton a "household name," Bush lacked the margin to rely on such openly divisive tactics again.

"Family values" had one other utility to Bush that certified it a big role in the fall campaign. By talking about his family, his children, and his wife of 47 years, Bush was carefully setting himself apart from his likeliest rival. Teeter had watched the Democratic race closely through the autumn of 1991, paying particularly close attention to Bill Clinton. The Arkansas governor worried the Bush camp, not only because he was smart and unusually good on television, but because he alone among his rivals had won reelection repeatedly in a statewide race. Clinton's candid talk about the need to make welfare recipients stay in school and find jobs chilled many Bush advisers, who worried that the Democrat would flank the president from the right on a hot-button issue of great appeal to voters in both parties and independents as well. He had been the chairman of the National Governors Association and led the centrist Democratic Leadership Committee. Bush and his aides put a high premium on politicians who, like Bush, had run repeatedly and traveled widely, believing that exposure to high-pressure politics and politicians toughened a candidate and made him harder to beat.

During 1991 Teeter and Sununu, then chief of staff, had made no attempt to hide their respect for Clinton; in an effort to provoke scrutiny from rivals and reporters, they reminded anyone who asked that Clinton was the challenger they most feared. The sooner he became the front-runner, they figured, the sooner he'd be cut down to size. That turned out to be more prescient than even they had imagined: the revelations about Clinton's alleged affair with Gennifer Flowers and his attempts to avoid military service as a college student had been well aired by early February 1992.

By the time Clinton survived New Hampshire, most top Bush advisers had concluded that Bush would face the Arkansas Democrat in the fall. They could barely contain their glee. The allegations of infidelity seemed enough to sink Clinton alone, but when the charges of draft dodging surfaced, Bush's campaign strategists were simply astonished by their dumb luck. Said one, "I thought the sex stuff was pretty close to deadly to begin with, just because most people don't live that way and even the few of them who do don't necessarily want the president to live that way. The draft stuff, shit, that's just blatant;

264

that's a legitimate issue, more legitimate than the sex stuff. Easier, too."

Just before the New Hampshire primary, a retired officer of the University of Arkansas ROTC had released a December 1969 letter from Clinton explaining his reasons for avoiding the draft, as well as an ROTC spot he once had coveted. In the letter Clinton explained that he had, after months of draft evasion, decided to "accept the draft in spite of my beliefs for one reason: to maintain my political viability." Though Bush told *The Boston Globe* in mid-February that attacks on Clinton's war record had been "quite unfair" and proved that reporters paid "too much attention to outside issues," his aides relished putting the draft issue to use in the fall. The letter safely removed Dan Quayle's alleged draft dodging from discussion in 1992; it set up an obvious comparison between the World War II bomber pilot and liberator of Kuwait versus "the man who ducked the ROTC."

But the letter also cemented what the Bush team expected would be the most potent weapon against Clinton: the man himself. The letter affirmed the Bush team's belief that Clinton could be defined as just another smooth-talking politician who couldn't be trusted. "The letter shows you that he was Slick Willie at age twenty-three," said one official working in opposition research. "He's got two big hickeys on him already, and there's undoubtedly more to come." Added another official in February, "You know, it's interesting. The Democrats' problem for years has been that because such a weird bunch of characters vote in their primaries and go to their conventions, they haven't been able to nominate anybody who could win. Then they finally look at a guy who ideologically wasn't so weird, but he goes out and takes a couple of bullets of another kind. You know, even if they heal up on Super Tuesday, he'll walk with a limp."

Clinton's willful survival through the early primaries and emergence in March as the Democratic front-runner nonetheless impressed the Bush campaign, where he came to be known variously as "the Robocandidate" or "the Energizer Bunny" ("he keeps going, and going and going . . ."). But when exit polls from the Connecticut primary on March 24 revealed that nearly half of the Democratic voters did not believe Clinton had the "honesty or integrity" to be president, Bush's subalterns began to breathe easier. Though Bush was running neck and neck with Clinton in national matchups, his advisers were beginning to see some obvious opportunities. "The good news is that the message is that George Bush has done a good job as president and can do a better job," said one senior adviser. "And besides, he's trustworthy."

". . . He'll Win by Default"

Connecticut's exit polls were no anomaly. Through March and April of 1992, as Clinton overcame California governor Jerry Brown and former Massachusetts Senator Paul Tsongas and seemed poised to clinch the nomination, his approval ratings continued to fall while his "negatives" crept steadily skyward. Clinton was in particular trouble with the independent voters he would most need to defeat Bush. A late April survey of 1,395 voters by the *Los Angeles Times* indicated that 50 percent or more of three key groups of voters in the state—those living in suburbs, those earning between $20,000 and $40,000 a year, and those aged 25 to 44—had unfavorable impressions of the Democratic front-runner. Bush could win the election without California; Clinton could not.

There were several ironies for Bush in the primary results. First, Clinton was carrying the kinds of negatives that Republicans had expected to generate for him after a predictable round of "definitional" smear tactics later in the election year. The Bush effort had hardly begun and Clinton's numbers were, to the professionals at Bush-Quayle headquarters in Washington, already looking pretty good, which was to say, bad. This unexpected development alleviated the need to hurriedly repeat the sorts of steps Bush took in 1988 to transform his race against Michael Dukakis from one about issues to one about "values." Revelations about Clinton's past—and his handling of those reports—had already taken care of that. "With absolutely no help from us," said a Bush-Quayle official in May, "he's looking as bad as Mike Dukakis did in 1988 after we were done with him. Nobody has ever seen a presidential candidate with negatives this high at this stage in the campaign."

Of course, Bush's own negatives were also high. Public dissatisfaction with his handling of his job was at or near an all-time peak in late spring. A Times Mirror study of 1,301 adults in the first week of May reported that 42 percent of the population held an unfavorable opinion

266

of Bush—the same percentage as four years earlier in the same survey. But Bush's political advisers believed these liabilities were "soft" negatives, the kind that can be reduced and reversed through a series of relatively simple counterdefinitional actions. Bush had overcome high "soft" negatives before: he had been perceived as a wimp at the outset of the 1988 campaign and turned that image around with a string of withering attacks on his rivals and CBS News anchorman Dan Rather. It stood to reason that the perception of Bush as a do-little defender of the status quo could be reconstructed with new rhetoric and imagery of vigorous action. Because they turned on credibility, Clinton's negatives would be harder to break down. Displays of strength and resolve are relatively easy to stage, especially for an incumbent. A reputation for honesty and integrity, however, is difficult to establish, especially for a challenger.

But the best news for Bush in Clinton's emergence was the possibility that most of the president's biggest drawbacks might not matter anymore. This was the most stunning piece of luck: after nearly four years in the White House, Bush's lack of convictions and thin cupboard of accomplishments paled in significance compared to the character problems Clinton had to overcome. Bush, who seemed to stand for nothing at home, found himself running against a man who stood for things most folks scorned. For Bush to find himself matched alone against someone whom most of his advisers—as well as many neutral observers—believed fatally flawed was the biggest break of the primary campaign.

Given this advantage, Bush naturally decided to lie low, telling his nervous advisers that the public was sick of politics for the moment and would not be ready to listen to an attempt to redefine himself nationally until late summer. Better instead to do as little as possible while the top Democrat self-destructed and wait until August—and the convention in Houston—for an incandescent redefining moment. As Skinner said in early April, "What you really need is a definitional speech in a forum where it would be widely accepted as a definitional speech, where it kind of recapitulates these things he wants to do. . . . It is very difficult to get people to focus on that kind of speech, with that kind of definition. In order to communicate it, you have to have an electronic audience."

Bush would therefore wait once more, using opportunities as they arose to lay out parts of his agenda to sympathetic special-interest groups—"narrowcasting," his aides called it—but leaving the big what-do-I-stand-for speech until late summer. Just as he had for nearly two years, Bush continued to believe that his reelection largely depended on renewed growth in the economy. By late April, the public was beginning to come around, as consumer confidence began to creep up—an early hint of higher approval ratings for Bush. The economy turned in a 2 percent growth rate in the first quarter of 1992 —its strongest showing since 1989. Other indicators, though not all, were also on the rise. Teeter breathed a sigh of relief in private conversations with top officials in April, explaining that voters' perceptions about the economy in the spring were historically more indicative of the vote in November than were soundings taken in August or September. As Teeter put it in public, "We'll come back as the economy comes back."

Not that Bush was geared to take strong action even if he wanted to. Skinner's reorganization of the White House had become, both inside and outside the administration, something of a laughingstock. Believing that a weak White House staff was all that stood between Bush and better approval ratings, Skinner brought in a handful of new senior aides in early 1992 to fill an array of administration positions, in some cases layering new bodies on top of old. From the Republican National Committee came two-time cabinet member Clayton Yeutter to serve as domestic policy czar; from Energy, Henson Moore became deputy chief of staff; from ABC News came Sherrie Rollins, who took over public liaison and intergovernmental affairs; and Marlin Fitzwater, the press secretary, was upgraded to communications "czar." On paper, Bush's staff looked battle-ready, if a little czar-heavy.

The problem with this heavying up was twofold. First, the new team had little to do. Despite attempts to maintain the appearance of White House control, much of the day-to-day decision making was transferred into the hands of the campaign team. Skinner, a former IBM salesman fond of the verb "interface," dissolved two long-standing policy councils into a single integrated body under Yeutter and circulated a lengthy document, complete with flowcharts, explaining who would sit on what subcouncils. As usual, much more thought was given to how it would work than to what it would do. One veteran policymaker laughed when he saw the directive. "It's perfect," he said. "After three years, we finally get a policy-making body, but we have no policy to make."

Skinner's other mistake was obvious to everyone who had ever worked for George Bush: the problem wasn't Bush's staff but Bush himself. In four years, the president had failed to define a domestic agenda or carry it out in a way that the public found effective or relevant. He had sought the job not to change the country but merely to serve it; he had campaigned not for a mandate but merely to win; he had organized his presidency not to accomplish anything so much as to get reelected; asked to name a single domestic policy goal he wished to accomplish in a second term, Bush couldn't narrow it down. "Single goal? Oh, there are several goals, and I've been spelling them all out. I think education reform certainly would be right up at the top of that. . . . It's awfully hard to single out one area, however. I'd like to be also in the same mode of trying to be sure this economy keeps moving and keeps strong, and you can't do that if we continue to add to the deficit. We're spending too much and the government's too big. But if you had to single out one, education covers so many of these fields, and our goals, to achieve those goals, cover them because I'm talking about—one of them is being ready to learn, and that's Head Start. Another one is a place where you can learn; that means drug-free schools. So when I talk about education, I'm talking about all those things."

In April, Bush took to rewrapping several domestic initiatives he had previously announced and reannouncing them all over again in public. As one conservative inside the White House put it: "Skinner comes in here and thinks our message isn't getting out, and so he concludes that it must be the fault of the messengers. Wrong. Our message isn't getting out because we don't have any message." Senior officials could barely keep a straight face when describing their boss as an "agent of change"; inside the White House, Bush's "five pillars of reform" were the source of endless mirth: "Five pillars—but holding up what?" went one running gag. Said one official, "The Five Pillars of Reform, the Three Happinesses—it's like a bunch of gringo Maoists got loose in the speech writers' office." The pillars themselves always seemed to be shifting: on any given day, Bush would choose from among any of seven or eight areas and designate the first five he could remember as "the pillars of reform." (Eventually, the architectonic metaphor had to be scrapped entirely when it was suggested that Muslims might find the reference offensive.) By April, White House officials were harking back nostalgically to the "good old days" of John Sununu. "Bush is probably going to win," said one campaign official, "but he'll win by default."

The only thing complicating Bush's stand-pat strategy was H. Ross Perot's impending entrance in the race. The Texas billionaire seemed well positioned to attack Bush and his dilatory record on the problems facing the country. Here was a *real* ass-kicking Texan who could challenge Bush's naturalized Lone Star credentials. His exploits as a can-do manager of a company he started with $1,000 trumped Bush's boasts that he once "met a payroll." Perot's startling gift for straight talk—about unwanted babies, he said, "I consider it irresponsible . . . to get drunk, get high, get laid, get pregnant"—pointed up Bush's tortured equivocation. Perot's character seemed beyond question, he took a backseat to no one in the family values department, and he had a well-known record of happily footing the medical bills of scores of children and military veterans. Perot's curious politics made him a prisoner of neither the Right nor the Left and thus a harder target for Bush's smear squadrons. But more than all that, he was a genuine outsider to Washington and politics in a year when any association with the federal city or its oldest profession was electoral poison.

Perot's pitch in a heatedly antipolitical year had more than a touch of genius. He spent much of the spring playing a reluctant Cincinnatus, insisting that he didn't *want* to run but adding that he *would* run if supporters took the time and energy to put him on the ballot in all fifty states—a relatively easy task that other third-party candidates before him had managed. During his lengthy courtship of the public in the interim, Perot stuck closely to the can't-anybody-here-shoot-straight script. In carefully spaced interviews on national television and radio programs, he accused the incumbent president of ignoring the nation's most pressing problems while buying off the public with a mixture of happy talk and deficit-financed bribery. And he said he would forgo the negative campaigning that had marked Bush's election-year performances in the past. "We will give them, the American people, a world-class campaign, and we'll give them something else. It will be a quality campaign. We won't do Willie Horton ads, we won't do this really obscene stuff that has been done in the primaries. Now that's all they can do, and that is a sad commentary on people, particularly those who are in power who don't believe anything, who don't stand for anything, who won't admit the problems of the country. Have you ever heard the president talk about the four-trillion-dollar debt? I haven't. Have you ever heard him come up with even a bad plan to work on it? I haven't. All you hear is Lawrence Welk music, 'Wonnerful, wonnerful, wonnerful,' and here we're spending four hundred billion dollars of your children's money this year to try to get you to vote for us again. If the American people want that, they don't want me."

But Perot's great strength—his political anonymity—offered Bush an opportunity to play the same card with Perot that he had expected to play with Clinton. Perot was not merely an outsider, but a man inexperienced at national politics at a time when the nation needed fundamental problems solved. "Perot's politics are actually pretty close to our own," admitted one top Bush campaign official, "but the difference is we can get it done and he can't." Taken another step, Perot was a loose cannon, a wild man on whom it was unsafe to gamble the lives and fortunes of an entire nation. Once again, Perot provided Bush a chance to turn his go-slow approach and innate caution into an asset in a year when the field seemed littered by much riskier contenders. Like Clinton, Perot was, as one senior campaign official put it, "a risk we cannot afford to take."

". . . If We Don't Scare 'Em . . ."

That Bush could reframe the 1992 race as a choice between risk and safety went a long way toward explaining how politically successful his status quo presidency had been. Bush was no longer against "change" per se; indeed, he was for it as long as it was marginal in scope and did not threaten the interests of his core constituents. But Bush had throughout his term stood firmly opposed to unnecessary risk and experimentation, and now he encouraged Americans to follow his lead as they pondered the next four years.

The strategy also revealed how economic hard times can scramble the electorate's mood. Pollsters and reporters who walked door-to-door in key precincts discovered that the poor economy of 1990 and 1991 had the effect not of radicalizing voters but instead of making them more conservative in many ways. Slow growth, combined with the loss of faith in government, only served to harden many Americans' belief that they can't afford to take risks. This was particularly true at a time when Communism had collapsed and a more competitive world economy was forcing rapid change in the life of the average American. As Rita Freeman, executive director of Social Democrats

271

USA, explained to E. J. Dionne of *The Washington Post,* voters "feel a little safer" with conservatives than liberals because, in part, "they figure the Right is less likely to go off the deep end." Even with incumbent congressmen resigning in record numbers and public discontent with politicians at all-time highs, the appetite for wholesale change was dangerously oversold. Bush campaign officials explained in background sessions with reporters that many voters seek first to protect the gains they have made and minimize the risks they may face in the future. This risk-averse constituency isn't necessarily in love with George Bush, but when it weighs the three evils, Bush doesn't appear to be as hazardous a choice as a Clinton or a Perot. As one senior campaign official put it, "Forty percent of the people will be with us if we just don't scare them. We need to get another 10 percent and one other person. And I don't care if we get another one after that."

By late May, Bush's advisers began to wonder if they needed even 50 percent to win. When Perot's standing in most polls rose to 35 percent or more, ahead of both Bush and Clinton and buoyed mainly by independents and other voters disaffected with the two major parties' nominees, the president's men mulled the notion of winning the White House with a thin plurality of voters. If Perot got in the race— as it appeared he would—and his support held, the victor in the 1992 campaign might attract no more than 34 to 45 percent of the vote. For Bush, this meant that wooing and retaining the Republican party's right wing, the country club set, and the most conservative Democrats could prove more crucial in 1992 than reaching out to moderates in the middle. It also meant that states where polls showed Bush was trailing Clinton in the late spring, such as California and Pennsylvania, were suddenly winnable in a three-man contest.

But Bush would also rely on what he knew to be the voters' deep reservations about the ability of government to do anything constructive in their lives. Twelve years of Republican rhetoric to that effect and a decade of political gridlock on Capital Hill had also helped convince Americans that government *couldn't* make their lives better, it could only make them worse. By that logic, it was hazardous to turn over the levers of power to someone who believed differently; Bush might not make things much better, but he wouldn't make things worse. When Los Angeles erupted in flames following the acquittal of police officers in the Rodney King beating case, Bush blamed the riots on Democratic social welfare programs dating to the 1960s, but failed to push aggressively for conservative alternatives. Reversing field that next day, aides rolled out data showing that spending on the poor for food stamps, housing, and Medicaid had increased on Bush's watch. Clinton began to complain about this circular reasoning, but was at a loss to dispute its obvious appeal. The Arkansas governor frequently lamented in campaign speeches that Bush had helped to convince Americans that "the government would mess up a one-car parade and you can't trust anybody in politics or in government." Clinton would often add, "Ironically, the more this Government fails us, the more disillusioned people get."

Bush lost no time ginning up new threats, foreign and domestic, in a fashion that burnished his credentials as the only trustworthy helmsman in turbulent times. Bush agreed to attend a global environmental summit in Rio de Janeiro in June only after his aides won concessions that they said preserved the United States' sovereign right to pollute as much as it likes. His senior military advisers warned that Germany and Japan might be forced to rearm if American troop deployments in Europe and Asia were curtailed. At home, the Los Angeles riots allowed Bush to dust off the Republican party's old law-and-order theme and remind voters in white suburbs that the enemy lurks within as well as without the nation's borders.

Bush's negative appeal to his risk-averse constituents helped to guarantee that he would launch no campaign for wholesale reform of the government or many of its more expensive habits in a second term. So did his lack of interest in a Republican Congress. He could hardly mount assaults on the entitlements or other subsidies of the middle class as long as he saw little self-interest in electing a Congress that was controlled by his own party. Without a game plan for reducing entitlements, there was little hope of bringing the federal deficit down from record levels. Without a deficit plan, Bush could hardly help stimulate private investment in research and development or re-channel funds from military spending into education, training, and public research and development. Instead, Bush returned in early 1992 to defending Cold War–era levels of military spending—even after the collapse of the Soviet Union—as a make-work jobs program for soldiers and military contractors. Completion of the modest projects Bush had set for himself—legal reform, regulatory reform, completion of the GATT round of trade negotiations—would benefit the country, but they were not by any measure the central challenges facing the nation. Clinton was on target when he predicted that in a second term Bush "would give us a little more of this, a little more of that, he'd tack around this issue and that issue. America will continue to lose ground but as painlessly as possible. He'll give us an anesthetic as we continue to slide."

Bush also lacks a clear rationale for a second term in part because the imperative that drove his first four years—reelection—will be moot on November 4, 1992. Absent the political goal of winning a second term, Bush would have no star to chart by. Already, the Bush White House is in danger of intellectual exhaustion after not four but twelve years in office. Many of the brightest Bush aides have no plans to stay around for a second term because they know the fun that goes with the heavy lifting of legislation is over. "You've got to get out of here soon," said one top official as he pondered his options in the spring of 1992, "because *nothing* is going to happen here in a second term." Even if Bush were inclined to lead vigorously, he would have a very brief window of opportunity in which to take action in a second term: almost immediately after the election, Bush would quickly begin to encounter splits within his party that would make the fault lines of his first term seem inconsequential by comparison. The race for the 1996 GOP presidential nomination is already under way: Dan Quayle, Phil Gramm, Jack Kemp, and Pat Buchanan have all begun to maneuver for position. If others, such as Dick Cheney, James Baker, Bill Bennett, Lamar Alexander, and Pete Wilson, opt to run, the second Bush administration will devolve into a hothouse of bickering factions. The fighting will not be covert, as it has been for the last year; it will be overt, unpleasant, and divisive, and will likely undercut any attempt to address America's problems.

A second Bush term would look a lot like the first: more of the same, only less. Bush would rely on his instincts, reacting to events as necessary. His goals wouldn't be bold, but then his actions wouldn't be imprudent. Like the experienced captain of a cruise ship, Bush would take care to coddle the first-class passengers, and though he would be indifferent to the vessel's course and destination, he could at least be trusted not to sink it.

ACKNOWLEDGMENTS

Many people helped to make this book possible, and while we would understand if none of them crave association with it, we would like to thank them anyway.

Henry Muller, *Time*'s managing editor, and John Stacks, *Time*'s chief of correspondents, encouraged and supported this project from its inception and allowed us to pursue it while we worked as White House correspondents. In addition to helping us with ideas, Washington Bureau Chief Stanley Cloud and Deputy Bureau Chief Margaret Carlson looked the other way as we missed meetings and skipped presidential trips to complete our work on this book.

Sam Allis, Joelle Attinger, Larry Barrett, Todd Brewster, Val Castronovo, Garry Clifford, Tom Curry, Hays Gorey, Dirck Halstead, Jerry Hannifin, Stan Kayne, Jef McAllister, Christopher Ogden, Walter Shapiro, Hugh Sidey, Strobe Talbott, Dick Thompson, Nancy Traver, Bruce van Voorst, Diana Walker, and our other colleagues at *Time* provided unstinting help, information, and encouragement. Lissa August, Don Collins, Jr., Joan Connelly, Brian Doyle, Cassie Furguson, Anne Moffett, Neang Seng, and Judith Stoler made our lives easier in innumerable ways. Don Collins, Sr., allowed us to ruin his weekends and made our computers do what we wanted. Wendy King was tireless as our researcher.

Wyatt Andrews, Michael Barone, Rita Beamish, Paul Bedard, Tom

De Frank, Ann Devroy, Maureen Dowd, Gene Gibbons, Larry Haas, David Hoffman, Brit Hume, David Lauter, John Mashek, Ann McDaniel, Tim McNulty, Michel McQueen, Jim Miklaszewski, Andy Rosenthal, Maureen Santini, Jerry Seib, Ken Walsh, Ellen Warren, John Yang, and other members of the White House press corps provided some of the best evidence in this book through their reporting and also allowed us to pick their brains for ideas, impressions, and anecdotes.

Ron Brownstein, Margaret Carlson, Michael Elliot, Christopher Ogden, Suneel Ratan, Strobe Talbott, and John Yang graciously agreed to read parts of the manuscript and did their best to save us from embarrassment. Whatever errors of fact or analysis remain are ours, not theirs.

Robert Barnett, our lawyer and agent, grasped the essence of this book long before the Gulf War, when almost everybody else thought Bush was boring.

At Simon & Schuster, Eric Steel shepherded us patiently through the maze that is modern publishing. Marcia Peterson was our unflappable copyeditor and grammarian.

Alice Mayhew, our editor, showed great skill, patience, and commitment in turning our manuscript into a book. We now know why she is considered the best in her business.

NOTES

"The Honor of It All"

16 *"Well, I don't know whether . . ."* Bush discussed his mandate at some length at a press conference in Houston on the morning after the election, November 9, 1988.

17 *Only half of America's families . . .* *Time*-CNN poll, October 23–25, 1989. Cited in *The American Enterprise*, November-December 1991, page 93.

18 *"There are already indications . . ."* Arthur Schlesinger, "Cycling Through U.S. History," *U.S. News and World Report*, December 1, 1986.

19 *"the most important problem . . ."* "The Public's Agenda," *Time*, March 30, 1987, page 37.

19 *One poll, taken in February 1987* CBS/*New York Times* poll, cited in *The American Enterprise*, January-February 1992, page 101.

21 *"Domestic policy can get us thrown . . ."* Bush quoted JFK in a speech to the American Legion, September 7, 1988.

21 *"Building a better America . . ."* Bush used "the water's edge" line in many speeches in 1988.

22 *"We don't need radical . . ."* Bush's announcement speech, Houston, October 12, 1987.

23 *"If by 'born again' one is . . ."* Doug Wead, *Man of Integrity* (Eugene, Ore.: Harvest House Publishers, 1988).

24 *Like their hero . . .* For a fuller treatment of Reagan Democrats, see Peter Brown, *Minority Party: Why Democrats Face Defeat in 1992 and Beyond* (Washington, D.C.: Regnery Gateway, 1991); and Thomas Byrne Edsall and Mary D. Edsall, *Chain Reaction: The Impact of Race, Rights and Taxes on American Politics* (New York: W. W. Norton, 1991).

25 *"didn't see any differences . . ."* David R. Runkel, editor, *Campaign for President: The Managers Look at '88* (Dover, Mass.: Aueburn House Publishing, 1989), page 112.

25 *"We need five or six issues . . ."* Ibid.

25 *When Atwater learned . . .* Atwater was not without some quarter. As governor, Dukakis had also signed a measure removing an old "unnatural acts" statute from the Massachusetts law books. When Pinkerton's gang of researchers stumbled on this, Roger Ailes suggested that Dukakis might be tagged as "pro-bestiality." Atwater balked at this suggestion, but a gang of college Republicans took up the case informally. Dressed up in bunny suits and other colorful animal costumes, they picketed a number of Dukakis events that fall, carrying signs that read "Hands off my body" and the like. At the time no one—neither Dukakis's aides, the traveling reporters, nor many in the crowds—could make sense of their presence.

26 *"you'd like to have sitting . . ."* Maureen Dowd, "For Bush on the Campaign Trail, the Style Is First Sour, Then Sweet," *The New York Times,* October 12, 1988.

26 *Bush entered the 1988 race . . .* David Rogers, "Bad News for Bush: High Negative Poll Ratings are Nothing to Shrug Off, Recent History Shows," *The Wall Street Journal,* June 23, 1988.

29 *"Although I've said . . ."* Gerald Boyd, "Bush Is Cautious about Deploying a Missile Defense Shield, *The New York Times,* August 26, 1988.

30 *"who wear fifty-dollar jeans . . ."* Bush spoke of sneakers and self-help in a speech to the Sacramento Comstock Club, October 4, 1988.

30 *"Let me give you some advice . . ."* Dowd, "Two Bushes on the Stump: One Tough, the Other Gentle," *The New York Times,* October 5, 1988.

32 *"I'd tell you 'Hee-Haw' . . ."* *Newsweek,* November 7, 1988, page 53.

33 *In some states* Evidence of Bush's deep thrust into Democratic turf can be found in CBS Exit Poll data.

33 *Compared with Reagan's showing . . .* Bush's defections are discussed in E. J. Dionne, *Why Americans Hate Politics* (New York: Simon & Schuster, 1991), page 316.

34 *"I can't keep everybody happy . . ."* Bush pondered his fate at voters' hands in an interview with black publishers, February 21, 1990.

35 *"The American people . . ."* Bush, in his morning-after press conference, November 9, 1989.

35 *"That's history . . ."* Bush discussed the campaign as ancient history in an interview with ABC News's Barbara Walters on "20/20," January 20, 1989.

"I Really Love My Job"

37 *"friendly takeover"* Sununu spoke of continuity with David Shribman, "Sununu, Bush Likely Choice as Chief of Staff, Would Bring Fervent Conservative Views to Post," *The Wall Street Journal,* November 17, 1988. Bush talked about continuity aboard *Air Force One,* March 17, 1989.

37 *In the three months* David Hoffman, "Differing Styles before the Media," *The Washington Post,* January 14, 1989.

39 *"too hyper"* Bush explained that he could never just take a day off in an interview with Brian Lamb of C-SPAN, taped December 20, 1991.

39 *the president was in such a hurry . . .* "Bush Outruns Football," *The Washington Post,* June 17, 1991.

39 *"got home from the inauguration . . ."* Marlin Fitzwater, in a speech to the National Press Club, March 3, 1989.

40 *"I'm here to answer your questions"* Terry Eastland, "Press Secretary Bush," *The American Spectator,* February 1990.

40 *"My view on Dan Quayle . . ."* Bush spoke of Quayle's confinement —and his own—in an interview with local television affiliates, June 15, 1991.

41 *"There's been a certain liberation"* Bush interview in *Time,* January 30, 1989.

41 *"Read my lips! Read my lips!"* *Newsweek,* November 18, 1988.

41 *"I learned an awful lot . . ."* Bush visited a day care center in Catonsville, Maryland, January 21, 1991.

42 *"a good deal of golf . . ."* John Yang, "Bush Relaxes with His Contradictions," *The Washington Post,* August 16, 1991.

42 *"What's the matter, Dakota . . ."* Naturally, Griffith and Johnson were later invited to the state dinner for the queen of Denmark. In 1992, Bush named the couple "official delegates" to the Winter Olympics.

43 *"It's easy to underestimate . . ."* Paul Gigot, "A Good Man in a Tiger Shoot," *The Wall Street Journal,* August 8, 1990, page A12.

44 *"If somebody comes out with . . ."* "In New Hampshire, They're Off!" *Time,* February 25, 1980.

44 *"Politics is no profession . . ."* Bush (with Vic Gold), *Looking Forward,* page 14.

44 *"I don't like to tell you . . ."* Bush, in C-Span interview, December 20, 1991.

44 *"This," she said, "is why wives . . ."* Ellen Warren, the *Miami Herald,* June 18, 1991. Also, see *Lamb* interview.

45 *In an eyes-only memo . . .* Tom DeFrank, "Playing the Media Game," *Newsweek,* April 17, 1989.

45 *"There are not enough stories . . ."* Fitzwater, in press club speech.

46 *In his first twenty-two months . . .* S. Robert Lichter and Richard Noyes, "Bad Press by Default," *American Enterprise,* January 1991.

47 *"I think sometimes that I . . ."* Bush talked of the bully pulpit and its powers in an interview with black publishers and editors, February 21, 1990.

49 *"I still get the same emotional . . ."* *Lamb* interview.

51 *"I want to answer your concerns . . ."* Richard Berke, "On Right, Signs of Discontent with Bush, *The New York Times,* May 1, 1990.

54 *When pop singer Gloria Estefan . . .* *The New York Times,* January 18, 1990.

55 *"Hasn't any one told you . . ."* Tom DeFrank, "Bush's Social Diplomacy," *Newsweek,* April 16, 1990.

"Watch What We Say . . ."

56 *Only seven weeks . . .* Bush denied "drift" and "malaise" in a press conference at the White House, March 7, 1989.

58 *No new president . . .* On the divided government that Bush faced, see, for example, Terry Diebel, *Foreign Policy,* Fall 1991, page 18; and David Broder, *The Washington Post,* September 29, 1991.

59 *These would include new legislation . . .* The disabled were a voting constituency quietly and ardently pursued by the GOP and estimated to number between 5 million and 34 million, depending on the definition of disability.

60 *"That's not just an agenda . . ."* Sununu's speech to the board of directors of the Freedom Forum, in Washington, December 11, 1991.

61 *"I don't think about my schedule . . ."* Bush's interview with *U.S. News and World Report,* published June 26, 1989.

62 *"In this kind . . ."* Gerald Seib and Michel McQueen, *The Wall Street Journal,* April 12, 1989.

62 *"government is too big . . ."* Bush's speech to supporters in Washington, February 12, 1992, among many others.

62 *he would not propose . . . spending cuts . . .* Bush's reluctance to publicly suggest spending cuts was on display, for example, during the closed-door budget summit of summer and fall 1990. Bush had Darman propose means testing of middle-class entitlements and other spending cuts that went beyond what House minority whip Newt Gingrich—who talks tough on this issue until it gets specific—and his fellow Republican congressmen were willing to support. Not much had changed since Murray Weidenbaum served as chairman of the President's Council of Economic Advisers under Ronald Reagan. Once, when Reagan assured Weidenbaum that budget deficits are useful because they dissuade liberals from voting for new spending programs, Weidenbaum replied, "Unfortunately, the deficit did not have that effect on conservatives." Weidenbaum recounted this exchange during the Reagan Oral History series at the University of Virginia's Miller Center, published in the center's spring 1990 report.

63 *"entitlements" or "mandatory programs" . . .* Bush spoke vaguely of "entitlements," for example, at the February 15, 1992, "Ask George Bush" session in Goffstown, New Hampshire.

63 *he attacked both his Republican . . .* Bush implied that Buchanan would make Social Security "voluntary," in a press conference in Knoxville, Tennessee, February 19, 1992. Bush also told the *Boston Globe,* in an interview published February 15, 1992, that "some are saying we're going to freeze, an across-the-board freeze. . . . And I don't think you can do that with Social Security recipients or Medicare or Medicaid recipients."

63 *the biggest taxer, the biggest spender . . .* For Bush's record on taxes, and a comparison to other presidents, see the February 21, 1991, study by William C. Dunkelberg and John Skorburg of the libertarian Cato Institute in Washington. This study found that largely as a result of Bush's 1990 budget agreement with Congress, total federal tax receipts as a proportion of national income (19.6 percent of GNP) will be higher during Bush's 1989–1992 term than during any previous four-year period in U.S. history, including the years of World War II.

For Bush's record on spending, see the February 27, 1991, study by Scott Hodge and the February 10, 1992, study by Daniel Mitchell, both of the conservative Heritage Foundation in Washington. Mitchell found that the federal government under Bush spent 25.2 percent of GNP—the largest share since 1946, and a sharp increase from the 22.1 percent share that Bush inherited in 1989. Stephen Moore of the Cato Institute reported in a February 4, 1991, study that Bush allowed domestic spending to grow at a faster rate than any president since Franklin Roosevelt: five times the pace under President Reagan and three times the pace under President Carter. Though Bush blamed Congress for this state of affairs, John Yang of *The Washington Post* demonstrated in a front-page article published on April 11, 1992, that Bush proposed budgets larger than those that Congress eventually passed.

Bush's regulatory record includes his promotion of amendments to the Clean Air Act, which cost the economy an extra $25–$30 billion a year, according to unpublished internal estimates of the White House Office of Management and Budget. Bush also championed the Americans with Disabilities Act, which required businesses and other institutions to adapt facilities for the handicapped at an annual cost of about $2 billion. *The Wall Street Journal* reported on January 22, 1992, page A14, that the number of regulations proposed and listed in the *Federal Register* rose 21 percent during Bush's first three years as president. It also reported that the number of proposed regulations in Bush's first two years exceeded by 17 percent the number in the previous decade. For further details on Bush's regulatory record, see op-ed articles in the *Washington Times* by Doug Bandow, January 24, 1992, and Thomas Hopkins, January 27, 1992.

63 *Bush, to his credit . . .* Figures on funding of AIDS research from the Budget of the U.S. Government, Fiscal Year 1993; also described by Bush in February 15, 1992, speech in Derry, New Hampshire.

64 *"it's better to let it sit there . . ."* Bush's August 10, 1991, exchange with reporters on the Cape Arundel Golf Course in Kennebunkport, Maine, among other occasions.

64 *Before 1980, he was pro-choice . . .* As a congressman from Houston in 1969, Bush chaired the House Republican Task Force on Earth Resources and Population Planning, whose final report in July 1970 proposed revising abortion laws "to eradicate the increasing number of unlicensed and unqualified practitioners who jeopardize the health and safety" of women seeking abortions. Bush confirmed that view when he told *Rolling Stone* magazine, in an interview published in March 1980, that he supported the Supreme Court's abortion rights decision in *Roe* v. *Wade.* A few months later when he was named Reagan's running mate, Bush reversed himself.

64 *mixed support for civil rights . . .* As a Yale senior in 1948, Bush led the campus fund-raising drive for the United Negro College Fund, a charity he supports to this day. Running for the U.S. Senate from Texas in 1964, however, Bush built his campaign around his opposition to the Civil Rights Act. As a first-term congressman in 1968, Bush revealed divided sentiments over the fair housing law. He voted to kill it on a procedural vote, then supported the law moments later on the vote for final passage.

65 *"an American Tory . . ."* "IGS Panel Assesses Bush Administration," *Public Affairs Report,* September 1990, page 5.

65 *"hate government"* Bush's speech launching his campaign for president on October 12, 1987, and often thereafter.

65 *". . . Civil Rights Act can never . . . succeed"* Bush 1964 campaign brochure is quoted in Jefferson Morley, "Bush and the Blacks," in *The New York Review of Books,* January 16, 1992, page 21.

65 *Bush exhibits . . .* On "bias for action" and its opposite, see Thomas J. Peters and Robert H. Waterman, Jr., *In Search of Excellence* (New York: Harper & Row 1982), particularly section beginning on page 119.

66 *"at the margins of practicable change"* Budget of the U.S. Government, Fiscal Year 1992, Part I, page 7.

66 *America cannot be strong . . .* Linking the domestic economy with military strength, Bush told the Knoxville Chamber of Commerce, on February 19, 1992, "If America is to succeed economically at home, we must lead abroad."

67 *During his first campaign . . .* On Bush's 1964 Senate race in Texas, see John R. Knaggs, *Two-Party Texas* (Austin, Tex.: Eakin Press, 1980), page 53.

67 *"We should repackage . . ."* The *National Review* symposium was entitled "The Republican Party and the Conservative Movement" and was published December 1, 1964.

67 *"I generally favor . . ."* Bush's University of Texas speech is quoted in Morley, page 21.

67 *"You know, John . . ."* Bush's regrets on "far right positions" recounted in "Campaign: The Choice," a *Frontline* documentary broadcast by PBS on November 24, 1988.

67 *"the smooth evasion . . ."* Franklin Roosevelt excerpt from his speech to the Democratic State Convention in Syracuse, New York, September 29, 1936.

68 *"Elect George Bush . . ."* Bush's "Watch the Action" ad appeared October 29, 1966, in *Forward Times,* a black weekly newspaper in Houston.

68 *"George Bush has proved himself . . ."* Democratic party chairman quoted in Morley, page 23.

68 *"God, I wish . . ."* Bush reversals on "voodoo economics" described by David Hoffman in *The Washington Post,* August 18, 1988, page 1A.

68 *"had gotten this enormous . . ."* Bill Green's conversation with Bush was reported by David Hoffman in *The Washington Post,* August 18, 1988, page A1.

69 *"there are times when the future . . ."* Bush delivered his inaugural address on January 20, 1989. Foreshadowing his one-page-at-a-time theme, Bush had told a "Jack Kemp Tribute Dinner to the Reagan Revolution and Supply-Side Economics" in Washington on December 1, 1988, that the Republican party's "success will be maintained . . . issue by issue, case by case."

70 *"They asked me the other day . . ."* Bush spoke of his first hundred days to employees of the Republican National Committee, January 18, 1989.

70 *"do no harm"* In defending his opposition to extension of benefits to the long-term unemployed in late 1991, and others of his economic policies in early 1992, Bush frequently used the phrase "do no harm." In a November 15, 1991, speech to the Fortune 500 Conference in Charleston, South Carolina, for example, Bush said, "Let me tell you what we won't do. The first rule of economic policy puts me in mind to the Hippocratic Oath: Do no harm." Also, in a March 9, 1992, speech to the National League of Cities Conference in Washington, speaking of urban problems such as broken families and welfare dependence, Bush said, "The government's first duty is like that of the physician: Do no harm." It's little wonder that Hippocrates should be a Bush favorite. The Father of Medicine's first aphorism, often abbreviated as "Life is short and the Art long . . ." continues in a Bushian fashion: ". . . opportunity fleeting, experiment dangerous, and judgment difficult." Bush also shares Hippocrates' emphasis on the role of exercise in good health. And the Bush who since late 1980 has opposed a woman's right to choose abortion would find support in the Hippocratic Oath, which unconditionally opposes abortion and euthanasia.

71 *"We could do worse."* Bush often said "we could do worse" in private sessions with his staff. He used similar formulations in public: for example, in an October 29, 1990, speech in Oklahoma City, he was unenthusiastic about the budget deal he had just struck with Congress but announced with a shrug that it "could have been worse."

71 *"I don't want to do anything . . ."* One of Bush's first postelection protestations that "I don't want to do anything dumb" came in an interview with *People* magazine, published in the edition dated December 26, 1988. He also repeated this injunction during an exchange with reporters about U.S.-Soviet relations, in the Oval Office on September 27, 1989.

71 *"I don't want to make . . ."* Bush wanted to avoid the "wrong mistake" in a news conference on April 24, 1990.

71 *"I don't want to"* Bush kept repeating "I don't want to . . ." at his press conference at Walker's Point, early on the morning of August 19, 1991.

71 *"What I don't want to do . . ."* Bush voiced his concern not to "make the situation worse," for example, in an October 28, 1991, teleconference with the American Gas Association.

71 *"My goal is to see . . ."* Bush emphasized "not doing anything dumb" to the economy during a press conference in Rome on November 8,

1991. He talked of the recession making business "leaner" and "more competitive" during a teleconference on November 15, 1991, with a Fortune 500 conference meeting in Charleston, South Carolina.

72 *"Just as important . . ."* Bush praised his economic package for "what it doesn't do" in a February 24, 1992, campaign speech in Bethesda, Maryland.

72 *U.S. military demobilize . . . "* Bush spoke against rapid demobilization, for example, at his November 9, 1991, news conference in The Hague.

72 *"the Smoot-Hawley days"* Bush's remarks during a trip to New Hampshire, January 15, 1992.

72 *appease Saddam Hussein . . .* Bush warned in a televised address from the Oval Office on August 8, 1990, against appeasing Saddam as Hitler was appeased. He vowed in a speech to the Reserve Officers Association in Washington on January 23, 1991, that "this will not be another Vietnam. Never again will our armed forces be sent out to do a job with one hand tied behind their back." Bush drew lessons from Carter's failed Desert One mission in several discussions with aides.

72 *"I wasn't a really good . . ."* Bush talked baseball with *USA Today,* October 5, 1989.

73 *"90 percent . . ."* Jim Baker has a prized photo of Bush falling down while trying to bowl, inscribed by Bush with the legend, "Ninety percent of life is just showing up."

75 *"A crisis suddenly emerges . . ."* William Schneider passage was published in *The Atlantic,* January 1990, page 40.

75 *"I have told you that I don't live . . ."* Bush discussed polls in his November 6, 1991, press conference at the White House.

77 *"we didn't get any new programs . . ."* Bush statement on preventing "new programs jammed down our throat" came in an interview with the authors on December 20, 1990.

78 *"of thinking that if we don't have a two-thirds . . ."* Fazio statement from *Congressional Quarterly,* July 27, 1991.

78 *In August 1991 . . .* Bush threatened to veto the transportation bill during an August 18, 1991, teleconference with the National Governors Association. His objections were addressed in Congress, and he signed the bill on October 28, 1991.

79 *"If he intends to veto . . ."* Kerry statement from *Congressional Quarterly,* July 27, 1991.

79 *"If you're looking for George Bush's . . ."* Gephardt's statement came in a press conference on November 22, 1991, at the Capitol.

80 *"prevent others from dealing . . ."* Mitchell statement reported by Adam Clymer of *The New York Times,* September 29, 1991, page A22.

82 *"There's not another single piece . . ."* Sununu's speech was to the second annual Conservative Leadership Conference in Washington, November 9, 1990.

". . . Not What We Do"

83 *"It is balanced . . ."* Bush called the budget agreement "balanced . . . fair, etc." in remarks announcing the agreement at the White House on September 30, 1990. He said it made him "gag" four weeks later, at a press conference in Honolulu on October 27, 1990. Then, three days later, he returned to his initial line, telling members of the Republican National Committee in Washington, "This budget agreement is unprecedented, it is long overdue, and in my view, it is essential."

84 *The president delivered . . .* Bush mixed attacks on Democrats and praise of them in his speeches in Oklahoma City on October 29, 1990, in Washington on October 30, and in Alexandria, Virginia, on October 31.

84 *Bush would enter . . .* Comparison of Republican electoral standing after the 1980 and 1990 elections is from David Broder, *The Washington Post,* September 29, 1991.

85 *"great frustration of having to deal with a Democratic . . ."* Bush's speech to the Utah Republican party in Salt Lake City.

85 *"Congress likes Bush . . ."* George Will wrote on Bush and Congress in his column published in *The Washington Post,* January 30, 1992, page A23.

85 *"The heart of Mugwumpery . . ."* Bartley's column appeared in *The Wall Street Journal* on February 13, 1992, on the editorial page.

86 *"Sold $7.7 billion in U.S. savings bonds . . ."* Internal memorandum from Ede Holiday, White House cabinet secretary, entitled "Administration 1990 Domestic Accomplishments," dated November 15, 1990.

87 *"the travel I have done on drugs . . ."* Bush complained of not getting credit for his domestic travel in an interview with the authors, December 20, 1990.

88 *"watch what we do . . ."* Mitchell's statement is quoted in "Watergate: Chronology of a Crisis," volume I, page 41, published by *Congressional Quarterly,* 1973.

89 *"how strongly I feel"* Bush's speech at Pease Air Force Base in New Hampshire, on January 15, 1992.

89 *"I think we were positioned . . ."* Bush talked of his "positioning" on human rights in China during a Washington news conference on December 1989.

89 *"I want to be positioned . . ."* Bush spoke of his "positioning" against David Duke in comments to reporters on *Air Force One* en route to Rome, Italy, on November 6, 1991.

89 *"What I want to do is look like . . ."* Bush's comments to reporters on March 5, 1992, quoted in *Time,* March 16, 1992, page 22.

90 *"putting me beyond . . ."* Bush refused to "be dragged beyond that" during a press conference in Denver, Colorado, on October 16, 1988.

90 *Then he reversed field* Bush vetoed the $6.4 billion unemployment extension bill on October 11, 1991, but signed a bill that cost $1 billion less on November 15. At the time, the so-called trust fund of regressive unemployment taxes collected from employers, and indirectly from workers, amounted to $8 billion. But as in the case of Social Security, the "trust fund" was no more than a bookkeeping device to persuade employers and workers that they were paying taxes into a fund that they might one day need to rely upon. In fact, those revenues were spent as soon as they were collected, on the general operations of government.

90 *"The idea that our young people . . ."* Bush is quoted defending his vote for the open housing law in Morley, page 24.

90 *"Nothing I've experienced . . ."* Bush talked of his exultation at debating his constituents in his autobiography, *Looking Forward* (New York: Bantam, 1988), pages 91–92.

91 *"It ought to be the happiness . . ."* Edmund Burke's statement on the role of a member of parliament was made in Bristol, England, in the 1770s. It is quoted by Nicholas King in *George Bush: A Biography* (New York: Dodd, Mead, 1980), page 59.

91 *"Nobody thinks you can be popular . . ."* Bush talked of the "ingredients" of the budget deal he didn't want during a press conference on 1990.

91 *"Have you ever changed . . ."* Bush's comment on "intellectual honesty" was quoted by David Hoffman in *The Washington Post,* August 18, 1988, page A1.

91 *Bush has defended his abortion switch* Bush talked of the number of abortions at a question-and-answer session with New Hampshire voters on February 16, 1992. See also Burt Solomon, *National Journal,* July 13, 1991.

91 *Thus, after reading* Den of Thieves Bush decried "greed" in an interview with *People* magazine, conducted December 16, 1991.

92 *"It is easy to lose track . . ."* Wildavsky's observation is from an op-ed column in *The Wall Street Journal,* November 25, 1991, page A12, adapted from his book *The Beleaguered Presidency* (New Brunswick, N.J.: Transaction Books, 1991), pages 301–346.

92 *"Why don't Republicans . . ."* Interview with authors on January 24, 1990.

92 *"Again and again . . ."* Gephardt's statement came in a Washington press conference on November 22, 1991.

93 *Bush took to blaming . . .* Bush blamed voters for not electing more Republicans in remarks to reporters at Pease Air Force Base on January 15, 1992, and made similar remarks in campaign speeches elsewhere.

93 *Sununu expanded the blame . . .* Sununu told Doug Harbrecht and Lee Walczak of *Business Week:* "Where [Bush] gets conflicting inputs is when he goes and talks to businessmen in different parts of the country. He talks to large business versus small business, and the advice quite often has self-conflicting components." This interview was conducted on November 20, 1991, and was published in the edition dated December 2, page 31.

94 *"put me down . . ."* Bush expressed "enthusiastic" support for the Gingrich tax-cut plan during a photo opportunity in the Oval Office on November 26, 1991.

94 *But Bush has yet* Penner and Collender were quoted by Alan Murray and John Yang, *The Wall Street Journal,* February 13, 1989, page A16.

95 *Federal spending under Bush rose . . .* Spending and tax figures are from Budget of the U.S. Government, Fiscal Year 1983, and from Heritage and Cato studies cited earlier.

95 *Total regulatory spending . . .* Bush's regulatory record is from *The Wall Street Journal,* January 22, 1992, page A14, and from articles by Bandow and Hopkins, previously cited.

95 *"we have more will than wallet . . ."* Bush denounced the measurement of concern in dollars in comments to reporters in the Oval Office on January 25, 1989.

95 *"a 120 percent increase . . ."* Bush bragged about his increase in spending in a Washington speech announcing his candidacy for reelection and a speech to the New Hampshire legislature, both on February 12, 1992; in "Ask George Bush" sessions in New Hampshire on February 15 and 16, 1992; and in a speech to the Knoxville Chamber of Commerce, February 19, 1992.

96 *"a poll-driven mélange"* Robert J. Shapiro, "Money for Nothing," *The New Democrat,* March 1992, page 19.

96 *"has been closing off American markets . . ."* James Bovard, *The Fair Trade Fraud* (New York: St. Martin's, 1991).

96 *"Jimmy Carter grain embargoes"* Bush spoke against grain embargoes in speeches to the National Association of Farm Broadcasters in Kansas City, Missouri, on November 12, 1987, and to the Agricultural Communicators Congress in Washington on July 11, 1988, among others.

96 *"There's not going to be net loss . . ."* Bush spoke of "redefinition" of wetlands during a January 16, 1991, press conference in Kennebunkport, Maine.

96 *"step back from the trees"* Bush's speech in Waterbury, Connecticut, on October 24, 1988.

96 *"the money to plant . . ."* Bush delivered his State of the Union address on January 31, 1990.

96 *. . . federal subsidies to the timber industry . . .* For details on Bush's tree program, and federal subsidies for the timber industry, see Karen Franklin, "Timber," *The New Republic,* January 2, 1989; Daniel Gross, "Seed Money," *The New Republic,* May 21, 1990, page 11; "Why Let Chainsaws Pare the Old Forests at All?" *The New York Times,* November 3, 1991, page E3.

97 *"I don't think the federal . . ."* Bush said he didn't think the government should "subsidize much of anything" in an interview with the authors, January 24, 1990.

97 *The biggest example . . .* Bush promised to create 30 million new jobs in his acceptance speech at the Republican convention in New Orleans on August 18, 1988, and repeated it often thereafter.

98 *"I am committed . . ."* Bush delivered his State of the Union address on January 31, 1990.

98 *He left it to Congress to find the money . . .* Bush promised a health care plan in remarks to reporters at the White House on November 6, 1991, and outlined that plan in his 1990 State of the Union address on January 31.

98 *Bush would not even bother . . .* The White House reported in a fact sheet on January 21, 1992, that about 622,000 children were enrolled in Head Start, or about 60 percent of those eligible. Sarah M. Greene, executive director of the National Head Start Association in Alexandria, Virginia, says her organization estimates that there are actually two million low-income children ages three and four eligible for Head Start, and that only 28 percent of them are being served.

99 *"I'm for unions; I'm for nonunions."* Bush on unions, quoted in Schneider, *The Atlantic,* January 1990, previously cited.

99 *"brave without being brutal . . ."* Bush's Pearl Harbor speech was delivered on December 7, 1991.

100 *"retain the support of your gun-owning constituency"* Feulner's memo to the president was dated March 15, 1989.

102 *The department found that the Helms* Details of Justice Department action against the Helms campaign were reported in the *Washington Times,* February 27, 1992, page A3.

103 *"Harry Truman . . ."* Bush invoked Harry Truman against the "special interests" in his speech at the Cowboy Hall of Fame in Oklahoma City, October 29, 1990.

103 *"kick ass"* The day after his 1984 campaign debate with Geraldine Ferraro, Bush uncharacteristically blustered (perhaps because he thought it might endear him to the hard hats among whom he was campaigning) that he had "kicked a little ass last night."

104 *"The elimination of drugs . . ."* Bush talked about the "demand side" of the fight against drug abuse to a small pool of reporters in the Oval Office on January 25, 1989.

104 *During his televised drug speech . . .* Bush's speech was delivered September 5, 1989.

104 *But . . . federal drug agents . . .* The story on the DEA sting operation that provided Bush with his bag of crack cocaine was broken by Michael Isikoff in *The Washington Post,* September 22, 1989, page 1A.

105 *"Has somebody got . . ."* Bush talked about "this drug guy" in remarks to reporters during a visit to Morse Tree Farm in Wells, Maine, on September 22, 1989.

105 *"number one" in the world* Bush's televised address to the nation about his national education strategy on April 18, 1991, and in other venues.

105 *(New York City public schools . . .)* Statistical comparisons of the public and Catholic schools of New York are from Sam Allis, "Can Catholic Schools Do It Better?" *Time,* May 27, 1991, page 48. These comparisons hold up for Washington, Chicago, and most other big-city school systems in the country.

106 *"our education goals"* Bush listed "education goals" as his top priority in an interview with the authors on December 20, 1990, and again during a press conference at the White House on April 10, 1991.

106 *"I got my wife . . ."* Bush was pressed on education at an "Ask George Bush" event in Nashua, New Hampshire, on February 16, 1992.

106 *"All the kids in America . . ."* Bush embraced the goal of college for all who are qualified, during a speech in Waterbury, Connecticut, on October 24, 1988.

107 *"the prevailing clichés . . ."* Windt was quoted by Burt Solomon in "Being a Good Manager Isn't Enough," *National Journal,* May 27, 1989, page 1316.

108 *"We're up against . . ."* Bush's press conference on the Israeli loan guarantees was held September 12, 1991, at the White House.

Color Me Bad

110 *"She's doing what I want done . . ."* Doug Brew, "Bush Does It His Way," *Time,* February 22, 1982.

110 *"Bush really needs a bad cop . . ."* Bush often spoke of catching javelins, but this reference came in a speech at a Belcamp, Maryland, housing project, February 14, 1992.

111 *"He compartmentalizes people . . ."* Eric Alterman, "Playing Hardball," *The New York Times,* April 4, 1989.

115 *"When you go through a tough time . . ."* Charlie Black spoke at length about the Bush–Sununu relationship on the "McNeil-Lehrer News-Hour," April 3, 1990.

116 *"Let that come from others"* Bush spoke of surrogates in his television interview with David Frost, January 3, 1992.

116 *"I think the Jewish community . . ."* Paul Bedard, "Skinner Takes off the Gloves," *The Washington Times,* February 25, 1992.

117 *intervened to weaken . . .* The back and forth over wetlands was explained in some detail in *BNA Washington Insider,* February 22, 1990, a newsletter published by the Bureau of National Affairs.

119 *"would ultimately fail"* Fred Barnes, "Sununu and Improved," *The New Republic,* May 29, 1989.

119 *"George Bush is a much . . ."* Laurence Barrett, "1000 Points of Spite," *Time,* October 15, 1990.

119 *leave "the pit bulldogs at the White House"* *The Washington Post,* October 9, 1990.

119 *"I have had thirty years . . ."* The Byrd lecture was recounted by Martin Walker, "The Pit Bull Who's Giving the White House a Bad Name," *Los Angeles Times,* April 21, 1991.

120 *"No, no, I probably am as bad . . ."* Sununu made these comments on "Meet the Press," October 14, 1990.

120 *"Where did I get . . ."* Michael Kelly first reported the Sununu–Lesher encounter in *Playboy,* November 1990.

125 *"My job is a seven-day-a-week . . ."* Sununu made this remark on "This Week with David Brinkley," June 16, 1991.

125 *"Obviously, I am very pleased . . ."* The White House attached a statement by Sununu, from which this quote comes, to the Gray report, which was released May 9, 1991. Eleven months later the independent Office of Government Ethics overturned some of Gray's findings and ordered Sununu to pay the government an additional $4,284.80.

125 *"You shouldn't be judged . . ."* Bush clarified his views on ethics in comments he made at the White House on June 19, 1991.

125 *Then Newsweek reported . . .* The stamp auction incident was first reported in *Newsweek*'s Periscope section entitled "On the Road Again," June 24, 1991.

126 *"That would be a concession . . ."* Sununu's dislike of the Metroliner was first reported in Evans and Novak as it appeared in *The Washington Post,* June 24, 1991.

126 *"Sununu is Sununu . . ."* Sununu's remarkable resilience was first noted by Ann Devroy in *The Washington Post,* September 9, 1991.

126 *"You're a liar!"* The Sununu–Devroy encounter was reported by Howard Kurtz in *The Washington Post,* November 11, 1991.

126 *"the president ad-libbed"* Sununu explained the genesis of the credit card ad lib in comments on "One on One with John McLaughlin," November 22, 1991.

Something to Believe In

132 *although Saddam was a "thug"* The exchange between Baker and Shevardnadze is from an interview with Baker on "The Gulf Crisis: The Road to War," a television series broadcast on the Discovery Channel, January 17 through February 5, 1992.

132 *An officer of the Defense Intelligence Agency . . .* Dispatch of the DIA officer was reported by Bob Woodward, *The Commanders* (New York: Simon & Schuster, 1991), page 222.

133 *After two terms . . .* *Newsweek* raised the "wimp" issue most prominently, if not first, in its cover on Bush entitled "The Wimp Factor," dated October 19, 1987. George Will called Bush a lapdog to Reagan in a column published in *Newsweek,* January 30, 1986.

133 *"For seven and a half years . . ."* Bush delivered his acceptance speech on August 18, 1988, in New Orleans.

134 *He encountered public resistance . . .* For a concise analysis of Bush's leadership of public opinion during the Gulf crisis, see Charles Krauthammer's column in *The Washington Post,* March 1, 1991.

135 *"I would simply say . . ."* Bush called the status quo "unacceptable" in remarks to reporters as he departed the White House for Camp David on August 3, 1990.

135 *"what is at stake in the Gulf"* Bush talked of preserving the United States position in an interview with the authors on December 20, 1990.

136 *"Who knows?"* Bush is quoted comparing himself with Teddy Roosevelt in a report by R. W. Apple in *The New York Times,* March 29, 1989, page A16.

136 *one of the strongest foreign policy . . .* During the Ford administration, Bush was CIA director, Baker was assistant secretary of commerce,

Cheney was White House chief of staff, and Scowcroft was national security adviser. Gates worked under Scowcroft in the Ford White House, then moved back to the CIA for all of the Reagan administration. Powell served as national security adviser to Reagan, where he had ample contact with Bush, Baker (who served as chief of staff and treasury secretary to Reagan), Gates, and Cheney (who by then was a ranking Republican member of the House). Little wonder that Quayle and Sununu never became full members of this club. They were invited to some meetings for the sake of appearance and to build their prestige in Washington, but they were also excluded from numerous sessions in which the toughest and most sensitive decisions had to be made.

138 *Bush treated the general . . .* Though Scowcroft was younger than Bush by one year, he had always looked and acted older. Scowcroft had far more experience and influence than Bush when both worked in the Nixon and Ford administrations.

139 *"There are certain decisions . . ."* Bush talked of Panama as a "warm-up" in an unpublished portion of an interview with Hugh Sidey on December 20, 1991.

139 *"strongly condemns the Iraqi military . . ."* The initial White House statement on the invasion of Kuwait was issued by the press office on the evening of August 1, 1990.

140 *when he heard that Iraq . . .* Bush's interview with the authors was on December 20, 1990, and excerpts were published in *Time*'s "Men of the Year" edition, dated January 7, 1991.

141 *Bush conferred with White House counsel . . .* Bush's conference with Gray was reported by Woodward, page 231.

141 *In "Doctor Slaughter". . .* Paul Theroux's novella "Doctor Slaughter" was published in *Half-Moon Street* (Boston: Houghton Mifflin, 1984).

142 *"It was apparent when you looked . . ."* Cheney talked about the map of the Middle East on the Discovery Channel special, previously cited.

143 *At a joint press conference . . .* The Bush–Thatcher press conference in Aspen was held on August 2, 1990.

147 *"I don't know"* Bush claimed not to know how long the Gulf deployment would last in his press conference on August 8, 1990.

147 *dropped a scheduled two-week . . .* Cheney's vacation plans were reported by Woodward, page 282.

148 *"I just am not one . . ."* Bush portrayed himself as a man of action, not words, in his August 11, 1990, press conference in Kennebunkport.

150 *"I don't see it right now"* Bush in his press conference on August 14, 1990, in Kennebunkport.

153 *It listed sixty-two calls . . .* Bush's telephone log for the first month of the Gulf crisis read as follows:

AUGUST

2 Mubarak, King Hussein, Fahd, President Salih of Yemen.

3 President Ozal of Turkey, Thatcher, Mitterrand, Thatcher again, Chancellor Kohl of Germany, Prime Minister Kaifu of Japan.

4 Fahd, Ozal, al-Sabah, Prime Minister Mulroney of Canada.

5 Kaifu, Mulroney, Ozal, King Hussein.
6 Mulroney, Prime Minister Andreotti of Italy.
7 Mitterrand, Mubarak, Salih, Mulroney, King Hassan of Morocco.
8 Emir Zaid of the United Arab Emirates, Sultan Qaboos of Bahrain, Ozal.
9 Thatcher, Prime Minister Hawke of Australia, Mulroney.
10 Mulroney, Mubarak.
11 Qaboos, Emir [Sheikh Khalifa bin Hamad al-Thani] of Qatar, Fahd.
12 President Assad of Syria.
13 President Perez of Venezuela, King Hussein, Kaifu, King Hussein again.
14 Ozal.
16 Ozal, Mubarak.
20 Ozal, Thatcher, Mitterrand.
22 Kohl, Prime Minister Mitsotakis of Greece.
23 Kohl, Hawke.
24 King Hussein.
30 Kohl, Mubarak, al-Sabah, Zaid, Ozala.
31 Fahd, Thatcher, Mitterrand.
SEPTEMBER
1 Mubarak, Salih.

154 *"In the aftermath of Iraq's . . ."* Bush addressed the UN General Assembly on October 1, 1990.

154 *"There's no change . . ."* Moments after delivering his UN speech, Bush disclaimed the opening to Iraq in remarks to reporters.

157 *"The President listened . . ."* Powell said that Bush "never hesitated" in an interview for the Discovery Channel special on the war.

157 *announcement of the new deployment . . .* Bush in a press conference on October 8, 1990.

157 *"The first thing we must do . . ."* Gorbachev's remarks were recounted by Baker and his top adviser on the Soviet Union and the Middle East, Dennis Ross, in interviews on the Discovery Channel special.

158 *"It would put us, frankly, in the position . . ."* Baker recalled comparing congressmen to the prime minister of Ethiopia in an interview for the Discovery Channel special.

158 *"convinced that the United States did not have the guts . . ."* Ambassador al-Sabah was interviewed on the Discovery Channel special.

159 *"Anything you did to generate support . . ."* Baker's remarks on coalition politics were from his interview on the Discovery Channel special.

159 *he would have gone to war . . .* Sidey asked Bush, in an interview conducted on December 20, 1991, what he would have done if he had failed to win the approval of Congress to use force against Iraq. "I'd have done it anyway," Bush said. "I had the power anyway."

160 *"Oh, I was just remembering . . ."* Bush recalled his plane being shot down in a chat with *Time* magazine photographer Dirck Halstead, on September 2, 1989.

160 *"War is never cheap or easy"* Bush warned against "euphoria" in his news conference on January 17, 1991.

161 *"We will make the fire . . ."* Saddam's speech was delivered on

April 1, 1990, and was monitored by the U.S. Foreign Broadcast Information Service.

161 *Saddam sought and received assurances . . .* Bandar's intermediation on behalf of Saddam was reported by Woodward, pages 199–204.

163 *Bush quickly had convened nine . . .* The officials who met with Bush on the evening of February 21, 1991, were Scowcroft, Baker, Cheney, Powell, Gates, Sununu, Quayle, Haass, and Fitzwater.

164 *"The Iraqis were just trying . . ."* Powell spoke of the Iraqis "stiffing" the world in his interview for the Discovery Channel special.

167 *"Yes, we want the suffering of . . ."* Bush spoke at Maxwell Air Force Base in Alabama on April 20, 1991.

168 *"the United States and the coalition"* Bush talked about "the internal affairs of Iraq" in remarks to reporters while playing golf in Islamorada, Florida, on April 3, 1991.

169 *"Do you miss the action . . ."* Bush quoted the Houseman character in a speech at Hickam Air Force Base on October 28, 1990. The reference comes from the movie *Three Days of the Condor*.

The Enemy Is Instability

172 *"an influential Stalinist group . . ."* Yakovlev's warning was reported by Francis X. Cline in *The New York Times,* August 17, 1992, page A1.

174 *"sympathetic to fostering . . ."* Bush spoke about the price of fostering American values abroad in a speech to the Mid-America Committee in Chicago on August 2, 1988.

174 *"the enemy is uncertainty . . ."* Bush emphasized that "the enemy is instability" in a joint press conference with German Chancellor Helmut Kohl at Camp David on February 25, 1990, and often thereafter.

175 *"but my mind goes back . . ."* Bush talked about "how it was a year ago" in a press conference in Kennebunkport on August 19, 1991, at 7:45 A.M.

176 *"Well, my gut instinct . . ."* Bush talked about Yanayev's "commitment to reform" in his August 19, 1991, press conference in Kennebunkport.

179 *"the Cold War is not over"* Bush spoke to the World Affairs Council of Northern California in San Francisco on June 29, 1988.

179 *"The ferment" in the Soviet Union . . .* Bush in his August 2, 1988, speech in Chicago.

179 *"Perhaps what is happening . . ."* Bush delivered his acceptance speech on August 18, 1988, in New Orleans.

179 *"Despite the drama . . ."* Bush emphasized the conventional imbalance in his August 2, 1988, speech in Chicago.

179 *"Soviet military spending . . ."* Bush spoke in Denver to employees of Martin Marietta on October 17, 1988.

179 *"This is no time to reduce . . ."* Bush said "This is not time to reduce our leverage" in a speech at the University of Michigan on October 19, 1988.

180 *"held himself back"* Bush's cautious approach to Malik is recounted in Nicholas King, *George Bush: A Biography,* pages 75–76.

180 *"I'm afraid you're very busy"* Bush recounts his shyness toward Mao in his autobiography, *Looking Forward,* pages 144–47.

180 *"intimidation" and "trepidation"* Bush confided to friends early in 1989 his "trepidation" at the prospect of dealing with Gorbachev, and he hinted publicly at this nervousness once he felt it was past, after the Malta summit, when he spoke at a dinner honoring House Minority Leader Robert Michel, on December 5, 1989.

181 *"a drugstore cowboy"* Fitzwater called Gorbachev a "drugstore cowboy" during the regular White House press briefing on May 16, 1989.

181 *"welcomed the changes"* Bush emphasized his "desire to see reform succeed" in a speech at City Hall in Hamtramck, Michigan, on April 17, 1989.

181 *"beyond containment"* Bush's commencement address at Texas A&M on May 12, 1989.

181 *"There cannot be a common European . . ."* Bush evoked a "Europe whole and free" in a speech in Mainz, West Germany, on May 31, 1989.

182 *"I deeply deplore . . ."* Bush emphasized his hope for "stability" in China in a written statement issued in Kennebunkport on the morning after the Tiananmen massacre, on July 3, 1989.

182 *"this is not the time . . ."* Bush held his first post-massacre press conference on June 5, 1989, in Washington.

183 *"all high-level exchanges"* The suspension of exchanges was announced in a written statement by Fitzwater on June 20, 1989.

183 *"negative forces"* Excerpts of the Scowcroft toast were reported out of Beijing by the Associated Press on December 9, 1989.

183 *"the first time we've had high-level . . ."* Baker lied about the first secret high-level visit to China during an interview on ABC-TV's "This Week with David Brinkley," on December 10, 1989.

184 *"Busher Who Rides Bicycle"* Bush reported his Chinese nickname in *Looking Forward,* page 137.

184 *"We love your adherence . . ."* Bush praised Marcos's "democratic principles" in a luncheon toast in Manila on June 30, 1981.

185 *"I feel under no rush"* Bush's comment, given in a press conference in Helena, Montana, on September 17, 1989.

185 *"this was the agreed timetable . . ."* Bush announced that he had agreed to a summit with Gorbachev, for the following spring or summer, in remarks to reporters at Cape Arundel Golf Course in Kennebunkport on September 23, 1989.

185 *He insisted . . .* Bush promised no "agenda" or "proposals" in remarks to reporters in the Oval Office on November 28, 1989.

186 *"I'd like to get . . ."* Bush held his NATO press conference on December 4, 1989.

186 *whether he thought it was time* Bush denied plans for a four-power agreement on Germany in a White House news conference on February 12, 1990.

187 *storming back to the press cabin . . .* Bush flew to Cartagena on February 15, 1989.

188 *Bush warily refused to comment . . .* Fitzwater explained the cautious approach toward East German emigration and the snub to Yeltsin in his briefing on September 13, 1989.

188 *"For all its risks . . ."* Eagleburger spoke at Georgetown on September 13, 1989.

189 *In a flat, constricted voice . . .* Bush spoke to reporters in the Oval Office the day the Berlin Wall fell, November 9, 1989.

190 *"We keep acting prudently . . ."* Bush emphasized his desire "not to exacerbate tensions" in an interview with Texas reporters in Dallas on November 10, 1989.

191 *"We are living in fascinating times . . ."* In reference to Eastern Europe, Bush, in a speech to the National Association of Realtors in Dallas on November 10, 1989. In remarks at a reception for Republican Claudine Schneider in Warwick, Rhode Island, on November 20, 1989, Bush turned to members of a high school band in attendance and said, "I'll say to you kids, you live in exciting times . . . when you have a shot, a clear shot, at living in a much more peaceful world."

192 *"Intellectuals in Eastern Europe . . ."* Kaminsky was quoted in the *Christian Science Monitor* on February 16, 1990, page 1.

192 *"Everything has been done late . . ."* Goble was quoted in *U.S. News,* dated January 31, 1992, page 20.

194 *"this is no time for appeasement . . ."* Kozyrev sent his appeal by telephone and fax on August 19, 1991, through the office of Allen Weinstein, president of the Center for Democracy in Washington.

194 *Bush's first press conference . . .* Bush spoke of how the coup plotters "underestimated" the Soviet desire for freedom in a news conference in Kennebunkport on August 21, 1991.

200 *Suspicious that Gorbachev . . .* Der Spiegel in October 1991 published excerpts from videotaped interrogations of Kryuchkov, Pavlov, and Yazov, in which all three said they long had harbored suspicions that Gorbachev was making secret deals with the United States. "Gorbachev often traveled abroad in recent years and frequently we had no idea what important issues he discussed there," Yazov said. "We naturally were not ready to increase our political, economic, and even military dependence on the United States." The *Spiegel* article was summarized in *The New York Times* on October 7, 1991, page A7.

200 *"When you think of the need . . ."* Hess was quoted by John Harwood in *The Wall Street Journal,* August 22, 1991, page A14.

Class President

203 *"the darling"* Yarborough's attacks are recounted by Bush in *Looking Forward* (New York: Bantam, 1988), page 48; and in Bearak, page 35.

203 *a "liberal"* Bush's counterpunch against Yarborough was reported by the *Dallas Morning News,* November 1, 1964.

203 *"the new Civil Rights Act . . ."* Bush was quoted defending "the other 86 percent" in the *Dallas Morning News,* October 28, 1964.

203 *"develop attractive job opportunities . . ."* Bush was quoted promising to help those "displaced from jobs" in the *Austin American,* September 25, 1964.

203 *"unconstitutional"* Bush was quoted on Wallace's electoral success in the *Dallas Morning News,* April 9, 1964.

204 *Jim Leonard, a native Texan . . .* Leonard's coaching of Bush is described by Jefferson Morley in "Bush and the Blacks," *The New York Review of Books,* January 16, 1992, page 20.

204 *"I generally favor the goals . . ."* The University of Texas speech was quoted by Morley, page 21.

205 *"I won't let them take it away from you"* Bush's acceptance speech in New Orleans, August 18, 1988, and often thereafter.

206 *"Presidency by Ralph Lauren"* Stanley's article appeared in *The New Republic,* December 12, 1988, page 18.

207 *"wants to give those who make $200,000 . . ."* Dukakis delivered his Labor Day speech on September 5, 1988.

207 *"By the 1920s most Americans . . ."* Dukakis delivered his Idalou speech on September 30, 1988.

207 *"there's an elite . . ."* Bush lambasted the "elite inside the elite" during a press conference in Denver on October 16, 1988.

208 *calling Dukakis "conceited"* Quayle was quoted in Stanley, page 20.

210 *"Any definition . . ."* Bush gave his "definition of a successful life," for example, in a speech to the American Society of Association Executives on March 6, 1990.

210 *"an America whole and good"* Bush's speech to community service leaders at the White House on June 12, 1991.

212 *"Certainly he cares about the poor . . ."* Walker and Ellis were quoted by Bearak in the *Los Angeles Times,* November 22, 1987, part I, page 34.

213 *"The marketplace . . ."* Bush declared that the market "cannot solve all of our problems" in the June 12, 1991, speech previously cited.

213 *"He just can't do it . . ."* Bush bemoaned the plight of a North Carolina businessman in his speech to the Small Business Legislative Council in Washington on February 5, 1992.

214 *calls himself "lucky"* Bush's acceptance speech in New Orleans, August 18, 1988.

214 *"painting oil rigs"* *Looking Forward* portrays Bush as a self-made man on pages 46–73.

214 *"You'll have a chance to run it . . ."* Bush's brother Prescott was quoted by Bearak.

214 *"George would've been just another carpetbagger . . ."* Williamson was quoted by Bearak.

215 *"I got a phone call from his father . . ."* Mills was quoted in *Congressional Quarterly,* January 14, 1989, page 56.

215 *"We never felt that Dad had any kind of wealth . . ."* Jonathan Bush was quoted by Bearak.

216 *"I wanted to induce my friends . . ."* Gramm was quoted by Eric Pianin in *The Washington Post,* February 3, 1992, page A4.

216 *Cutting this tax . . .* Projected benefits of a cut in the capital gains tax are from studies by the Congressional Joint Committee on Taxation.

216 *"reward investment . . ."* Bush spoke to the Philadelphia Chamber of Commerce on January 30, 1992.

216 *"If the horse is fed amply with oats . . ."* Galbraith's reformulation is from his book *The Culture of Contentment* (Boston: Houghton Mifflin, 1992), page 27.

217 *"There are also revenue aspects of it . . ."* Bush defended his capital gains proposal in a White House press conference on July 28, 1989.

218 *Neither Reagan nor Bush cut taxes . . .* The tax statistics are from the Budget of the United States: Fiscal Years 1992 and 1993, and from reports by the Joint Committee on Taxation, Social Security Administration, Heritage Foundation, Cato Institute, Citizens for Tax Justice, and Progressive Policy Institute.

219 *"I think it's a disguise . . ."* Bush discussed the Moynihan plan in a White House press conference on January 24, 1990.

219 *"I don't want to see the benefits . . ."* Bush directly accused Moynihan of endangering Social Security benefits in an interview with the authors on January 24, 1990.

220 *"the legislature and the executive . . ."* Bush spoke of "the system" in a speech to the American Society for Public Administration in Washington, October 24, 1991.

221 *The leading Democratic plan . . .* Analysis of the Bentsen tax plan is from the Joint Committee on Taxation and Citizens for Tax Justice.

222 *the Reagan-era debt* Costs of interest on the national debt and thrift bailout are from Budgets of the United States: Fiscal Years 1989 through 1993, and studies by the Heritage Foundation and Cato Institute.

223 *"generational accounts"* Budget of the United States: Fiscal Year 1993.

223 *$43 billion annual subsidy . . .* For details on tax subsidies, see the Congressional Budget Office's report entitled "Reducing the Deficit: Spending and Revenue Options, February 1992."

224 *the Bush household budgets* Other examples and details of Bush's perks were reported by Fred Barnes in *The New Republic,* September 2, 1991, page 22; and Dana Priest in *The Washington Post,* March 31, 1992, page A7.

225 *"You travel anywhere . . ."* Bush talked about worldwide respect for the U.S. in a speech to political supporters in Oklahoma City, March 6, 1992.

225 *their own hourly wages* . . . Comparative wages were reported by the U.S. Bureau of Labor Statistics, "International Comparisons of Hourly Compensation Costs for Production Workers in Manufacturing, 1975–90," November 1991.

225 *In 1990 he paid 30 percent* Comparisons of Bush's taxes with those of an average family are from *Money* magazine, January 1992.

226 *One New Hampshire businessman* . . . The businessman wooed by the Bush campaign in 1980, and ignored in 1992, was interviewed by Kenneth Cooper in *The Washington Post*, January 21, 1992, page A1.

226 *"I understand there's two . . ."* Bush referred to his fund-raisers in remarks to reporters on *Air Force One* en route to San Francisco, February 25, 1992.

226 *"George Bush is in trouble . . ."* Nofziger was interviewed in *Newsweek*, March 2, 1992.

227 *"There wasn't anything subtle . . ."* Bush wrote of his dream to "make a lot of money quick" in *Looking Forward*, page 58.

227 *"I want to reward . . ."* Bush linked the American dream with the capital gains tax in a speech to the annual meeting in Washington of the Small Business Legislative Council, February 5, 1992.

Managing the Decline

229 *"The nation faces this year . . ."* Portions of Bush's comments, in a nationally televised response to LBJ's 1968 State of the Union message, were reprinted by *The New York Times*, January 28, 1968.

230 *"Let's face it . . ."* Bush made this joke at the annual Gridiron dinner in Washington in April 1989.

231 *"entire net foreign asset position . . ."* Benjamin M. Friedman, *Day of Reckoning* (New York: Random House, 1988), page 227.

231 *The deficit, expressed as a percentage* . . . The relationship between the deficit and private savings was discussed in Gene Koritz, "Why Long Rates are Resisting the Pull of Economic Gravity," *Business Week*, December 23, 1991, page 20.

232 *"We are about to enter an era . . ."* Rudman, who announced in March 1992 that he would resign from the Senate, made these comments in an interview with *Time*'s Nancy Traver, March 25, 1992.

232 *Meanwhile America's competitors overseas* . . . "Competitiveness Index 1992," by the Council on Competitiveness, July 1991. See also "Gaining New Ground: Technology Priorities for America's Future," Council on Competitiveness, March 1991. The privately funded council shares a name with the Quayle body but is in no way connected with it.

232 *"two very different ideas . . ."* Bush, in his acceptance speech at the Republican National Convention, New Orleans, August 18, 1988.

233 *"While citizens in the United States still . . ."* "Competing Economics—America, Europe, and the Pacific Rim,'' Office of Technology Assessment, October 1991, page 5.

233 *"We've had a very consistent . . ."* Rohatyn made his comments on ''This Week with David Brinkley,'' February 22, 1992.

233 *"I've started going into the numbers . . ."* Bush disclosed his alarm at the size of the deficit in an interview with *Time,* January 30, 1988.

234 *"a manageable first step"* The story of the 1989 budget negotiations is told in full detail by Lawrence J. Haas in *Running on Empty: Bush, Congress and the Politics of a Bankrupt Government* (Homewood, Ill.: Business 1, Irwin, 1990).

235 *"What is at stake here . . ."* Bush comments were reported in *The Wall Street Journal,* May 5, 1990.

235 *$5 billion in entitlement cuts . . .* The reluctance of the House Republicans was first reported in *Time,* October 15, 1990.

237 *"I'm not interested in talking . . ."* Bush made his comments about the budget deal in a press conference at the Waldorf-Astoria in New York, October 1, 1990.

238 *"I ask you to consider immersion . . ."* Bush spoke to the fifty-ninth annual convention of LULAC in Dallas, July 6, 1988.

239 *"When we seal the free trade agreement . . ."* Bush spoke in Chicago, September 20, 1991.

240 *"A major change in the way . . ."* Watkins's comments were reported by John Burgess, ''Agencies Devising Plan for Federal Labs to Help Increase U.S. Competitiveness,'' *The Washington Post,* December 10, 1991.

241 *"an idea whose time has come"* Bush spoke in a ceremony at the White House, and his comments were reported in ''Shhh. Now This Idea is Okay,'' *Time,* December 23, 1991.

241 *"The only thing I can say . . ."* Quayle's offer was reported by Kirk Victor, ''Tale of the Red Tape,'' *National Journal,* March 21, 1992.

242 *"They only want enough substance . . ."* Gore's comments were reported in ''Need Friends in High Places?'' *Time,* November 4, 1991.

243 *"It's important because . . ."* Lee Smith, ''High Level Support,'' *Fortune: The American Century,* 1991, page 52; see also *The Washington Post,* February 15, 1990.

244 *The CEOs he had invited . . .* The relative salaries of American CEOs and their Japanese counterparts were discussed in detail in *The Wall Street Journal,* December 31, 1991.

244 *Nor did the fact that many . . .* Michael Parrish, ''Is Bush Taking the Right People to Japan?'' the *Los Angeles Times,* January 1, 1992.

245 *"The economy at best is in a lull . . ."* Boskin made his comments in a speech to American Council for Capital Formation, November 9, 1990.

247 *If a relative handful disapproved . . .* Ten percent of those surveyed in early April 1991 by *The Wall Street Journal* and NBC News said that Bush's visage deserved to be chiseled into Mt. Rushmore.

247 *"The fear and uncertainty . . ."* Bush made these comments in a speech to a Joint Session of Congress, March 6, 1991.

247 *"it is difficult to escape . . ."* Mullins's comments were reported by

The Wall Street Journal, June 6, 1991; Greenspan's by *The Washington Post,* June 6, 1991.

249 *"If you raise interest rates . . ."* Bush's comment to Greenspan was first reported by Jack Nelson, "Bush Talks with Many, Shares Power with Few," the *Los Angeles Times,* November 6, 1989.

250 *the GOP money men . . .* James Risen and Douglas Jehl, "Backers Stun Bush into Focusing on Economy," the *Los Angeles Times,* October 20, 1991.

250 *"You notice when tax cuts . . ."* Bush spoke in Rome on November 6, 1991.

251 *Bush's poll numbers dipped . . .* *Time,* December 9, 1991.

251 *a "state of decline"* The *Wall Street Journal*/NBC News poll was taken December 6–9, 1991.

251 *"the George Mitchell" recession* Quayle's comments about the recession were reported in *The Wall Street Journal,* November 19, 1991.

251 *"We can't sit back . . ."* Bush made his comment in Bradenton, Florida, December 3, 1991.

"I'll Do What I Have to Do"

253 *"number-one priority . . ."* Bush made clear jobs were his top priority in his annual Christmas message, December 23, 1991.

253 *"I think people now know . . ."* Bush vowed to do "what I have to" in a television interview with David Frost, January 3, 1992.

254 *"We are going to lift this nation . . ."* Bush repeated his "This will not stand" line in his State of the Union message, January 28, 1992.

254 *Secretary of Housing and Urban Development Jack Kemp* Kemp made the "gimmicks" comment on CNN's "Newsmaker Saturday," February 1, 1992.

255 *Darman told Congress . . .* Darman explained this in detail in the Director's Introduction, Budget of the United States Government, Fiscal Year 1993.

255 *Bush's plan "is 180 degrees off . . ."* "How Not to Build a Recovery," *Business Week,* February 17, 1992. See also Howard Gleckman, "Why Bush's Budget Shuffling Doesn't Add Up to Growth," *Business Week,* February 17, 1992.

255 *"stop the ones that will hurt growth . . ."* Bush spoke about regulation in the State of the Union Message, January 28, 1992.

255 *"I understand that politics is . . ."* State of the Union Message, ibid.

256 *Bush proposed to accelerate outlays . . .* David Rogers, "Bush's Pro-Growth Spending Plan Shows Conflict with Budget-Cutting Record," *The Wall Street Journal,* February 6, 1992.

256 *"Here are the options . . ."* Hillary Stout, "Bush Backs Off Plan to Propose Medicare Cuts," *The Wall Street Journal,* February 6, 1992.

257 *" 'This will not stand,' the president said . . ."* "In the Starting Gate," *The Washington Post,* February 13, 1992.

257 *"But the message is—I care."* Bush made this comment in remarks to an Exeter Town Meeting, January 15, 1992.

257 *Bush denied that he had ever . . .* Bush, interview with the *Boston Globe,* February 16, 1992.

258 *"If you belong to the Exeter-Yale GOP . . ."* Patrick Buchanan, cited in *Time,* March 2, 1992.

259 *the "biggest mistake"* Bush renounced the 1990 budget deal in various interviews, mostly with Atlanta-based journalists on the eve of the Georgia primary, March 2, 1992.

259 *"So often," he said, " politicians do . . ."* Bush made these remarks to the home builders, Charleston, South Carolina, March 5, 1992.

259 *New Hampshire won . . .* Robert Pear, "White House 'Funnel' Gets Help for States with Primaries Nearing," *The New York Times,* March 10, 1992. Also Bob Davis and John Harwood, "Bush Plans to Offer Pollution Credits to Firms That Buy, Then Junk Old Cars," *The Wall Street Journal,* March 9, 1992.

260 *"It is time for Congress . . ."* Bush marked the deadline in a speech to Republican lawmakers, in the East Room, March 20, 1992.

260 *"We are the change . . ."* Bush's hour-long Rose Garden press conference, April 10, 1992.

261 *"We liberated the entire world . . ."* State of the Union message, January 28, 1992.

262 *"By the grace of God . . ."* Ibid.

262 *"If we can change the world . . ."* Bush fine-tuned the point in the March 20, 1992, East Room speech, written by former speech writer and OMB deputy designate, Robert Grady.

263 *"I think people understand when Barbara . . ."* Bush spoke of family values in remarks to employees of Liberty Mutual Insurance, Dover, New Hampshire, January 15, 1992.

263 *Racial code . . .* This point is made by Thomas Byrne Edsall and Mary D. Edsall, *Chain Reaction* (New York: W. W. Norton, 1991), page 216.

265 *"quite unfair . . ."* Bush spoke of rival attacks on Clinton's war record in the *Globe* interview, March 16, 1992.

266 *A late April survey . . .* Unreleased data from a *Los Angeles Times* poll taken April 23, 1992, to April 26, 1992.

268 *It's perfect . . ."* "Why Is This Man Smiling," *Time,* March 16, 1992.

269 *"Single goal?"* Bush, in Rose Garden press conference, April 10, 1992.

269 *"George Bush is probably . . ."* Janice Castro, "Asleep at the Wheel," *Time,* April 6, 1992.

270 *"We will give them . . ."* H. Ross Perot's interview with David Frost, April 24, 1992.

271 *Pollsters and reporters . . .* David Lauter, "Pennsylvanians Hesitate to Snap at 'Change' Bait," *Los Angeles Times,* April 27, 1992.

272 *"feel a little safer"* E. J. Dionne, "Europe Has Lesson for U.S. Democrats," *The Washington Post,* April 21, 1992.

273 *"the government would mess up . . ."* Gwen Ifill, "Questioned about Trust, Clinton Turns Angry," *The New York Times,* April 24, 1992.

274 *"would give us a little more . . ."* Robin Toner, "Clinton Lays Plans for November with Survivor's Calm and Confidence," *The New York Times,* May 4, 1992.

INDEX

303

Demarest, David, 38, 46, 57, 124, 239
Democratic Leadership Committee, 264
Democratic National Committee, 239
Democrats, Democratic party, 64, 67, 74, 75, 99, 102, 109, 120, 175, 198, 224, 240, 242, 243, 246
Bush's popularity as seen by, 38, 43
compromise strategy and, 57–62, 69, 75, 77, 78, 85, 88, 91, 92, 94
Congress dominated by, 56, 57–58, 69, 83–84, 85, 92, 260
coopting domestic initiatives of, 58, 77–78, 85, 88, 92, 99
Gulf War and, 84, 85, 157, 210
Hispanic voters and, 238–39
labor unions and, 239
Los Angeles riots blamed on, 272
minority favoritism ascribed to, 24
in 1988 election, 15, 16, 18, 19–20, 24–27, 28–34, 205, 207–8, 219–20
in 1992 election, 63, 200–201, 261, 262, 263, 264–67
Reagan Democrats and, 16, 24–27, 28, 29, 30, 31, 32, 33, 34
recession blamed on, 251, 254
Social Security taxes and, 120, 218, 219–20
Deng Xiaoping, 183
Den of Thieves (Stewart), 91–92
"deputies," 195–96, 197
Desert One, 72, 284*n*
Deukmejian, George, 250
Devroy, Ann, 126
Diefenderfer, Bill, 92
Dionne, E. J., 272
Doctor Slaughter (Theroux), 141
Dole, Robert, 109, 112, 114, 119, 128
domestic policy:
compromise on Democratic initiatives on, 58, 77, 85, 88, 92, 99
follow-through lacking in, 97–102
foreign policy contrasted with, 92–93, 108, 134, 136, 169, 210, 236, 261, 262
as low priority, 12, 48, 57, 65, 70, 77, 79, 83, 85, 86–88, 269
1988 election and, 21
Reagan vs. Bush on, 19
reelection strategy and, 58, 60, 62, 81, 269

symbolic approach to, 12, 57, 70, 85, 88, 97
"talking points" strategy for, 57–62, 77, 80–82, 83
veto of Democratic initiatives in, 77–80, 222
voluntarism as solution in, 209–13
see also specific issues
"Don't Worry, Be Happy," 17–18
Dowd, Maureen, 54
Drexel Burnham Lambert, 17
drugs, 17, 18, 21, 45, 58, 60, 63, 80, 83, 86, 87, 88, 89, 95, 103–5, 210, 253, 262, 263, 269, 288*n*
drug summit (1990), 103–4
Duberstein, Ken, 116
Dukakis, Michael, 11, 20, 25–26, 29–30, 31, 32–33, 57, 76, 89, 133, 178, 179, 205, 207–8, 220, 222, 266, 278*n*
Duke, David, 89, 101
du Pont, Pete, 22

Eagleburger, Lawrence, 137, 149, 162, 183, 186, 188, 243
Eastern Europe, 12, 52, 71, 76, 133, 173, 174, 175, 177, 181, 187, 188, 190, 192, 193, 196, 200, 248
Economist, 77
education, 11, 17, 19, 22, 27, 28, 30, 32, 43, 58, 59–60, 83, 84, 87, 89, 95, 98, 101, 103, 105–6, 210–11, 213, 214, 253, 254, 255, 260, 269, 273, 288*n*
Edwards, Edwin, 89
Edwards, Mickey, 121
Egypt, 52, 72, 142, 146, 153, 163
Eisenhower, Dwight D., 80, 103, 136, 177, 200
election of 1988, 15–35, 44–45, 54, 56, 60–61, 62, 76, 111, 128, 212, 215, 222
anti-Soviet rhetoric in, 178–79, 181
Bush's campaign promises in, 15, 20, 21–22, 24, 28, 29–33, 59–60, 96, 97–98, 106, 196, 220, 229, 237, 238
class divisions exploited in, 204–9
Democrats in, 15, 16, 18, 19–20, 24–27, 28–34, 205, 207–8, 219–20
"kinder and gentler" agenda in, 28, 30, 31, 32